Acknowledgements

This book would not have been possible without the time, trust, and support of many people. I am deeply grateful to all those who, in different ways, participated in, enabled access to, and collaborated with me throughout this research. At the heart of this work are the mothers, sisters, and aunts of young men whose stories are told here, the young men themselves, and their wider communities. I am especially thankful to Glodi, Angelique, Sasha, and Venesha for making this work possible, and I remain indebted to you in so many ways. Thank you to Selam Gebrekidan for supporting the research process in crucial ways.

I also wish to acknowledge the institutions that allowed me to observe and learn from them: the police, the courts, local authority bodies, and other government institutions. I am particularly grateful to Rabah Kherbane, Hugh Davis, Osman, and Kate Bex for facilitating access to trials and engaging in legal discussions with me. Thank you to Reece Grant for taking the photographs featured in this book.

At the London School of Economics, I received invaluable support from the Department of Anthropology, the Law School, and the International Inequalities Institute. I am especially grateful to Rita Astuti, Niki Lacey, Deborah James, Peter Ramsay, and Mike Savage for their mentorship and encouragement at the LSE. Thanks also to Catherine Alexander for steadfast support and collaboration over the years. Thank you to David Gellner for mentorship and guidance. My current academic home at the University of St. Gallen in Switzerland and my team in the Department of British Cultures have given me the space and community to complete this work. I owe special thanks to Suzanne Enzerink for supporting me in so many ways in the writing process, and for reading the manuscript with care.

I want to thank my collaborators: Thank you to Roxana Willis for unwavering support with this book and for so much more. Thank you, Victoria Klinkert, for our collaboration in recent years; thank you to Martha McCurdy for research support including at the early fielwork stages of this book and later at St. Gallen; and thank you to Jasaron Bajwa, Catriona Gotz, Thomas Herzmark, and Smera Rehman for research assistance. Jas, special thanks to you for 'translating' my ethnography into legally intelligible writing for our parliamentary submission.

Thank you, Maja Hojer Bruun, for shared writings experiences in Skagen and for support throughout. Thank you to Liz Fekete and the team at the Institute of Race Relations for the collaborations and conversations that sharpened my thinking towards the end. Lauren Wroe and Patrick Williams—I learnt a lot from you through our joint writing project on county lines. And thank you to the team at OUP—and in particular to Kezia Johnson—for supporting this book project, from the early stages through to the production process. I am indebted to my editors and the anonymous reviewers whose feedback has significantly strengthened the manuscript. Thank you to Sara Appel and Sally Parker for your respective editorial and indexing support.

To my family and friends, thank you for sticking it out with me in the long process of writing the book. I am especially grateful for the chats and time spent with Adam, Alice, Ana, Andrew, Catherine, Charlotte, Clara, Chunbok, Glodi, Hanna, Izzy, Insu, Jakob, Jess, Johanna, Chun Hu, Jan-Hendrik, Kris, Maira, Maja, Marco, Marie, Marthe, Meredith, Mino, Nabila, Olly, Raul, Rebecca, Rita, Roxana, Sandra, Sarah, Sasha, Saul, Selam, Stephan, Suke, Suzanne, Yumi, and Youngran—and so many others. To Tom—thank you for everything, and for helping us hold things together, when life happens on top of work in unexpected ways. Mia, thank you for a lifetime together as twins. Kyung, and Olaf—thank you for support, gimbab, and kimschi. And finally, to Haku, Kuno, and Miku: you are the best kids I could have ever hoped for. Without you, this book might have been published much sooner!

Contents

1
From Enemies to Slaves?

Introduction

Glodi was five years old when he moved to England from the Democratic Republic of Congo. He remembers being on the plane to London, sitting in a row next to his mother and his younger sister. They were finally joining their father, who had come to the UK a few years prior to work. Glodi remembers the sense of excitement he felt when hot food was served on the plane; the touch and smell of the lemon-scented wet wipe that the air hostess handed him—he had never seen one before. He was bickering with his sister when an older white man seated in front of him turned around, rudely telling Glodi's mother to get her children under control. As his mother responded in Lingala, the man shouted at her to speak English. Glodi did not understand what had just happened. He did not care. At Heathrow airport, his father, a tall man with a bright smile, was waiting for them. To this day, Glodi remembers the feeling of his father's arms around him as he greeted his son after years apart. 'This is going to be different', his mother had said when they disembarked the plane. 'But I promise you it will be amazing'.

Glodi's father took them to a small flat in South London on a large inner-city social housing estate. Like many other estates across England, it was built by the government decades ago to provide housing for working-class populations. But over the decades, following de-industrialization and government disinvestment, the estate had fallen into poverty and structural decline. Families living in the neighbourhood were struggling to get by. Glodi's father, a painter and decorator who had come to Britain in search of a better life, worked long hours to pay the rent and bills. At times, there was little food in the house, when his father had not been paid. In the winter, the flat was cold when there was not enough money for heat. In school, Glodi struggled to fit in. The children made fun of his accent and demeanour for

Drugs, Race, and the Politics of Modern Slavery Law. Insa Lee Koch, Oxford University Press.
 DOI: 10.1093/9780198899631.003.0001

being ‘fresh off the boat’. Glodi was cross-eyed until he had surgery in his teenage years, and the children were merciless in their bullying. ‘I learnt that in order to get by, I had to fight’, Glodi remembered. He was repeatedly excluded from school lessons as a punishment for his disruptive behaviour.

When he was a bit older, Glodi turned to what he refers to as ‘hustling’ to get by. Aged eleven, he was selling doughnuts and drinks in the schoolyard that he bought from a nearby supermarket. With this income he would buy himself lunch and contribute to groceries at home. When he turned thirteen, he began to sell marijuana. By that point, the ‘hood’, as he calls his estate, had long become home. Glodi commanded respect; he is tall and muscular and had a reputation for being tough. Soon, Glodi stopped attending school on a regular basis, and stayed out for long hours, leaving his parents worrying where he was. When his mother found out he was dealing marijuana, she kicked him out of the house. Aged fifteen, Glodi now found himself on the street. He constantly moved around—each night staying somewhere different, sometimes ‘sofa surfing’ with friends, other times finding refuge in stairwells on his estate or on night buses. One day, a friend introduced him to a man in his early twenties who offered him a job and a spare room. Glodi was in no situation to say no.

This was Glodi’s introduction to selling Class A drugs—heroin and crack cocaine—for an established drug dealer. Based in London, his new employer had a dedicated phone line set up to take orders for users in Hastings, a seaside town about sixty miles southeast of London. Glodi became a runner; his job was to stay in Hastings and follow directions from his boss, directly selling drugs to users. For the first time, Glodi was earning money and, while in Hastings, his boss provided him with a roof over his head. But this new life came at a cost. He lived with the constant threat of attacks from rival dealers; on one occasion he was badly stabbed, suffering serious injuries. He could not call the ambulance for fear of being arrested. Back in London, on one of the rare days he attended school, the teachers found a BB air gun and scissors in his backpack. For this, he was permanently expelled. Selling drugs then became his only occupation, and he spent long periods of time away from London. In 2010, aged just seventeen, Glodi was arrested and charged with intention to supply Class A drugs. He refused to give up the name of his boss, pleaded guilty to the charges, and was sentenced to three years at a young offender’s institution. He was sent to Cookham Wood prison, one of the country’s most notorious youth detention facilities, known for its high levels of inmate and staff violence.

When Glodi was released in 2012, about to turn nineteen, he was determined to turn his life around. He applied for a job at McDonald's and was invited for a group interview. He listened to the other interviewees relate their work experience, but given the illegal nature of his employment until that point, he could not share his own CV. He did not get the job. Nor did he get anything else he applied for. Glodi felt trapped in his life, 'everyone else had moved on', he recalled, 'and I couldn't even get a job at McDonald's'. Then, one day, when Glodi was leaving a supermarket, a white Mercedes pulled up next to him. It was his old boss. He invited Glodi to a Caribbean restaurant for lunch. While sharing food, he thanked Glodi for not having revealed his identity to the police, but informed him that he still owed 4,000 pounds for the drugs and money that the police had seized when he was arrested. His boss offered Glodi a deal: he could work off his debt, and in turn, Glodi would be promoted to a safer position within the business. He would control the drugs phone line, taking requests from users and directing them to runners who would deliver the drugs. For Glodi this was an offer he could not refuse: one step up from doing the most dangerous work of 'running' drugs on the streets while settling his debt. Glodi accepted, and was back in the business, again.

o

Glodi's experiences speak to a new reality present in the news, policy reports, and emerging case law: that of predominantly teenage boys and young men who have been involved in the illicit drugs trade becoming 'modern slaves' and 'victims of criminal exploitation'. Behind this development lies an emerging set of responses to what the government has termed 'county lines'—the name given to regional networks of Class A drugs (mostly heroin and cocaine) that it sees as expanding from larger cities, like London, to market, rural, and coastal towns. 'County lines', the dominant narrative tells us, is a new and particularly harmful drugs distribution model—one that works through extractive relations, as mostly male teenagers and vulnerable adults are lured into the trade by others higher up the chain, often under false pretences of money, social rewards, and friendship. New recruits are made to perform the most menial and dangerous labour of 'running' the drugs, transporting them to their places of destination and directly selling them to users on the streets. Often, these recruits are subjected to relations of debt bondage by those higher up in the chain, making it impossible to ever leave the drugs trade.

What makes this narrative of 'county lines' drug dealing so astonishing is that those at the bottom rung of the drugs economy are now thought of as victims who should be safeguarded despite—or precisely *because* of—the crimes they have committed. Here, people's involvement in criminal activities is no longer seen as a cause for their punishment, at least not straightforwardly so. Rather, law enforcement, the courts, and frontline professionals are now talking of these people as potentially vulnerable individuals—as modern slaves—in need of protection from the full force of the criminal law. This expansion of legal victimhood becomes even more astounding when considered against the fact that the newly discovered slaves hail from the same post-industrial and multiracial urban neighbourhoods that, only a few years prior, had become the target of the government's 'war on gangs'. In the aftermath of the civic uprisings that followed the police killing of a young, unarmed man named Mark Duggon in 2011, the government had come to construct urban Black and working-class boys and young men from inner-city housing estates as 'gang' members. The surveillance, monitoring and (pre-emptive) policing that was licensed by the government's 'war on gangs' echoed deeper colonial logics of fighting the racialized enemy within (Williams, 2015; Nijjar, 2018; Williams and Clarke, 2018; Koram, 2019).

And yet, today, it is precisely this same demographic of boys and young men who are discovered as modern slaves. Central to this shift 'from enemies to slaves' has been the *Modern Slavery Act 2015*: a piece of legislation initially introduced to respond to growing public concerns over trafficking primarily at Britain's national borders. Under this legislation, individuals identified as victims of exploitation have a defence in law for certain crimes, including for drugs offences of the kind Glodi committed as a young runner. The opposite, however, is also true: individuals accused of facilitating these crimes can be prosecuted in Britain's criminal courts not only for drugs offences, but as human traffickers who can potentially face life in prison. Ten years on from when the *Modern Slavery Act* became law, those implicated at the bottom rung of Britain's regional drugs economy have been recognized as the largest group of modern slaves, often spoken about as victims of 'criminal exploitation' (Centre for Social Justice and Justice&Care, 2024). A new cultural zeal has been awakened, as police officers, social workers, local authority officials, lawyers, and judges are learning to speak and act upon the mandate to identify these victims, extend safeguarding solutions, as well as prosecute those who are believed to be behind these crimes.

This book is an ethnography of the unfolding institutional, moral, and legal landscape of anti-slavery efforts in what is now commonly seen as a national crisis of county lines. I explore what happens when a demographic of people previously seen as enemies are reconceived of as victims and slaves, and how enemy logics become invoked, reproduced, and cemented in both case law and institutional responses even in the face of their newly found juridical victimhood. In doing so, I tell a bigger story about state power, racism, and the law in what is often said to be a post-racial world. How, I ask, can we make sense of the government's discovery of 'modern slaves' in the figure of the 'exploited' drug dealer? How does the liberal tale of redemption that now professes to save the most vulnerable 'from themselves' and 'for their own good' silence the workings of state-induced social suffering? In what ways does this state-induced social suffering speak to deeper colonial logics of racial exploitation and legacies of transatlantic slavery that are silenced by the government's emphasis on 'exploitation' and 'slavery' of a new kind? What forms of state power, including knowledge practices, monitoring, pre-emptive policing, and prosecution strategies, have been licensed in the name of doing good? And finally, what does this tell us about the discovery of modern slavery not just as a juridical development, but as a political project-in-the-making at a time of deep conjunctural crisis?

To answer these questions, I conducted more than five years of ethnographic research, analysing the emerging modern slavery jurisprudence as it relates to those implicated in the illicit street-level economy of heroin and crack cocaine. Beginning in 2018, I worked closely with young men and their families, followed law enforcement staff and frontline professionals, spent time with defence lawyers and prosecution teams, and interviewed high-level government officials and politicians from across the spectrum. This involved conducting multi-nodal and multi-sited fieldwork: I spent much time in the homes and communities from which young people working in Britain's street-level economy hail; shadowed officials in police stations and the local government offices where modern slaves are now identified and safeguarding options implemented; ended up for months inside Britain's criminal courts where, for the first time in history, trials under the *Modern Slavery Act 2015* are now heard; and travelled from the capital city of London to the 'provinces' and back again, tracing the movements that county lines drugs distribution networks are said to be taking. Throughout, I have worked most closely with the family members of individuals identified 'at risk' of modern slavery (either as victims or as perpetrators), side-by-side with their mothers, sisters, and aunts, who continue to advocate for their children and young kin when professionals have often given up on them.

What has emerged from this multi-sited, multi-scalar, and multi-actor ethnography is a murky, at times counterintuitive picture that complicates the claim that we are witnessing a shift from enemies to slaves. I have no doubt that many professionals whom I spent my time with were committed to acting upon their new mandate to improve the lives of individuals who had committed offences and were now identified as vulnerable. And yet, their professed aim to become guardians of care cannot be divorced from the structural context in which they moved—and which includes the government's prior 'war on gangs', steep inequality and austerity cuts, and a deeply racist criminal justice system. As I came to know more families at the receiving end of these policies, I realized how pervasive the sense was that they were being 'set up to fail'. Not only did interventions designed to safeguard children often do nothing to protect them in the long run, but drugs runners who ostensibly met the government's criteria of exploited victims continued to be criminalized, and their family members' pleas for justice silenced. This murky picture was reinforced as I moved to the courts, where distinctions between victims and 'gang' members, between slaves and traffickers, remained vanishingly thin, as legal battles over evidence tended to boil down to a technocratic assessment of 'exploitation' and 'trafficking'.

Drugs, Race, and the Politics of Modern Slavery Law argues that the fraught workings of modern slavery policies bring into sharp relief the fallacy of a tale of redemption that purports to save the most vulnerable in post-racial Britain. As such, the ethnographic picture that I present is symptomatic of a liberal conceit writ large—one that, at various moments in time, has presented Black, racialized, and working-class communities as in need of saving both 'from their own kind' and 'for their own professed good' (Kempadoo, Sanghera, and Pattanaik, 2005; Kempadoo and Shih, 2022; O'Connell Davidson, 2022). In Britain today, this tale of redemption makes it possible to recognize individuals' *de jure* vulnerability while at the same time denying and deepening the state's *de facto* production of their classed and racial domination. Or to put it differently, redemptive logics impose an idea of 'criminal exploitation' onto the 'structural exploitation' that Britain's racialized and working-class communities are made to endure at a time of entrenched economic and political crisis. And yet, it is also this structural exploitation that brings to the fore the legacies of Britain's colonial past of transatlantic slavery and racial exploitation, a past that has been abdicated by the tale of 'new' or 'modern' slavery and exploitation. At precisely the moment when the British state has embraced the fight against slavery, it has done so not to address its history of racial empire, less even its afterlives in state racism today, but to resurrect the image of the slave master in the body of racialized and working-class youth as the enemy within.

Discovering modern slavery on 'home ground': Beyond narratives of crisis

'More than two hundred years ago, the British House of Commons passed historic legislation to make the slave trade illegal. But sadly, the grim reality today is that slavery still exists in towns, cities and the countryside across the world. And be in no doubt, slavery is taking place here in the UK' (HM Government, 2014, p. 5). These were the words with which Theresa May, then Home Secretary, introduced the government's modern slavery strategy in 2014, announcing the *Modern Slavery Bill* that would become an Act of Parliament the following year. Widely applauded by government officials, politicians, and law enforcement as a world-leading Act, the legislation contains several important provisions. On the one hand, it specifies the offences of slavery, servitude, forced or compulsory labour, and human trafficking, increasing the maximum punishment available for these offences to life in prison. On the other hand, the legislation provides a defence for those who commit certain offences due to having been exploited. The legislation also specifies several other provisions, including the confiscation of assets of those who commit modern slavery crimes, civil orders for those convicted of modern slavery offences and those 'at risk' of committing them, and a new government position, that of the Independent Anti-Slavery Commissioner whose duties include promoting good practice in the prevention, detection, investigation, and prosecution of modern slavery offences and the identification of victims.

The passing of the *Modern Slavery Act* has marked a distinct shift in the landscape of British politics and law: a recognition that modern slavery is a grave crime happening not only in cross-border trafficking scenarios, but on 'home ground', within British borders. Concerns over modern slavery and human trafficking had been running strong on the international scene since the 1990s, when the anti-trafficking lobby revived older fears around 'sex trafficking' in a cross-border context. Yet, a decade into the new millennium, the rhetoric shifted as modern slavery was no longer treated as an immigration crime alone at the national borders, but as an issue happening also on "home soil' inside Britain. In 2013, the Centre for Social Justice, an influential conservative think tank, published a high-profile report entitled 'It still happens here' (2013) that urged the government to move away from a narrow understanding of modern slavery as a cross-border trafficking crime alone. The report proved influential in the ensuing parliamentary debates that led to the *Modern Slavery Act* and a host of other policies addressing modern slavery through the courts, local government bodies, and at the frontline. Ten years on, the drive to eradicate slavery on 'home soil' has only become more urgent, as reports have highlighted that the most prevalent form of modern slavery—'criminal exploitation'—involves British nationals who have been exploited within national borders (Centre for Social Justice and Justice&Care, 2024; House of Lords Modern Slavery Act 2015 Committee, 2024).

The growth in the number of modern slaves 'on home ground' has in large part been due to boys and young men like Glodi. In other words, a rapidly growing number of individuals are reported as involved at the bottom rung of regional drugs distribution networks, now called county lines. Identified as an 'emerging business model' in 2015, the National Crime Agency (NCA) spoke of a 'growing body of intelligence, emerging in particular from London and the South East [whereby] vulnerable young people are being exploited in order to facilitate the running of street level drug dealing'. County lines was defined as 'a national issue involving the use of branded mobile phone "lines" [used] by groups to extend their drug dealing business into new locations outside their home areas' (NCA 2015, p. 1), with heroin and crack cocaine being identified as the main substances supplied. Subsequent reports have characterized provincial, market, and rural towns as being 'flooded' by the arrival of urban dealers expanding beyond the over-saturated drugs markets in the cities. But these town populations, represented as law-abiding, unsuspecting, and innocent, were not the only identified victims: 'criminal exploitation' or 'child criminal exploitation' was said to be ripe, as children and teenagers were believed to be 'trafficked' into the drugs trade by those higher up the chain.

Soon, the government came to argue that county lines was present across the entire country, observed now by every single police force in the UK (National Crime Agency, 2017, 2018), with the most recent figures published by law enforcement sources placing the number of 'unique lines' at 6,644 (National County Lines Coordination Centre and National Police Chief's Council, 2024, p. 15). In 2018, the government officially recognized 'criminal exploitation' as a form of modern slavery, and mentioned county lines drug dealing as the primary area where this exploitation takes place (Cooper et al., 2017). A ratcheting effect has taken place as politicians and law enforcement, backed up by UK media outlets and also increasingly documented in television shows and films,[1] have come to emphasize the

[1] See *County Lines* (2019) Directed by Henry Blake, UK: Meerkat Films.

distinct nature of this 'poly-crisis' involving drug dealing, violence, and modern slavery, and the need for urgent response and policing. A steady supply of reports and academic scholarship has similarly testified to the exceptional nature of this regional form of drugs trafficking, highlighting the exploitation of children and vulnerable adults as a defining feature of this trade (Coomber and Moyle, 2018; Home Office, 2018; Ofsted, 2018; Robinson, McLean, and Densley, 2018; Stone, 2018; Ministry of Justice, 2019; Turner, 2019; Spicer, 2020; Spicer, Moyle, and Coomber, 2020; Windle, 2020; Centre for Social Justice and Justice&Care, 2024).

Notwithstanding the urgency with which the crisis of modern slavery and county lines has been sounded, it bears emphasizing that it remains virtually impossible to record county lines activity with any accuracy, less even the connection between county lines and modern slavery. For a start, county lines is not a recorded offence. As Densley et al. have pointed out, county lines has operated as an 'all-encompassing terminology' based on police intelligence, allowing for 'drug dealing practices of practically any entity to fall under [its] rubric' (Densley, 2023, p. 2). Its discovery, as we will see in this book, was inextricably tied to intelligence supplied by the institutions that were responsible for enforcing the government's prior 'war on gangs' (Wroe, 2023; Koch, Williams, and Wroe, 2024). What is more, if 'county lines' remains a nebulous concept based on policing realities rather than self-evident facts, then the same is true for 'modern slavery' (Broad and Gadd, 2023; Carvalho et al., 2025; Craig et al., 2019; Fudge, 2025). As O'Connell Davidson (2022) reminds us, in a situation where slavery has been legally abolished, defining what constitutes 'slavery' and 'human trafficking' is bound to be a slippery exercise. This is arguably even more so the case where slavery is approached through its criminal 'proxy'—the idea of 'criminal exploitation'—which has been thrown in the midst.

Indeed, policing sources have acknowledged the difficulties of recording county lines, noting that its recording is based on a 'somewhat subjective assessment' (National County Lines Coordination Centre and National Police Chief's Council, 2024, p. 32). Academic commentators too have begun to critically interrogate the county lines phenomenon (e.g. Densley et al., 2023; Spicer 2020; Koch et al., 2024; Windle et al., 2020; Atkinson-Sheppard, 2024). And yet, dominant commentary has stopped short of theorizing the implications of county lines' contingency. Here, I take up precisely this inquiry. Indeed, as a social phenomenon, the projected crisis of county lines is not dissimilar to that of 'mugging' analysed so famously by Stuart Hall and his colleagues in *Policing the Crisis* (2013) nearly a half-century ago. Focusing on an emerging moral panic in the media, law enforcement, and judicial bodies, Hall et al. argued that concerns about 'street muggers' were not attributable to an objective rise in numbers: mugging was not a recorded offence in English law and policing. Rather, it was statistically manufactured by police taking a 'pick n mix' approach to what counted as mugging: bashing together different categories of crime and projecting a new crime—'mugging'—into existence' (Day and Bean, 2022, p. 50). Hall et al.'s concern was to show how the emergence of this moral panic repurposed tropes about Black criminality at a time when rising strikes, Black power movements, growing unemployment, and an economic crisis had called into question Britain's post-war welfare consensus.

Far from letting criminal categories stand in 'all [their] common-sense immediacy' (Hall et al., 2013, p. 2), Hall et al. then urged their readers to place them within the context of 'wider social forces and conjunctures' (2013, p. 3). Here, I follow their refusal to let criminal categories stand in their common-sense immediacy. Rather than 'proving' or 'disproving' their objective existence and patterns of victimization, I interrogate the contingency of allegedly self-evident categories by placing them within the wider context contributing to their solidification. Some of the concepts that are central to my analysis are more structurally similar to 'mugging' than others: like mugging, 'county lines', and 'criminal exploitation' are not (yet) recorded offences[2]. By contrast, and unlike mugging, 'modern slavery' and 'human trafficking' have been legally codified. Yet, as criminal categories, these concepts also lack any stable reference point in the outside world, and their fusing with county lines and criminal exploitation in policy language and practice has further destabilized their meanings. I take this instability as my point of departure, to investigate how the discovery of county lines operates as a techno-moral mechanism that acts as a mechanism for state building at a time of deep crisis. But before I develop the contours of this argument, it is necessary to address a major challenge that I anticipate at least some readers at this stage will raise: that 'race' and 'racism' have nothing to do with this.

[2] At the time of this writing in April 2025, the government had announced codifying 'criminal exploitation' through legislation (see Chapter 8).

What's race got to do with it? On numbers, state racism, and enemy logics in the law

When presenting this research to academics and practitioners, I have repeatedly been confronted with the question of what 'race' and 'racism' have to do with county lines and responses to it. Sometimes, it has come from conservative circles, other times from self-professed liberal audiences. Sometimes, it has been asked defensively, other times outright aggressively. Academic responses have been among the most critical. When I submitted a co-written article about this subject to a social work journal, it was rejected by the editor for being 'morally unconscionable'. When the same article was later published by the journal *Race & Class* (Koch, Williams, and Wroe, 2024) and *The Guardian* covered it in a news story (Townsend, 2023), the social media response on the part of those critical of it ranged from claims that we were fabricating facts about racism to criticisms that we were wilfully blind to the real harm that county lines activity is causing. Similarly, an anonymous reviewer of my book proposal on behalf of a major University publishing house insisted that I was making a series of misplaced 'niche arguments about racial injustice and neo-liberalism'. The reviewer quoted statistics of Albanians (presumably racialized by the reviewer as white) being victims of county lines and modern slavery, concluding that my arguments are neither grounded 'in theory or practice', are driven by the 'polemics of critical race theory', and 'might actually be offensive to people working in the field'.

The argument that county lines is beyond race reflects a broader assumption shared by government institutions based on the belief that Britain is a post-racial country, where institutional racism is a thing of the past (Nijjar, 2022; Elliott-Cooper, 2023; Kudnani, 2023). It is often argued, for example, that county lines can affect *anyone* (regardless of their skin colour or 'race'), and that hence, safeguarding and policing responses cannot possibly be discriminating on the basis of ethnic and racial origin (or indeed for that matter, any other axes of intersectional inequality, such as class or gender). Often, the contrast that is drawn in these conversations is with law enforcement practices under the government's now failed 'war on gangs', and the more blatant forms of racial targeting that were authorized in its wake, including with respect to stop-and-search practices, profiling, and prosecution tactics (Williams, 2015; Williams and Clarke, 2016, 2018; Nijjar, 2018; Koch, Williams, and Wroe, 2024). In the words of a senior detective in one of the country's largest police forces, tackling county lines is about 'dismantling networks of exploitation rather than arresting individuals', and 'networks' don't know 'any skin colour'. Said another detective, in the presence of other senior officers during a meeting arranged to present major findings from my fieldwork: 'I cannot possibly see how the policing response to county lines can be said to display any racial bias'.

Let me unpack some of these claims by considering the publicly accessible data on county lines as well as drugs policing. It is true that intelligence returned from police forces suggests that those now caught under the policies come from a variety of ethnic and racial backgrounds. In its 2016 annual assessment of county lines, the National Crime Agency stated that groups originating from London are 'predominantly' Black British or 'Afro Caribbean'; groups from Liverpool and Manchester are often 'white'; and those from Birmingham are of 'Asian ethnicity' (2016). Similar language was mirrored in a more recent government briefing, which states that 'people from all ethnicities and nationalities are targeted and the demographics of victims of exploitation vary across England and Wales', with some areas reporting an over-representation of people from 'black and mixed ethnic groups' while in others, the victims 'are mainly white' (Home Office, 2023, p. 6). And yet, data from multi-agency safeguarding partnerships has also indicated a significant over-representation of Black young people in county lines cohorts at a rate of six times more than other ethnicities (Wilson et al., 2021; see also Wroe, 2021). This disproportionality, particularly among boys and young men, was also noted in the most recent county lines assessment jointly published by the National County Lines Coordination Centre and the National Police Chief's Council. The numbers from metropolitan areas are particularly concerning, with the proportion of Black individuals reported as involved in county lines being as high as 60.1 per cent against a national population of 10.5 per cent Black people (2024, p. 23).

The figures become even more dire when we consider the broader critical commentary on racial disparities in drugs enforcement more broadly (Eastwood, Shiner, and Bear, 2013; Shiner et al., 2018; Williams and Clarke, 2018; Koram, 2019; Woolley, 2021). When county lines policing responses were initially rolled out, official sources continued to report on the extreme racial disproportionality within the criminal justice system. Throughout 2019–20, for example, all racially minoritized groups were over-represented in police-recorded searches for drugs (33.8 per cent) when compared to their proportion in the general population (an estimated 15.6 per cent). Comparatively, white people were underrepresented in police searches for drugs, accounting for 50.4 per cent of searches for drugs against their proportion in the population (84.4 per cent) (Allen, 2021). This, despite the fact that drug use is most prevalent amongst white university/college students, who acquire their drugs through friends, neighbours, colleagues, or family members (Koch, Williams, and Wroe, 2024). Labour MP David Lammy's assessment of racial bias within the criminal justice system further uncovered disproportionality at every stage, from prosecution to sentencing and resettlement. Discrepancies were found to be particularly pronounced in the case of drugs convictions and sentencing, with the report finding that the odds of receiving a prison sentence were around 240 per cent higher for Black and minority ethnic offenders than for their white counterparts (Lammy, 2017).

But more importantly even, we cannot reduce our discussion about race and state racism to an exercise in numbers. While mainstream analysis has focused, in the words of Philips and colleagues, 'on the numerical incidence of race and disproportionality in criminal justice outcomes, defaulting to a positivist lens of quantification', this does not tell us anything about 'race's complex material and symbolic manifestations in the intersection with crime, control, and social order' (2020, p. 428). Writing about criminology, they argue that notwithstanding the fact that 'governing', 'categorisations', and 'social order' have been central issues in the discipline, concerns over race and ethnicity have been mostly relegated to its margins (see also Phillips and Bowling, 2003; Bosworth, 2004; Agozino, 2019; Aliverti, 2021; Cioccini and Greener, 2021; Fatsis, 2021; Parmer, 2017). We can make a similar point about the police's constructions of county lines, and the mainstream academic commentary that has accompanied it. Here, issues of ethnicity and race have been relegated to the periphery of the debate, constituting a mere footnote or afterthought (if that) to mainstream narratives. The outcome is that these mainstream narratives have remained what Philips et al. call 'analytically white'—defined by a consistent failure 'to situate contemporary formations of crime and its institutional controls within historical racial configurations constructed as part of the dominant social order' (ibid.; 428).

Acknowledging, then, how constructions of social order and law are bound up with racialized 'other'ing means to acknowledge the weight of the past. Indeed, Europe's internal enemies were constituted through racial categories produced by imperial conquest, whereby distinctions of colour joined those of religion and culture to distinguish the rulers from the ruled (Stoler, 1995, p. 27). Britain was established in 1707 as a state that already held colonies, thus making it an imperial state from its inception—and one that would expand into the world's largest empire at its height, powering Britain's capitalist economy (Bhambra, 2021; Elliott-Cooper, 2023). But the colonies were not just sites for resource extraction and exploitation; they also provided 'a location for experimentation and innovation that transformed the exercise of governmental power at home and configured the institutionalization of imperial knowledge' (Gilroy, 2004: 46, cited in Aliverti, 2021, p. 306). Britain's expansion in the Americas, Australasia, Africa, and India provided the figure of a racialized 'other'—an enemy figure—against which honourable men and women in the metropolis were constructed. The making of Black criminality in the context of the transatlantic slave trade—of which Britain was a central player—was central to this. Black men were seen as hyper dangerous, and Black women were seen as sexually promiscuous and morally deviant (Gilroy, 2004; Elliot-Cooper, 2019: 542–544). These enemy constructs were central to the law, directly informing ideas of (in)justice (Gilroy, 2004), justifying penalties to subdue subjugated populations and territories (Black et al., 2021), and giving rise to distinct technologies of state violence across both the colony and metropole (Axter and Danewid, 2025).

Importantly, too, imperial constructs that framed colonized populations as enemies 'leaked' beyond the boundaries of space and skin to attach themselves to other individuals and populations who were believed to lack respectability. This included the British poor (Skeggs, 1997; Tyler, 2015). Sure enough, they were still placed in a morally superior position to colonized subjects, a process exhibited through the Poor Laws in the metropolis and the 'whitening' of Britain's working classes on the frontiers of settler colonies (Elliot-Cooper, 2019). And yet, they too have been the subject of intense othering and disciplining. As Robbie Shilliam (2018) has shown in his comprehensive analysis of 'race and the undeserving poor', power brokers in Victorian England also made ideological distinctions between the 'deserving' and the 'undeserving' poor, by associating the undeserving with African slaves and the deserving with English propriety. The former, often vagabonds and travellers, were thus symbolically 'blackened' and policed as an internal threat to the wider moral fabric. What is more, far from disappearing in contemporary times, these processes of racialization and policing have only deepened as Britain's working-class communities have become the object of intense moral defamation under neo-liberal policies, a point brilliantly illustrated in Willis' ethnography of life in a multiracial working-class community (2023).

As a growing literature in critical legal scholarship has shown, race and racism have remained key instruments in state domination long after the formal end of transatlantic slavery and empire (El-Enany and Bruce-Jones, 2015; Koram, 2019; de Noronha, 2020; El-Enany, 2020; Bhattacharyya et al., 2021; Black et al., 2021; Elliot-Cooper, 2021; Fekete, 2022; Nijjar, 2022; Willis, 2023; Laub, 2024). The 'afterlives' of slavery are clearly evidenced in the continuous construction of enemy figures that present racialized people as a threat to be contained and punished. We have already seen how, in *Policing the Crisis*, Stuart Hall and his colleagues analysed the turn to 'law and order' in the 1970s as an outcome of moral projects designed to shore up popular consent at a time of deep state crisis. The British press, reinforced by the establishment, conjured an idea of a country under threat in the figure of the 'mugger' that was transposed onto the urban Black working-class youth. Since Hall et al. wrote their account, the figure of the racialized enemy has been conjured time and again, giving rise to distinct patterns of policing and punishment—including with respect to 'the political rioter' in the 1980s (Gilroy, 1987), 'the Muslim terrorist' in the wake of 9/11 (Parmar, 2011), 'the Asian grooming gang' in the 2000s (Bhattacharyya et al., 2021; Cockbain and Tufail, 2020), and 'the illegal migrant' (de Noronha, 2020). But it is in the figure of 'the urban gang member' central to the government's 'war on gangs' (Williams, 2015) that the story of this book comes home: out of this enemy figure, 'modern slaves' and 'human traffickers' became reconstructed and projected into Britain's body politic.

In short: to deny a priori that 'race' as a tool for social control has no role to play in the dominant tale of modern slavery and county lines would mean to fundamentally mischaracterize state racism today. This is not to say that county lines is just about minoritized youth. To repeat the obvious, I do not deny that individuals racialized as non-white are safeguarded as victims, nor do I argue that a person racialized as white cannot be at the receiving end of punitive policies. This book shows how both of these things are true. However, I also take seriously the point that many of those identified as both victims and perpetrators count among the demographics that have long been racially coded as law's constitutive 'other'. I analyse how individuals minoritized as non-white continue to be treated as criminals by frontline workers, law enforcement, and the courts; how even when they are safeguarded, the solutions offered often do nothing to improve their lives; and how their families' struggles for justice are silenced or even criminalized. And I show, in a continuation of Shilliam's (2018) and Willis' (2023) discussion, how poor white individuals and associates of minoritized defendants end up being 'blackened' as they are associated with drug-dealing activities. Many have argued that race and racism remain key instruments in state domination today. This book argues that this remains so even if—or perhaps *because*—enemy logics have worked their way into a liberal language of redemption that professes to save the most vulnerable.

Critiquing redemption: when enemies become victims

Much of the ground-level work for the arguments I am advancing in this book has been laid out in the critical anti-trafficking literature. This literature has shown that 'neo-abolitionist' efforts, as I call them here, that present modern slavery as 'the epitome of a moral wrong' (Brace, 2018, p. 4) have a distinct racialized legacy that reflects colonial logics of white saviourism (Kempadoo, Sanghera, and Pattanaik, 2005; Anderson, 2013, 2018; O'Connell Davidson, 2015, 2022; Brace and O'Connell Davidson, 2018; Kempadoo and Shih, 2022; Shih, 2023). 'Neo-abolitionist' fears have emerged at various points, including in the nineteenth century in the form of a moral panic around 'white slavery' and, about a hundred years later, in the late twentieth century, in the figure of the 'trafficked migrant'. In each of these moments of 'apparition' (O'Connell Davidson, 2015), anti-trafficking policies and legislations were invoked in highly selective ways. Far from addressing European histories of colonialism and racial slavery, less even the structural exploitation that continued to be a lived reality of those at the sharp end of racial capitalism, neo-abolitionist discourses have typically presented modern slavery as a crime emanating from communities considered a threat to the workings of liberal political and economic institutions. As such, neo-abolitionist initiatives have also gone hand-in-hand with, and deepened, processes of criminalization, justifying tougher immigration, border control, and racist policing—the very structures that, in Saidiya Hartman's words (2008), we can identify as the 'afterlives' of racial empire and transatlantic slavery.

These efforts to 'save' the vulnerable—whether 'fallen sisters' during the 'white slavery panic' (Kempadoo, Sanghera, and Pattanaik, 2005, p. xi), or, hundred years later, 'trafficked migrants' from the global south—did not mark the end of anti-slavery efforts. Rather, in this book I am concerned with what I call modern slavery's 'third apparition': the British government's discovery of modern slavery in the figure of the county lines drugs dealer. This discovery had certainly not been anticipated by the drafters of the *Modern Slavery Act 2015*. As we saw above, county lines was only discovered by the National Crime Agency the same year the Modern Slavery Bill became law. The connection between 'county lines' and 'modern slavery' was first made by law enforcement keen to prosecute drug dealers for more than just their drugs crimes (Spicer, 2020), taking advantage of the longer sentences that come with human trafficking offences, the possibility of injunction orders upon conviction, and the stigma of being labelled a trafficker (which, according to police, was akin to being called a 'paedophile'). Now, the same institutions previously responsible for implementing the 'war on gangs' were instructed to tackle exploitation and modern slavery. In the years to come, the language of 'gangs' became fused with that of 'county lines', 'criminal exploitation', 'human trafficking', and 'modern slavery', as one term came to stand in for the other, giving rise to distinct knowledge practices, multi-agency partnerships, pre-emptive policing, and new defence and prosecution strategies.

The reconceptualization of 'gang' members no longer just as criminals but as potential victims of exploitation, trafficking, and slavery was in tune with what has been described as a broader 'vulnerability zeitgeist' or 'spirit of the time' (Brown, 2014). As social policy and legal scholars have argued, the idea that vulnerable individuals should be spared punishment and instead be safeguarded—even where they have offended—has entered social and criminal justice policy making with an astonishing speed in recent years (Fitzgerald and Munro, 2012; Brown, Ecclestone, and Emmel, 2017; Brown, 2019; 2014; Ramsay, 2012), and across vast areas of policy making, including in housing, migration detention, national security, health, and criminal justice policy (Heath-Kelly and Gruber, 2023; Ticktin, 2011; Fassin, 2011; Aliverti and Tafwiq, 2025). And yet, for virtually all of the professionals I encountered in the course of my research, safeguarding vulnerability in the case of drug dealers was described as a completely unchartered territory, one that challenged their deep-seated assumptions about how to attribute responsibility, blame, and guilt. 'We need a fundamental culture change', is how one law enforcement officer put it, 'to recognize offenders as victims'.

Through sheer luck and coincidence (see below), I was able to witness, in the aftermath of the passing of the Modern Slavery Act, a new moral and juridical reality-in-the-making as drug dealers were being re-inscribed through a language of victimhood and modern slavery. Professionals were trained to 'safeguard' the newly discovered vulnerable; defence lawyers were instructed to run the 'modern slavery' defence; and, as the first prosecutions were brought under the Act, precedent was being made, proving that drug dealers could indeed be prosecuted for human trafficking charges. I initially thought of these happenings as akin to a process of 'making up' of people. I borrow the term from Ian Hacking (2006), who used it to capture how possibilities for personhood come into being as an outcome of bureaucratic and state processes. Hacking shows how, in nineteenth century Europe, labels such as the 'schizophrenic' or the 'gambler' emerged as a manner of classifying conditions that had their origins in industrial and state bureaucracies. Similarly, in my realm, new possibilities for thinking of drug dealers as slaves and their traffickers were being created as officials from all walks of life were creatively engaging with trafficking language and policy, with vast amounts of funding, resources, and training being put into such efforts.

Over time, however, as my ethnographic project developed, I became convinced that what was at stake was also a state-building project—that the tale of drug dealers 'transforming' from enemies to victims did not just serve to 'make up' new persons but functioned as a mechanism for expanding, reinforcing, and producing an excess of state power at a time of deep political and economic crisis. Just like in earlier moments of 'neo-abolitionist' activity, modern slavery initiatives had targeted marginalized populations whose labour and movements were considered a threat to the workings of liberal economic and political institutions. Here once more, the individuals deemed in need of saving were those whose loyalties to the state or a formal employer were in question: 'suspect' populations' of Black, minoritized, and working-class youth implicated in the illicit economy of drugs, and the social relations of interdependence, hierarchy, and debt that made business work. I began to think that what made these relations so threatening to the authorities was that they were imagined, in Battacharyya et al.'s words, 'to play by their own, different rules, and therefore to be acculturated within some other moral order or system of authority, embedded in an alternative and unknowable form of social organisation'. This provided the conviction that 'this alternative system should at the very least be visible to the state and the nation, facilitating an industry of interpreters, investigators, rehabilitators and enforcers, in a typical colonial/anthropological mode' (2021, p. 49).

This book offers an account of the lived experiences of young people and their families, the industry of professionals who now identify and respond to victims and perpetrators of modern slavery, and the forms of 'techno-moral governance' (Acosta, Bruun, and Koch, 2025) that are licensed in its wake. My intention is not to attribute malicious intentions to the professionals who are now tasked with the mandate to do good. Nor do I want to depict a picture of Foucauldian power relations that presents those engaged in anti-slavery efforts as passive conduits of disciplinary logics. And yet, like in Savannah Shange's study of 'carceral progressivism' (2020), I am interested in how allegedly progressive or social justice driven agendas end up reproducing punitive logics that come at the expense of the most marginalized populations. Thus, I explore how enemy logics that run through the law become replicated despite—and often because of—the good intentions of individual officers, lawyers, and judges. To be clear, when using the term 'enemy', I do not mean the same thing as 'criminal', although the two terms often overlap. As argued above, to speak of 'enemy logics' is to get at a deeper colonial logic that has consistently constructed certain racialized categories as the antithesis of justice and the nation, expanding martial logics by waging 'wars' on those populations on both external and internal fronts (Nijjar, 2018, 2022). Here, I explore how this logic of fighting the enemy within is resurrected and further deepened through a liberal discourse that is professing to safeguard, protect, and care.

As the book progresses, it will become clear how exactly these murky and contradictory practices echo colonial logics at the heart of the state. For one, as noted, the story of redeeming the vulnerable echoes a 'white saviour complex' (Kempadoo and Shih, 2022) that had been a central part of colonial 'civilising' missions. This white saviour complex is present when government rhetoric propagates a story that sees county lines drugs dealers as in need of saving from their own communities and kin. But colonial echoes are also central to the practices of techno-moral governance (Acosta, Bruun, and Koch, 2025) developed by officials who are mandated with the role to fight modern slavery today. As professionals step in to identify, safeguard, and police county lines as modern slavery, they do so in ways reminiscent of a colonial/anthropological mode of 'seeing like a state' (Scott, 1998) by rendering informal social relationships legible through the lens of pathos and crime. And finally, as I will argue in the final chapter, the very act of reviving the language of 'exploitation' and 'slavery' can be understood as an exercise in 'colonial aphasia' (Stoler, 2011) that further distances Britain from its own imperial histories of transatlantic slavery at a time when its political, legal, and economic institutions have come under widespread attack, and when racial justice movement members like Black

Lives Matter have pointed at the continuous existence of state violence and police racism today. At precisely the moment when the British state has embraced the fight against slavery on 'home soil', it has done so not to address its history of racial empire, less even its afterlives today, but to resurrect the image of the slave and their master in the bodies of Black, racialized, and working-class youth.

Let me come back to Glodi, the young man with whom I introduced this book. We saw that Glodi began working again for his old boss after being told that he had a debt to pay off. This time, in a sea-side town about eighty miles from London called Portsmouth, Glodi began 'holding' the line, that is, taking phone calls from drug users and directing them to runners who delivered the drugs. One day, when he was on his home estate in London, the police burst through the door (see the image at the front of the volume for a picture of Glodi on his estate). 'We are arresting you for human trafficking and drug dealing!' they told him. Glodi remembers how surprised he was. For him, human trafficking was about international people-smuggling—people being crowded into the back of lorries. This is not what he did, he was a drug dealer, working in a business with and for others. Yet, his fate was sealed. In 2016, while he was serving a long prison sentence for drugs charges that he had pleaded guilty to, he was charged with human trafficking offences too, alongside two co-defendants in what the government would consider its first ever 'test case' into modern slavery. A prolonged legal battle followed. In 2019, a conviction for human trafficking was secured. Precedent had been made: Glodi had gone from being a drug dealer whose history of dealing neatly fitted the 'exploited victim' or 'modern slave' designation, to become Britain's first ever human trafficker—effectively a 'slave master'—in a county lines case.

Ethnography, positionality, and advocacy-based research

In April 2018, I returned to my long-term field site—a place I call Park End, a large urban council estate of 13,000 residents located on the outskirts of a major town in southeast England, about an hour's drive from London (Koch 2018). I spent much time with Lindsey, a white, British working-class mother and community organizer, who had lived most of her life on the estate. One day, while sitting with a cup of tea around Lindsey's table in the kitchen, her phone rang. It was her sister Sue. Lindsey soon had tears streaming down her face. 'What will happen to you all now?' she whispered. When she hung up the phone, there was a long silence before she shared, 'My sister has spilled the beans'. Lindsey explained that her sister's fifteen-year-old son, a white boy named Lee, had been dealing drugs for the past couple of years on behalf of others. The people he was working for had sent him to different towns across the country to sell drugs, on occasion obliging him to carry a gun to guard the drugs. Lee was scared about just how serious his involvement with drugs had become, and had confided this fact to his mother. Terrified and not knowing how to help her son, his mother had gone to the police and told them about the gun. She now expected her son to be channelled into the criminal justice system but, as she had said to Lindsey, she would rather see Lee 'in prison than dying on the streets'.

And yet, Lee did not face the wrath of the criminal justice system—at least not yet. In the weeks that followed the phone call, we learned that the police were treating the 15-year-old boy as a victim of 'criminal exploitation' and as a 'modern slave' in need of protection. Lee was placed in the care of a 'multi-agency' team of social workers, law enforcement, and local authority workers. They would pay the family regular visits, pick up Lee 'for chats', and remain closely involved in the family's daily life. Less than a year after his disclosure to the police, the authorities moved Lee, together with his entire family, to a new house at the expense of the state, located about an hour's drive from Park End, and ostensibly for Lee's own protection. Lee's journey, which I followed mostly through his female family members, marked the beginning of a multi-sited, multi-scalar, and multi-network ethnography that took me from the families to the police stations and local authority offices to the courts and, throughout, back to the families, and to some of the young men who had been through the criminal justice system.

Due to the open-ended nature of this ethnography, it is difficult to add up the number of interlocutors I worked with, or the length of time I have spent with them. But to give at least a basic sense of the fieldwork, beginning in 2018 I have researched county lines through the lens of families like Lee's, including during a four-month stint in the Park End community that I had already lived in for a number of years in the past. In 2018, I also shadowed law enforcement officials and frontline workers in the same town, having obtained formal permission from the relevant government agencies to do so. From 2019 onwards, much of my research has been in London, identified by the government as the major hub of county lines export. There, I have worked closely with, and interviewed, law enforcement, frontline workers, politicians, experts trained in identifying modern slavery, and prosecution and defence lawyers. I also continued to be in close contact with, and reach out to new, families. Between 2018 and 2021, I followed six full-length trials in Crown Courts, spending a total of about twelve months in England's courts in Oxford, Portsmouth, and London; and from 2021 onwards, I monitored many more trials through the media. During the period of the global Covid-19 pandemic and its aftermath, much of the research (including court proceedings) took place virtually. Since I began working with families, some young men have also left the illicit economy and/or prison, thus making it easier for me to work with them.

Throughout this research, my own stable reference points have been my relationships with the women who are family members, often the mothers but also sisters or aunts, of the boys and young men who have been discovered as being at risk of exploitation in county lines. I have known some of these women for a long time, including Lee's family members, whom I first met in 2009. Others I met more recently, often through chance encounters at grassroots events. While the women come from all walks of life, they share some markers of identity: they have primary care duties for the young men involved in the illicit economy, are aged between their mid-thirties and fifties living in the country's deindustrialized neighbourhoods, with familial histories of migration located in Britain's colonial domination. My closest interlocutors included: Lindsey, a white woman, mother of mixed-heritage white British and South Asian children, and aunt to fifteen-year-old Lee; Lisa, a white British woman and mother of twenty-year-old, mixed-heritage white British and Caribbean T.; Tami, a Black woman of Caribbean descent who raised K.S., her sixteen-year-old younger half-brother, himself of mixed-heritage Caribbean and Nigerian descent, almost as her surrogate son; and Valerie, a Black woman of Caribbean descent and mother of twenty-five-year-old M. All of them share an experience of feeling virtually left alone with their children's exposure to, and dependence on, both the illicit economy and the criminal justice system.

It is appropriate at this point to say something about my own positionality. I do not claim to have any way of knowing what it feels like to be in the position of the families that I have become close to over the years; my own privileged life setting us in many ways apart. But there are also points of connection that I believe made the research possible and created enduring friendships. My gender and the fact that over the course of this research, I gave birth to my three sons, counted among those points of connection. Some also commented on my racial heritage. As a mixed heritage

Korean German and first-generation migrant to the UK, I too have had lifelong experiences of being racialized as other than the white majority. For at least some of the mothers that I worked with, the fact that, in the words of Tami, 'I have colour in me' meant that they felt able to share experiences that, she insisted, white people 'don't get'. In the highly sanctioned settings of the courts, my affiliation with the women and the children they cared for also meant that I became further racialized, such as when the court staff during K.S.'s murder trial insisted that I was a 'family member', and effectively banned me from returning to the court room. In Park End, my prior residence and friendship with people as well as the fact that my first book had been well received by the community meant that families welcomed me back in. I have described elsewhere what it meant to become accepted by and in a community that has been stigmatized for its multicultural working-class roots (Koch, 2018).

Most of all, I believe it was my commitment to not just compiling research, but to offering hands-on support and advocacy work that made much of this book possible. The disjuncture between the state's own narrative of redemption and the actual realities of the continuous failure to safeguard are most forcefully illustrated in the mothers' desperate attempts to get their children's stories heard. As an anthropologist who also holds a fully qualifying law degree, I was often more familiar with, and able to navigate, the legalistic jargon that can infuse professional language. As such, I frequently found myself helping family members write up 'case histories' of their children, putting pressure on professionals, or even just explaining the modern slavery policies to families who struggled to understand what was going on. Over time, this work became both more time-intensive and emotionally involved, as I found myself accompanying family members to formal meetings, sitting with them in court proceedings, doing prison advocacy work for their children, and getting involved in publicity work. I started introducing myself to professionals as an 'advocate' of the women and sometimes also of their children (where the latter had given me consent). As a legal term, the title of 'advocate' also had the added benefit of giving me access to bureaucratic and confidential files, something that was particularly helpful when interacting with prison institutions.

I think of this work as a kind of political labour in a situation where voicing criticisms of the government's 'modern slavery' policies is nearly impossible—a point that I return to in Chapter 8. And yet, doing such work can also backfire, not least on the families who I have tried to support. In Chapter 4, I describe how my and Tami's presence in the public gallery during the murder trial of her brother K.S. became an object of suspicion for the court, eventually leading to a court-imposed ban on attending the remainder of the trial under threat of arrest. Apart from the risks that this posed to us, Tami felt strongly that the court had achieved what they wanted all along: that is, to isolate the defendant, K.S., from any family support and hence critical witnesses during what she experienced as a deeply unfair trial. In another episode recounted in Chapter 8, my intervention on behalf of M., a twenty-five-year-old man serving a long prison sentence, was followed by the young man being 'informally' punished by guards on the prison wing. In Glodi's case, he found that he was suddenly recalled to prison in 2023 a few months after he had been released on license, having served half of his sentence. The recall also happened after I, alongside journalists and social media commentators, had contributed to his efforts to make his story known publicly.

There is no way of proving a causal relationship between my advocacy efforts and the state's targeting of the young men and/or their family members. At the very least, however, these examples illustrate, once more, the creeping authoritarianism that has accompanied the government's impetus to care, and hence directly engage the core arguments I explore in this book. They also raise urgent questions about the need to build solidarities from the bottom up. Once more, I return to these questions in Chapter 8. For now, I want to limit myself to one last note on anonymity. For reasons of protection, I have anonymized most individuals in this book. In some situations, this creates a certain awkwardness, such as when fictionalizing the names of legal professionals and defendants in publicly accessible trials. However, because my discussion combines trial notes with more personal and informal times spent with various individuals, this appeared necessary. When introducing the children that the women I worked with cared for, I followed the women's own practices of naming them, some by their (fictionalized) first names, others by their initials, yet others by their surnames. This creates a certain inconsistency in naming practices throughout this book; yet it is one that reflects the vernacular through which I first encountered them.

The only interlocutors that I have not anonymized are those whose media coverage I discuss in the book as well as, related to this, the individuals who appear in two trials, including defendants and lawyers. First, the defendants and lawyers in the trial of Miller and others that I discuss in Chapter 5 have not been anonymized. This is due to the fact that I also draw on media coverage of this trial to illustrate a broader point about how young men like Miller have been represented, stigmatized, and criminalized not just by the law, but in the wider social imagination. Second, due to the importance of the trial as a precedent-setting case and hence the impossibility of anonymizing it, I have also not used any fictional names for individuals who appear in Glodi's trial, with the exception of the victims identified by the prosecution in this case. However, in both of these instances, I have limited myself to my notes on publicly accessible court data, formal interviews with the individuals concerned, and a few very basic ethnographic snippages. As concerns Glodi himself, I have shared details of his story that were already in the public domain and/or checked with him that he is happy for me to write about them. While the result is undoubtably less than perfect, my hope is that at the very least the individuals identified feel comfortable with this outcome.

Chapter outline

This book tells the story of what happens when individuals previously criminalized as drug dealers are discovered as potential victims and slaves—and what this tells us about racial statecraft in an allegedly post-racial world. Chapter 2 provides the contextual backdrop for the remainder of the book. Contrary to the dominant story of newness, the discovery of 'modern slavery' on home soil was not unprecedented, nor did it come out of nowhere. Rather, it revived the saviourist logics of earlier neo-abolitionist efforts on the national political and legislative scene, as the British government's 'war on gangs' became repurposed to protect 'vulnerable' children from 'criminal exploitation', 'modern slavery', and 'human trafficking'. This shifting logic was further breathed into life by professionals who came to see themselves as protecting both their broader constituencies and vulnerable drug dealers from the exploitative acts of 'hard-core criminals'. And yet, the state's binary of victim and perpetrator, slave and trafficker, also breaks down when we turn to the voices of those caught up in the street-level economy of heroin and crack cocaine. I argue that far from constituting a neutral, less even a benevolent narrative, the story of 'saving' the vulnerable in contemporary Britan has resurrected a colonial logic of redemption that constructs Black, racialized, and working-class youth as in need of saving from themselves, for their own good.

Chapters 3 and 4 place this narrative of redemption in a broader political economy context, one in which the idea of criminal exploitation is contrasted to the structural exploitation endured by racialized working-class communities. These chapters foreground the voices and experiences of the boys, young men, and their closest female family members. Chapter 3 takes the reader back to where I was first introduced to 'modern slavery': to Park End, a deindustrialized social housing estate. In this community, decades of neo-liberal dispossession and the government's recent turn to austerity politics deepen a logic of racial extractivism that has long been exercised against its residents. Since many young people feel they have no choice but to enter the illicit economy, the welfare state's failure to offer a more sustainable pathway to young drug dealers and their families needs to be placed against this backdrop. Chapter 4 shifts the focus from the welfare state's failures to the workings of a deeply racist criminal justice system, which continues to criminalize young people as 'gang' members while attacking the mothers and female carers who fight on their behalf. At the heart of these two chapters is the social suffering confronted by those at the margins, and that bring into relief the workings of a disjunctive democracy that has extended a colour-blind narrative of justice and care while allowing substantive inequalities and racist injustices to flourish in its midst.

Chapters 5, 6, and 7 shift the ethnographic lens from the grassroots back to the 'industry' of professionals now tasked with identifying, acting upon, defending, and prosecuting those implicated in modern slavery. Chapter 5 is concerned with the array of frontline professionals who have the first duty of call. These professionals see the modern slavery agenda as a genuine opportunity to safeguard the most vulnerable. Yet, their efforts to distinguish slaves from perpetrators also introduce heightened forms of monitoring while generating racialized knowledge about 'suspect' communities even—or perhaps especially—where no formal crime has been committed. Chapter 6 moves from the front line to the criminal courts. Once more, for the defence lawyers with whom I worked, acting on the court's duty to prevent victims of human trafficking and modern slavery from suffering undue punishment offers an opportunity to protect their clients. But as different government bodies struggle to pin down what exploitation looks like, defence lawyers' attempts to get clients acquitted can also backfire. Taken together, the chapters argue that efforts to eradicate modern slavery can best be understood as exercises in 'techno-moral governance' (Bornstein and Sharma, 2016) that deepen, rather than alleviate, enemy logics at the heart of the law.

Like the frontline workers and the defence lawyers we encountered in the last two chapters, the prosecution lawyers and investigators to whom I turn in Chapter 7 were driven by a commitment to protect those they consider vulnerable to exploitation. This chapter examines the case that made precedent in English law: the conviction of Glodi, the young man introduced at the start of this chapter, alongside his co-defendants Karamera and Alford in what was the first-ever conviction of county lines dealers for human trafficking in a jury-led trial. While the case was widely celebrated as a landmark decision, my ethnography reveals a more complicated story. Focusing on the difficulties that the prosecution team faced in bringing the charges, I detail how investigative officers and prosecution lawyers not only struggled to graft singular logics of victims and perpetrators onto complicated social hierarchies, but changed their assessment of who was to be seen as a victim and who should be prosecuted for drugs and/or human trafficking. These difficulties were carried over into the trial, where phone data provided strangely sterile evidence in lieu of actual voices from the identified child victims. I argue that these challenges do not merely evince technical problems in prosecuting modern slavery cases. Instead, they bear witness to a political project-in-the-making: one that has resurrected the image of a new and ultimate enemy within. In Britain today, the impetus to protect vulnerable individuals has conjured the figure of the law's unfathomable 'other'—the modern-day slave master in the body of racialized and working-class youth.

Chapter 8 provides the concluding epilogue. In 2021, the UK government's Commission on Race and Ethnic Disparities claimed that institutional racism is a thing of the past. This statement came the year after global Black Lives Matter movements, sparked by the police murder of George Floyd in the US, challenged the enduring realities of police racism that are grounded in imperial histories of racial slavery and dispossession. In this concluding chapter, I argue that the discrepancy between the different understandings of 'racism' put forward by the government and social movement members respectively, encapsulates the key contradiction at the heart of this book: namely, the contradiction between the liberal anti-racism endorsed by the narrative of salvation at the heart of modern slavery policies, and the realities of state racism that continue to live on in the policing, safeguarding and prosecutions of communities caught up in 'county lines'. And yet, resistance is also possible. I return to three central narratives that have framed the book's analysis: the perspective of Glodi, the first young man to be convicted of human trafficking charges in a jury-led trial concerning county lines; that of the mothers and other female family members who fight on behalf of the boys and young men; and that of the ethnographer herself. Across these different domains, we can see a kind of counter-hegemonic political labour at work that functions as an everyday, lived, bottom-up critique of the state's liberal logic of salvation.

2
County Lines as Modern Slavery: Saving Vulnerable Communities 'From their Own Kind'

Introduction

In the spring of 2018, during a research trip back to my long-term fieldsite, a post-industrial council estate about an hour's drive from London (Koch, 2018), I found myself drawn to a controversy that was occupying this town's regional as well as the national media: the murder of Harun Jama. On 3 January 2018, the sixteen-year-old from Birmingham had been in Oxford, a middle-sized city located about seventy miles from his home. It was not his first visit: only a week prior, Harun had been arrested by Oxford police on suspicion of dealing drugs. A drugs package had been seized off him during the arrest, placing Harun in a drug debt 'to a gangster higher up the chain' for whom he had been dealing (Seaward, 2021). Now, Harun had come back to Oxford to pay off the debt by selling more drugs. He would never settle the debt. Around 7.45pm, Harun was found on a towpath of the river Isis near the centre of town. He had been stabbed multiple times. He was rushed into hospital but later pronounced dead. Three years later, an inquest determined that Harun had been unlawfully killed (Seaward, 2021). Nobody has, to this date, been charged for the killing (BBC, 2024; Norris 2024; Seaward, 2023).

The murder of this boy, a stranger to the town with apparently no local connections or friends, was the subject of much debate amongst frontline professionals, local authority workers, and police officers across the county. For them, the unexplained killing served as a reference point to talk about what they saw as the growing threat of 'county lines'. 'County lines' is the name given by the British government to what it sees as the expanding

Drugs, Race, and the Politics of Modern Slavery Law. Insa Lee Koch, Oxford University Press.
 DOI: 10.1093/9780198899631.003.0002

economy of heroin and crack cocaine spreading from cities to smaller market and coastal towns, due to a saturation of drugs markets in urban conurbations. It works by using runners—teenagers like Harun—who deliver, store, and sell the drugs directly to users, following the orders of others higher up in the chain, often under conditions of coercion and debt bondage. Since its discovery in 2015 (National Crime Agency, 2015), the government has argued that tens of thousands of young people are involved in this trade, generating an overall annual profit of over £800,000,000. Over a thousand different drugs lines were said to be in operation around the time when Harun was murdered (Ministry of Justice, 2019), though the most recent figures published by official law enforcement sources have placed the number of 'unique lines' at 6,644 (National County Lines Coordination Centre and National Police Chief's Council, 2024, p. 15).

When Harun's murder happened in 2018, the issue of county lines had begun to be extensively covered in the news as a national threat, seeping into public debate at a fast pace. One person who was instrumental in tabling county lines as the 'number one issue' in the town where I was doing my fieldwork was the local police force's so-called 'problem solving officer', itself a new role that had been created a few months prior to develop a more 'holistic' approach to problems of violence, drug dealing, and 'criminal exploitation'. This role was occupied by Laura, a white British officer in her thirties. Keen to speak to me about the challenges that Harun's death had brought to the forefront, she invited me to come 'and have a chat' in the back offices of the town's police station. I soon followed up and went to see Laura one morning. As soon as we sat down, Laura started talking: 'County lines are probably the biggest challenge we're facing', she said. 'The drug dealers are coming in from the big cities. You take one out, and another comes straight in, and it isn't in house anymore, they're travelling all over, and it is just becoming massive, and it's spiralling out of control. And with that, all the violence is increasing dramatically, they come with their firearms, their knives and swords'.

The case of Harun Jama was an illustration of this escalating crisis. As Laura continued to explain, the police strongly suspected that Harun was a victim of 'criminal exploitation' by county lines dealers who were forcing him to work off a drug debt. The police had received intelligence that he had been working for a drugs line coming from his home city, Birmingham, and the suspicion was that he had been killed by members of a rival drugs line who were defending their turf. Indeed, earlier in the day, before he was killed, Harun had been seen selling drugs to the homeless population in Oxford. Laura explained that the police—together with the support of other local agencies—had entered Harun into the government's mechanism for identifying modern slaves and victims of human trafficking, the so-called 'National Referral Mechanism' (NRM), a few months prior. The NRM is a bureaucratic body housed in the Home Office, Britain's border and law enforcement agency, that identifies and supports victims of modern slavery and human trafficking. At the time of Harun's death, the police had still been awaiting the final decision from the NRM as to whether Harun was a modern slave. Laura was confident that Harun was indeed a slave: 'He just ticks all the right boxes', she said, 'an unaccompanied minor, in a town he doesn't know, with drugs on him'.

Harun's status, suspended ambiguously in media and police talk between murder victim, potential slave, drug dealer, and 'gangster' from the city, intrigued me. It also provides a starting point for analysing the most recent shifts in the government's modern slavery agenda. In the last chapter, we saw that soon after the implementation of *The Modern Slavery Act 2015*, it became clear that the largest group of modern slaves discovered by official mechanisms today are boys and young men who have committed drugs crimes in what the government has identified as the expanding regional drugs trade of county lines: teenagers like Harun who deal drugs on behalf of others, often travelling to vicinities away from their home cities to sell drugs directly onto street users. These teenagers—and in some instances adults—are no longer considered 'gang' members to be policed under the government's 'war on gangs' but instead as victims in need of saving. And yet, this discovery of drug dealers as modern slaves begs many questions. How do we make sense of the discovery of modern slavery among urban, working-class, and racialized youth involved in the illicit street-level economy? What had to happen, in policy thinking and practice, to make it possible to reconceive of this demographic no longer 'just' as drug dealers, but as slaves in need of redemption? And what does the picture look like when we shift the focus from the perspective of professionals to the lived experiences of those now targeted as either slaves or their exploiters?

In this chapter, my aim is to unpack the 'making' of county lines drug dealers as both victims and perpetrators of modern slavery offences. To be clear, I do not wish to deny that the patterns of victimization now analysed under the labels of county lines, criminal exploitation, and modern slavery do not happen in real life, and the next chapters will discuss this in more depth. Rather, I am interested in the 'how' and the 'what': in how the county lines narrative became logical to think with, and what it tells us about the workings of state power. Contrary to the story of newness, the discovery of 'modern slavery' on home soil was not unprecedented, nor did it come out of nowhere. Rather, it brought the logic of earlier neo-abolitionist efforts to the national political and legislative scene, as the British government's 'war on gangs' was repurposed to incorporate a language of protecting vulnerable children from the 'criminal exploitation', 'slavery', and 'trafficking' committed by others from within their communities. And yet, the state's binary of victim and perpetrator, slave and trafficker, also breaks down when we turn to the voices of those caught up in the street-level economy of heroin and crack cocaine. I argue that far from constituting a neutral, less even a benevolent narrative, the story of 'saving' the vulnerable in contemporary Britan has resurrected a colonial logic of redemption that constructs Black, racialized, and working-class youth as in need of saving from themselves, for their own good, with dramatic consequences for those targeted by policing and legislative efforts.

Ethnographically, this chapter introduces some of the constituencies that I worked with, and that I will return to at different moments throughout this book: modern slavery trainers who are individuals typically with a background in policing or charity work who now train others to spot and respond to the signs of modern slavery; professionals who enforce and implement these policies 'at the front line'; and the young men who are themselves implicated in the illicit economy. I accessed the first cohort of professionals through snowballing techniques, usually at the hands of the professionals who had attended modern slavery training sessions. As for 'frontline' professionals, I draw upon a four months' stint of ethnographic research carried out with local government officials and law enforcement in a town identified as a major 'importing' hub for county lines activity coming from the cities of Birmingham and London (Chapter 5). I was given permission to shadow the local police force and local authority departments in 2018. Finally, I juxtapose these official narratives with the story of Glodi, the young man introduced at the start of the last chapter who, in 2019 and alongside his two co-defendants, became Britain's first-ever drug dealer to be convicted of human trafficking laws in a jury-led trial (Chapter 7). Before introducing my ethnography, however, I will first situate my account within the history of neo-abolitionist efforts on both the national and international scene, and how such efforts were revived in the government's repurposing of its 'war on gangs' on the domestic front.

A brief detour into the history of neo-abolitionist efforts: from 'white slavery' to the 'trafficked migrant'

Notwithstanding the language of newness that has subtended current policy narratives, initiatives that claim to eradicate human trafficking as modern slavery are not unprecedented (Kempadoo, Sanghera, and Pattanaik, 2005; Anderson, 2013, 2018; O'Connell Davidson, 2015, 2022; Brace and O'Connell Davidson, 2018; Kempadoo and Shih, 2022; Shih, 2023). The critical anti-trafficking literature has traced the origins of this 'neo-abolitionism', as I refer to these efforts here, to the period following the abolition of the transatlantic slave trade. Functioning as a disciplinary force deployed to maximize the exploitation of workers and repress resistance to capitalism, the slave trade saw a total of 10 million Africans forced on a deadly journey across the Atlantic. This trade in human beings was only abolished by Britain in 1807, and slavery itself in 1833, at a time when it had ceased to be as profitable and resistance from among slave colonies become rampant. Yet, the same Act that abolished slavery across the British empire also contained a provision for the financial compensation of slave owners for lost property. The British government borrowed £20 million to compensate its 46,000 slave owners, which amounted to 40 per cent of the Treasury's annual income. The loan was one of the largest in history, and the British taxpayer only paid off that debt in 2015. Enslaved people, by contrast, did not receive anything and moreover were compelled to provide forty-five hours of unpaid labour per week for their former masters, for a further four years.

It was within this context that neo-abolitionist efforts first emerged in Britain, marking what O'Connell Davidson has referred to as modern slavery's 'first apparition' (2016). Yet, concerns over the return of slavery did not target the former slave owners who had benefited from the compensation scheme. Nor did these efforts attack the 'coolie system', the system of indentured labour which was introduced to compensate for the loss of slave labour and which took workers from colonial India to the West Indies to power the expansion of extractive industries after the official end of slavery. Neither those 'who employed indentured labourers, nor the shipping companies, recruitment agencies, money lenders, and others involved in the state-sanctioned trade of moving them [through the coolie system]' were of concern to neo-abolitionists (2016, p. 59). Rather, fears of trafficking re-emerged in relation to individuals who moved without the permission of the state or a formal employer, clandestinely or not. The abolition of the transatlantic slave trade had also generated large scale displacements on a global scale, which coincided with the internationalization of wage labour. This included the movements of Indian and Chinese people within the British empire but outside the coolie system (Kempadoo, Sanghera, and Pattanaik, 2005, p. xii). It also included growing numbers of European women crossing borders in search of new opportunities.

In what constituted a repurposing of bourgeois imperial scripts around feminine sexuality, these people became imagined as 'masterless', 'dependent', and as 'unfit for full freedom', on account of their race or gender (Kempadoo, Sanghera, and Pattanaik, 2005; O'Connell Davidson, 2016). Policy and legislative efforts on the domestic scene soon came to focus on what is known in the literature as the problem of 'white slavery' (Bristow, 1977; Walkowitz, 1980; Gibson, 1986; Doezema, 1999). In a rhetorical move that not only denied the economic opportunities that European women were seeking, but conflated the diverse types of work pursued, white women who travelled, typically into the colonies (Fudge, 2025), became depicted as trafficked into prostitution, often at the behest of foreign men. References to the transatlantic slave trade were common, as 'the degraded black slave was replaced by the demoralized white woman' (Irwin, 1996). Between 1885 and 1912, Britain passed a string of statutes to control this traffic on the domestic arena. *The Criminal Law Amendment Act 1885* instituted a first definition of a trafficked woman. But it also increased the police's hold over the lives of working-class women (Walkowitz, 1980). As the focus began to shift from preserving the purity of respectable English girls to protecting 'the state and society from the threat posed by foreign girls' (Lammasniemi, 2017, p. 72), controlling immigration became key. *The Aliens Act 1905* marked the start of systematic immigration control. While primarily targeting Jewish migrants from Eastern Europe, it created complex 'powers of surveillance and repatriation over foreign women suspected of prostitution' (ibid: 73).

The frenzy over 'white slavery' also marked the beginnings of international cooperation, supported by Western European and US middle-class feminist reformists who sought to 'save' their 'fallen sisters' (Kempadoo, Sanghera, and Pattanaik, 2005, p. xi).[1] It did not last, however. After 1914,

[1] A 1921 League of Nations Report lamented the fact that 'women, for the most part underage, were engaged for lucrative posts and then always in complete ignorance of the abominable lot which awaited them, were transported to foreign countries and finally flung penniless into houses of debauchery' (League of Nations 1921, cited by Gallagher, 2010, p. 56). Between 1904 and 1933, four international conventions were passed with the aim of

European migration effectively halted due to World War I, and the 'white slavery' campaign lost its momentum. It would not be until the 1990s that concerns over trafficking resurfaced again, this time at the hands of international bodies such as the United Nations, and supported by a broad lobby of charities, philanthropists, businesses, churches, and Western feminists. This 'second apparition', as O'Connell Davidson has referred to the resurgence of anti-trafficking concerns (2016), happened once more in a context of heightened movement and displacements. Across much of the global north, the post-war democratic settlement had given way to neo-liberal policy making, resulting in widespread deindustrialization, outsourcing of manufacturing bases to the global south, and processes of 'accumulation by dispossession' that drove up global inequalities (Harvey, 2007). Forms of traffic that 'had formerly been sanctioned but closely controlled by the state [were now] deregulated' (O'Connell Davidson, 2016, p. 60), resulting in a massive upsurge of migration on a global scale. The end of the Cold War further added to increased mobility (as well as Western fears of uncontrolled migration), as formerly communist states opened their borders for the first time.

In this late twentieth century climate, prominent campaigners like Kevin Bales, co-founder of the organization *Free the Slave*—the American sister organization of the *UK's Anti-Slavery International*—came to insist that there 'are more slaves today than all the people stolen from Africa in the time of the transatlantic slave trade' (2012, p. 9). Just like in its earlier incarnation, anti-trafficking concerns had not focused on the structural exploitation and forced displacements within a system of global capitalism. This time, too, Western states did not consider cross-border traffic in people per se an immoral undertaking. After all, forces of globalization insist on free trade, while neo-liberal policies favour unqualified access by transnational corporations to natural resources and raw materials predominantly in the global south. Rather, the dominant discourse reinvented the problem of trafficking in the figure of the 'trafficked migrant' who had been exploited

suppressing 'white slave traffic'. The focus continued to be placed on deporting foreign prostitutes as a measure to reduce trafficking supply, with almost no attention given to the demand side of prostitution (Gallagher, 2010, p. 58). In 1949, the newly created United Nations consolidated its various instruments into a single document: the *Convention for the Suppression of the Traffic in Persons and the Exploitation of the Prostitution of Others*, a legally binding instrument that identified as a perpetrator anybody who 'to gratify the passions of another procures or exploits the prostitution . . . even with the consent of that person' (United Nations 194: Art. 1). This document also recognized men along women and children as potential victims.

at the hands of 'organized criminal networks' from the former East and the global south. In what Woods (2013) has described as a continuation of the 'colonial gaze' in the African context, not only were parents, village elders, and organized criminal networks identified as human traffickers, but entire nations reconceived of as exporting countries that stood in, once more, for the uncivilized other. Trafficking now also became linked to a broader set of issues, including money laundering, gun and drugs running, and people smuggling, all seen as a threat to the legitimate economies and political institutions of Western countries, and to their national sovereignty and security (O'Connell Davidson, 2015).

A number of international provisions were enacted in the early 2000s.[2] Of these, the *Protocol to prevent, suppress and punish trafficking in persons, especially women and children* (often referred to as the 'Palermo Protocol') provided the first international definition of trafficking as a process involving recruitment, transportation, and control organized for purposes of exploitation,[3] and has been described as the 'linchpin' of the global campaign to end modern slavery (Fudge, 2025). The stated purpose of the Palermo Protocol is threefold: to prevent and combat trafficking in person; to protect and assist victims of trafficking; and to promote and facilitate co-operation among states through mutual legal assistance and law enforcement co-operation (Legislative Guide cited by Gallagher, 2010, p. 79). In practice, the Protocol enhanced, first and foremost, state control and law enforcement powers. In the early 2000s, concerns over trafficking amplified with the attack on the Twin Towers and the ensuing 'war on terror'. As 9/11 became 'read as an even more direct and deathly threat to Western liberal democracy than "organized crime", terrorism was added to the bundle of

[2] This included the *UN Convention on Transnational Organized Crime*, which was adopted by General Assembly resolution 55/25 in 2000 and which replaced the 1949 United Nations Convention cited above, and three additional protocols: the *Protocol to prevent, suppress and punish trafficking in persons, especially women and children*; the *Protocol against smuggling of migrants by land, sea and air;* and the *Protocol against the Illicit Manufacturing of and Trafficking in Firearms, their parts and components and ammunition.*

[3] The definition of trafficking reads as follows: 'Trafficking in persons shall mean the recruitment, transportation, transfer, harbouring or receipt of persons, by means of the threat or use of force or other forms of coercion, of abduction, of fraud, of deception, of the abuse of power or of a position of vulnerability or of the giving or receiving of payments or benefits to achieve the consent of a person having control over another person, for the purpose of exploitation. Exploitation shall include, at a minimum, the exploitation of the prostitution of others or other forms of sexual exploitation, forced labour or services, slavery or practices similar to slavery, servitude or the removal of organs' (United Nations 2000: Art. 3a).

security threats supposedly presented by or linked to trafficking' (O'Connell Davidson, 2015, pp. 4–5). If human trafficking had previously been seen as a threat against a person, it now became explicitly viewed as a threat against the state, authorizing ever tougher immigration controls, stronger law enforcement, and greater powers for border guards (Anderson, 2013, 2018; Fudge, 2025; O'Connell Davidson, 2015).

The number of states making human trafficking a specific crime increased from 20 per cent in 2000 to 90 per cent in 2015 (Fudge, 2025: 38). In 2015, the UN also adopted the eradication of forced labour, human trafficking, and modern slavery by 2030 (Target 8.7. of its *Sustainable Development Goals*). This commitment on the part of the UN has been joined by an ever-growing proliferation of bodies—in both the public and the private sector—that profess to eradicate modern slavery, often framing these issues through a discourse around women's rights and human rights. As Fudge points out, the rhetoric is one of humanitarianism, even if the effect of these policies is to reinforce territorial sovereignty over national borders. But concerns over human trafficking have not remained confined to debates around national borders. As the next section will show, in contemporary Britain, human trafficking is no longer exclusively seen as a cross-border issue, but also as a grave crime on 'home ground'. I argue that like in earlier periods of slave-making, anti-trafficking efforts on the domestic front have revived a colonial logic of redemption as now young predominantly racialized and working-class youth are seen as in need of saving from themselves, for their own good, in the so-called crisis of 'county lines'.

'Anyone can be a slave': the slave on 'home ground'

'Hands up for those of you who think they know what a modern slave is!' Nicola's voice cut through the room. A silence followed, as the audience remained motionless, looking unsure of themselves. It was a warm morning in June 2018, and I was sitting at the back in the so-called judge's room, a dark, oak-panelled room with wooden tables in the Mayor's office, a heavy Edwardian building located in a Midlands town, and the same town where I had come across the murder of Harun Jama. I had come to attend the county's first ever modern slavery training session, delivered for frontline officials and local authority workers. Despite the sunshine outside, the leaded glass in the deep bay windows created a dim atmosphere, and the old paintings of military figures on the wall were a visceral reminder of how empire and the wealth amassed through the transatlantic slave trade and colonial endeavours continued to be interwoven into the first ever training session on 'modern slavery' run for the town's frontline professionals. And yet, this imperial history would only feature in its absence in the training session today. The training was funded by the local police force and delivered by Nicola, a white British woman in her thirties who worked for a domestic violence charity that had recently expanded its focus to 'modern slavery' and 'human trafficking'.

About thirty people were gathered in the room that morning, many of them white British women and men who worked across a number of law enforcement and safeguarding professions in the town: police officers dressed in their working uniform (though some were also dressed in civilian clothes), housing officials, social workers, probation officers, charity workers, two researchers including myself, and a Magistrate judge who was writing his doctoral thesis on the government's response to victims of modern slavery. Nicola greeted us with a bubbly smile, telling us how passionate she was about the topic. 'I can talk about modern slavery all day!' she exclaimed with a nervous laugh. 'It's my favorite conversation for a dinner party'. Turning more serious, she added that today we would be hearing about some pretty grim case studies. Humour was her coping strategy, and we should not be offended if she made jokes: 'When you don't use humor, you cry', she explained. To get us thinking about today's session, she continued, she wanted to invite us to join her on a brainstorming exercise. She asked, 'When you hear the word "human trafficking", what does that make you think of?'

After a few moments, the audience began shouting out keywords: 'Car washes! Women! Movement! Exploitation! Unwilling! Bondage!' Nicola nodded approvingly. 'What about modern slavery: what does that make you think of?' she continued. 'History', someone interjected. 'Yes, exactly! History!' Nicola repeated, her voice now trembling with excitement. 'It makes you think of your history lessons in school. People working in fields, chains, plantations . . . But you're wrong: and *that's why* we stuck the modern bit into it, to say it's different from old slavery. Today's training is not about history, it's about something that is happening in Britain today'. The room fell silent, as the audience was processing the information they had just been given. Nicola concluded her introductions with one last question: 'What nationality does "slavery" make you think of?' 'Albania!' 'Eastern Europe!' 'Somalia!' 'Sundanese!' 'Indian!' The answers started coming in. Nicola looked triumphant. 'Would you be surprised', she asked with a meaningful pause, 'if I tell you that the largest numbers of slaves are actually British?'

Nicola's introduction to the topic of the training was illustrative of a new moral and legal reality in the making: that of 'modern slavery' on 'home soil'. In Britain today, the issue of human trafficking—now recast as 'modern slavery' to give it a 'distinctly British inflexion' (Fudge, 2025: 165)—has been re-discovered as an urgent problem in need of fighting. This is not to say that human trafficking did not feature before on the domestic policy agenda: the UK had been an early signatory of the Palermo Protocol, and in the early 2000s, implemented a string of statutes that integrated human trafficking into immigration law.[4] Yet, the government's interest in human-trafficking issues remained relatively low in these years (cf. Anderson, 2013). In 2011, a newly elected Conservative-led government reluctantly adopted the 2011 *Council of Europe Convention on Action Against Trafficking in Human Beings,* feeling that it demanded too much in the way of victim protection (Fudge, 2025: 165). The same year, it published *Human Trafficking: The Government's Strategy*, which identified four priorities, including a renewed focus on prevention overseas, a stronger border at home, tougher action on the perpetrators, and better identification and care for victims. The role of the National Crime Agency (NCA), which would come into force in 2013, would be to connect and direct local, national, and overseas action to detect and disrupt human trafficking and to strengthen border arrangements. The stated goal was to stop 'illegal immigrants' before they got to the UK by putting in place a scheme at the visa application stage that would help identify victims and offenders (ibid.: 170).

Then, in 2013, a sea change happened. An influential right-leaning think tank called the Centre for Social Justice set the tone for a more expansive debate on human trafficking—no longer just as an cross-border crime but as a crime within Britain's borders. It published a report entitled 'It happens here: equipping the United Kingdom to fight modern slavery', which presented modern slavery as a grave crime encompassing human trafficking, slavery, servitude, and forced labour. Its preface stated that 'slavery

[4] The *Nationality, Immigration and Asylum Act 2002* introduced a set of offences of 'trafficking in prostitution' under s. 145, which would become incorporated into *The Sexual Offences Act 2003* and reframed as 'trafficking for sexual exploitation outside of prostitution'. This Act created growing awareness around labour trafficking (Anderson, 2013, p. 141). The emphasis of trafficking for purposes of prostitution changed with the *Asylum and Immigration Act 2004*, which introduced a new offence of 'trafficking people for exploitation', but it still retained its focus on trafficking as an immigration crime.

is the ultimate state of impoverishment', describing the 'hard-fought history' of 'a number of nineteenth-century British politicians [who] sought to abolish the international slave trade' as one of 'our Parliament's finest achievements'. And yet, 'the tragic trade continues on its destructive path. And it happens here'. The report argued that that the dominant policy construction of modern slavery as an immigration crime 'sends completely the wrong message': 'Increasingly we are seeing that UK nationals are also forced into modern slavery, without crossing any international border. Victims of modern slavery have had a crime committed against them and our response must be the same as it would be towards any other victim of crime, regardless of their country of origin' (ibid.: 12).

The report proved highly influential during the ensuing parliamentary debates, contributing to the setting up of a joint committee to consider a draft modern slavery bill, which became the *Modern Slavery Act* in 2015. The goal of the Act has been described as boosting the state's coercive power (Fudge, 2025: 177). It consolidated the existing legislation on human trafficking, divided modern slavery into a number of subcategories (which, alongside human trafficking also include domestic servitude, forced and compulsory labour, as well as confusingly, a standalone offence of modern slavery), and took it from the immigration context into the criminal law. With the passing of the legislation, the stage had been set for ever growing numbers of slaves to be discovered within Britain. In 2022, the National Referral Mechanism, the government's mechanism for recording trafficking victims and modern slaves, reported an all-time high of 16,938, with an additional 4,580 adults being entered into a separate system for suspected adult victims who did not consent to going through the NRM process. Dark figures are estimated to be much higher. For example, the anti-trafficking charity *Walk Free* which describes itself as an 'international human rights group focussed on the eradication of modern slavery, in all its forms, in our lifetime', stated that according to the 2023 Global Slavery Index, on any given day there are 122,000 people living in modern slavery in the UK.[5]

Like in the earlier moments of 'slave making', and as further unpacked in the next chapter, concerns over trafficking had become pressing at a time of social upheaval, marked by austerity politics, growing inequalities and,

[5] Walk Free https://www.walkfree.org/global-slavery-index/country-studies/united-kingdom/ [accessed 2 October 2024].

in 2016, the referendum on leaving the European Union. In this polarizing political climate, reviving the fight against modern slavery allowed the Conservative government to build cross-party political support and to reinforce 'a narrative of moral authority, liberty, and British exceptionalism' (Fudge, 2025: 169). Once more, like in the earlier discourse on human trafficking, exploitation did not refer to the structural conditions that the most disenfranchised communities confront at the hands of the market and the state. Rather, slavery was reconstructed as a grave interpersonal wrong emanating from within migrant and racialized working-class communities, and far worse than the transatlantic slave trade (in turn represented in highly anachronistic terms) would have ever been. This language was explicitly invoked by Kevin Hyland, then Independent Anti-Slavery Commissioner, a high-ranking government position created by the *Modern Slavery Act 2015*, when he told an audience of mostly middle-class professionals in 2018: '40 Million people across the world are suffering from modern slavery, people in London and in Congo . . . 13 million people were involved in the transatlantic slave trade. In our times, this is just in one day'.

The professionals I spent time with during my research similarly made a point of distinguishing what they called 'old' slavery from contemporary suffering. For example, at an online training workshop on modern slavery run for frontline professionals by the prominent anti-trafficking charity *Stop the Traffick Foundation*, Kate, our white trainer, showed us PowerPoint slides containing screenshots of newspaper headlines about modern slavery accompanied by images that she had taken from major newspapers, including the Guardian, the Evening Standard, the Mail Online, and the Sun. The images showed people in chains, their hands tied up—images that, as would become clear, Kate took to be representative of what she called 'old slavery', referencing the history of the transatlantic slave trade. Giving us a moment to take in these images, she asked: 'What do all of these pictures have in common?' She collected some answers from attendees before answering her own question:

> I could say what ties it all together—the pictures all show ropes, people with hands bound, chains. I am here to tell you that modern slavery doesn't look like this [a red 'X' appeared on top of the slide]. If there is one thing you take away from today, let it be this. Modern slavery doesn't look like this. There are some cases where people might be tied up, and physical strength used, but if you're being threatened or your family is or you believe you are trapped in debt bondage and if you work a bit harder

> then actually you will be able to pay off money you think you owe and be able to be free or send money home to family, those are the kinds of thing that keep people in place. There is no need for their hands to be bound. It's really depressing when the media shows these images—as long as we see modern slavery as this we don't see this.

Like in the earlier moments of neo-abolitionist efforts discussed above, the distinction drawn here between 'modern' and 'old' slavery served to relegate the transatlantic slave trade to some distant past, in some far away place, and to completely deny its integral connection to the exploitation of racialized bodies in the pursuit of capitalist and imperial interests. Common as this tendency is in the British public (Gilroy, 2005), it provided the backdrop against which 'new' slavery could be imagined as far worse, more widespread, and more urgent than 'old' slavery had ever been. Thus, unlike the old system of slavery which was in the open, and about 'plantations', 'shackles', and 'chains', modern slavery was presented as personal, intimate, and invisible. Modern slavery, I was told repeatedly, typically operates in the realm of psychological manipulation: a slave was a vulnerable person who had been taken advantage of by another under false pretences of money, comfort, friendship, or love. While physical coercion could be a part of the relationship too, the key to understanding modern slavery was its emotional hold. In fact, the most genuine slaves were those who did not even realize that they had been exploited; while a person who too readily asserted their own victimhood might be 'faking it'.

If victims did not know that they were victims, then the onus fell on those around them to identify and to save them. And this, in turn, created a duty to be 'vigilant'. Professionals explained to me that being vigilant meant to always be 'switched on' and 'present', to 'be mindful of the fact that things are not always what they seem', and to 'refuse to look away'. At modern slavery training sessions, attendants were instructed to be mindful of the possibility of modern slavery wherever they went: the person sitting next to you on a bus or in the train, the person serving you coffee or a meal in a restaurant, or the person washing your car at a car wash could be trafficked and exploited. The mantra of many professionals was 'to better be safe than sorry', even if this meant getting it wrong at times, or getting oneself involved in awkward situations—such as when a victim refused to accept their victimhood, and experienced the offer of redemption as an unwanted intrusion. As Nicola had told us during the training workshop: 'You get this a lot with Albanians for example who work at car washes . . . They will tell you this [their work situation] is better than anything they have ever had before, and that they don't want to give it up. They don't know any better'.

In short, in contemporary Britain, slavery has been discovered once more as an urgent threat facing the nation: this time not in the figure of the female 'white slave' or the 'trafficked migrant', but as the slave-as-anyone who has been trafficked and exploited within Britain. This is what modern slavery trainers emphasized again and again when insisting that 'slavery does not know any skin colour', that it is 'beyond nationality or race', and that 'it can affect anyone' (and indeed, at the modern slavery training session with Nicola, she would conclude the day by confessing to the room that she too had once become a slave when kept in an abusive relationship with her ex-husband). And yet, the story does not end here: for if according to modern slavery trainers and professionals, today anyone can be a slave, then the government has reported that the largest group of modern slaves today are those implicated in the illicit economy of 'county lines'. It is here that the government's previous 'war on gangs' has been repurposed into anti-trafficking initiatives and policing, giving rise, as I shall show, to a murky politics of redemption that now professes to save Black and minoritized working-class youth from themselves and their own good.

The county lines drug dealer as slave par excellence

It was a cold morning in January 2019. I was back in the same town where, more than six months earlier, I had first interviewed Laura about the murder of Harun Jama and heard law enforcement officials speak of the incoming threat of 'county lines'. This time, I had come to attend a parents' evening held to inform parents about the dangers of 'child criminal exploitation' in 'county lines'. The evening would be held in the large assembly hall of a secondary school located next to the town's largest council estate, a neighbourhood which had been blighted by industrial decline and which I'll call Park End (Koch, 2018). I had been invited to come along by Nick, a colleague of Laura's and a police officer working on outreach activities. He was also the school's allocated police officer, and he would regularly spend time on the school's site. Forty years old, balding, white, and usually dressed in plain clothes while on duty, Nick described himself as a 'middle-aged guy who doesn't have much street cred'. He was originally from a big city, but after an attack that he only narrowly survived and left him with lasting

PTSD, he had decided that he needed a change. This is what had brought him to the town, where he had started working for the local police force a few years back.

The evening of the event we drove together from the police station to the school in Nick's private car. Cramped in the back between two other officers who were joining the event, I listened to Nick tell us how passionate he was to address criminal exploitation in the town. He told me that the school we were driving to had recently seen an upsurge of children getting involved in county lines, often recruited by older people who were coming into town from other cities and picking up children from outside the school gates, driving them off in expensive cars. The children would often go missing for days, if not weeks, Nick explained, before being picked up by police sometimes hundreds of miles away in drug users' homes or on the streets. Nick felt strongly about the issue; the welfare of children was close to his heart and something that he felt personally invested in. He was keen to raise awareness around this issue so that parents would be more 'vigilant' and be able to 'spot the signs'. But more so he was passionate about changing the way that his own colleagues thought of these children, not as criminals but as victims who needed protection. Nick said. 'The key thing for me is [to understand] that the drug dealer might have been exploited and is actually a victim who needs safeguarding, even if he has committed a serious crimes'.

Nick's reflections on county lines, criminal exploitation, and the challenges that they posed to what he called 'traditional police culture' are representative of the most recent policy development in the modern slavery story: namely, the discovery of county lines drug dealers as modern slaves. As we saw in the last section, the *Modern Slavery Act* moved modern slavery out of the immigration context and into the domestic criminal law. Not long after the passing of the legislation, it became clear that the fastest growing group of slaves recorded by the NRM were individuals moving within the street-level economy of drugs: the so-called victims of criminal exploitation—often children—in the county lines drugs economy discovered by the government the same year that the *Modern Slavery Act* was enacted (National Crime Agency, 2015). In 2019, a cross-party review into the *Modern Slavery Act* argued that the number of potential victims identified in the UK had more than doubled in three years; and that the proportion of children identified had increased in the same period to nearly 45 per cent, in large part due to the rise in county lines and other forms of criminal exploitation (Home Office, 2019b). In 2024, the Centre for Social Justice published a high-profile report entitled 'Criminal exploitation: modern slavery by another name' arguing that criminal exploitation was by far the most prevalent type of modern slavery today and urging the government to amend the title of the *Modern Slavery Act* to 'Modern Slavery and Exploitation Act'.

Now, to understand how the connection between county lines, criminal exploitation, and modern slavery happened in policy thinking and policing practice, it is necessary to return to the government's prior 'war on gangs'. I will discuss the ramifications of the 'war on gangs' in more detail in Chapter 4. Suffice to say here that it had been implemented by the government in response to the civil uprisings that followed the police's killing of a young unarmed Black man named Mark Duggan on 4 August 2011.[6] While the uprisings were driven by complex reasons, including by deep-seated frustrations with police racism, austerity politics, and public sector cuts (Lewis et al., 2012)—issues I will turn to in the next two chapters—the government had solely placed blame with what it saw as a problem of 'gang and youth violence' emanating from inner-city housing estates. Its official policy enshrined in the *Ending Gang and Youth Violence Programme* or EGYV (HM Government, 2011) institutionalized a programme of greater police powers alongside closer collaborative working and information sharing between agencies, including those engaged in safeguarding, and resulting in ever more pre-emptive policing, surveillance, and targeting of Black working class youth (Koch, Williams, and Wroe, 2024; Nijjar 2018; 2022; Williams, 2015; Williams and Clarke, 2016).

In 2015, county lines entered the UK policy and policing agenda through the same institutional channels that were responsible for executing the government's anti-gangs strategies. A culmination of local 'problem profiling' and 'mapping' work carried out by local authorities under the EGYV programme was evaluated as 'highly significant' in identifying the 'emerging' phenomenon of county lines. A specialist team of experts had been seconded to the EGYV to build a picture of this 'emerging pattern of youth violence and drug trafficking'. In its baseline assessment, the NCA spoke of a 'growing body of intelligence, emerging in particular from London and

[6] As Day and McBean have pointed out, after Duggan's death, the police were supported by several institutions—the Independent Police Complaint's Commission, the media, and the political establishment—'to surround his death in confusion, if not lies' (2022, p. 40). Mark was presented as a 'gang member' in the media and a criminal with intent to cause imminent harm. A 2014 inquest found that Mark had not, as asserted by the police, been holding a gun when he was shot, but that regardless, his killing by an officer was lawful.

the South East [whereby] vulnerable young people are being exploited in order to facilitate the running of street level drug dealing'. In a follow-up briefing, the NCA suggested that thirty police forces were now experiencing these supply practices, with an additional five reporting county lines as an 'emergent crime' (2016). London was cited as the most popular 'exporting hub' (2016, p. 6). By 2017, NCA stated that they believed county lines to be a concern for all police forces across England and Wales, with 270 different groups said to be operating nationwide (National Crime Agency, 2017). This was believed to be a 'conservative estimate', and in 2018, the NCA confirmed that the number of known lines was around 2,000 (National Crime Agency, 2018; Spicer, 2020, pp. 27–28).

As county lines was elevated to the level of a national threat, policing responses to it became integrated into the government's anti-gang story. Crucial to this development was the idea of 'criminal exploitation' or 'child criminal exploitation', defined by the government as a situation 'where an individual or group takes advantage of an imbalance of power to coerce, control, manipulate or deceive a child or young person under the age of 18', 'even if the activity appears consensual' (HM Government, 2018, p. 48). The *Ending Gang and Youth Violence* programme was rebranded in 2016 to *Ending Gang Violence and Exploitation* programme or EGVE (HM Government, 2016). This set out what it called 'the new challenge: gang related exploitation of vulnerable young people and adults' (2016, p. 2). It named 'tackling county lines'—further specified as 'the exploitation of vulnerable people by a hard core of gang members to sell drugs'—as the top of its six priority areas (2016, pp. 2–6). Two years later, in 2018, the Home Office published a typology of modern slavery. Here 'criminal exploitation' was identified as a type of modern slavery, with county lines mentioned as its main modus operandi (Cooper et al., 2017, p. 35). The typology included a 'pen portrait' of criminal exploitation, namely where 'victims are forced to take part in gang-related criminality most commonly relating to drugs but also including knives and firearms . . . Gangs force victims who are often children and vulnerable young people to move drugs and money to and from the urban areas'.

Once the connection between county lines, criminal exploitation, and modern slavery had been made in policy thinking, it took on a reality of its own. Through the centring of county lines and criminal exploitation in the government's narrative of modern slavery, each experienced a ratcheting effect, with one reinforcing the language of exceptionalism and crisis that had been central to the other. As already noted, government sources started reporting an exponential increase in modern slaves due to county lines activity, further naturalized by the media, policy reports, and legal guidelines (e.g. Cooper et al., 2017a; Ofsted, 2018; The Centre for Crime and Justice and Justice and Care, 2024), and featuring in a growing body of academic commentary (Coomber and Moyle, 2018; Home Office, 2018; Ofsted, 2018; Robinson, McLean, and Densley, 2018; Stone, 2018; Ministry of Justice, 2019; Turner, 2019; Spicer, 2020; Spicer, Moyle, and Coomber, 2020; Windle, 2020; Centre for Social Justice and Justice&Care, 2024). In 2018, the government funnelled £3.6 million into the National County Lines Coordination Centre on top of funding already allocated to strengthen the law enforcement response through closer collaboration between police and multi-agency work. In 2019, the Home Office launched its *County Lines Programme* (2019a). The programme was buoyed with a £145 million investment for three years, on top of the £65 million invested to tackle what the Home Office called 'the most violent and exploitative distribution model yet seen'.

Modern slavery in county lines drug dealing did not just exist in the policy documents, reports, and funding structures of central government agencies, however. Police officers and other local authority workers on the ground had also begun to speak this language when I shadowed them in 2018 and 2019. Let me return to Laura, the police officer with whom I opened this chapter. The time she invited me to the back office in her police station to discuss the case of Harun Jama was also the start of a prolonged conversation about county lines. Indeed, the murder of this teenager, a stranger to Oxford with apparently no local connections and hence no reason for being there other than to supply the local population with drugs, was the subject of much debate amongst frontline officials, local authority workers, and police officers across the regional police force. While there were question marks around the circumstances of his murder, his death was commonly seen as a harbinger of a new form of evil that was coming from the big cities, and that was attributed to the saturation of drugs markets in the cities. What made county lines different from other modes of drugs trafficking, Laura explained to me, was that this was about venturing to new territories or areas—places like Oxford, where Harun had been murdered, and which, she believed, had historically been sheltered from 'city gangsters'.

Laura explained to me what the process of setting up a drugs line in the provinces looked like: as strangers to the localities in which they would turn up, the success of city dealers depended on, first and foremost, their ability to attract a new customer base among a highly volatile population of drug users who typically already had dealers who they relied on. An experienced drug dealer, perhaps in his early or mid-twenties, from a larger city would turn up in a town by car or public transport, and 'scope out the scene': he might 'hang out' in the town centre, which typically has a high density of drug users (particularly within the homeless population); he'll then approach users, to ask them 'if they are smokers' or 'want gear'. Typically, drugs would be offered for free on that first occasion, and drug users would be invited to bring 'all of their mates along' to also receive free drugs. In return, the dealer would ask for drug users' phone numbers and save them on the 'deal line' phone. Once given access to users' phone numbers, the drug dealer had secured his most valuable commodity: the contacts to whom he would advertise his drugs through his deal line by sending out 'marketing messages', or mass messages advertising his gear, including special deals: 'two for one', 'one for 10£, two for £15'. The dealer would then go back to the city to return with a bigger supply of drugs that would be sold to his newly recruited clients. This to-and-fro, connecting city and province, would become a regular trafficking route for both drugs and runners.

'These people are colonizers', is how another officer put it who had similarly explained to me the process of setting up a 'county lines' drugs line. He was not the only person who used the language of 'colonization', 'invasion', or 'conquering'. Racially loaded images of a *terra nullius*, or a savage state of nature, were repeatedly drawn on to describe how 'gangsters' from the city were taking over provincial places. Tyler has shown how, in the dominant British imagination, 'the "inner city" signifies a multicultural image of the nation fragmented by class and ethnicity' (2012, p. 5). This is encapsulated in the figure of the young Black man: hooded, masked, or pictured in mugshots, and involved in 'knife crime' (Bhattacharyya et al., 2021, p. 41). By contrast, the 'village' (and we can say, by extension the 'province') is associated with a 'white, rural, and essentially middle-class ideal of Englishness' (Tyler, 2012, p. 5). This was visualized in official police posters that presented incoming county lines as a racialized threat, while those at the receiving end were often depicted as white (see Figure 2.1). In the tales of colonization and conquest, drug dealers from the cities were routinely imagined as bringing violence, chaos, and even death to town populations who, in turn, became socially flattened: to local drug users whose properties were taken over for purposes of drug dealing and storing (in a process known as 'cuckooing'); to local teenagers who might be hired to carry out the drug dealing; and to the larger town population writ large imagined as middle class and innocent.

Figure 2.1. Posters produced by the National Crime Agency warning of the dangers of county lines. County lines is imagined as a racialized threat, with incoming city 'gangsters' imagined as Black, and town residents as white.
Source: © National Crime Agency.

Importantly, law enforcement did not just imagine town populations in the 'provinces' as victims. Teenagers from the cities like Harun Jama, who, on one account, were harbingers of evil could, on another, be re-imagined as victims too: as vulnerable individuals who had become caught up in exploitation, trafficking, and modern slavery at the hands of others higher up the chain. In fact, it was precisely the possibility of victimhood among urban drug dealers that served to further 'dangerize' them, for those inflicting the harm—a harm far worse than drug dealing—came from within their own circles. Like in the depictions of modern slaves we have already encountered, criminally exploited children were depicted as having been 'groomed' or 'brainwashed' under false pretences of money, luxury, or some social reward by those they had trusted; only to be subjected to coercion and drug bondage when they wanted to exit again. Their superiors—often only a few years older than the runners—were presented as cunning and ruthless, they would pick on their own friends or friends' children, neighbours, and 'looked-after children' (living in care), or those without parental authority or 'male role models' around them. As one police officer said, reflecting on a drug dealer he had come across:

> He would recruit kids from a young age. There was a kid living on a housing estate, year 5 [school year], he picked him out 'cos he was smart. There was no dad around, mum was struggling. He gives the boy money to buy [things]. The boy is recruited. Have you seen the Godfather, the

kind of Cosa Nostra type of guy? He is looking out for kids, turns up on the estate, says to the kids, 'Get yourselves an ice-cream, all of you'. Dee said: 'I used to go out of my way to help people. I didn't want anyone to snitch on me'.

These themes were brought home to me when attending the parents' evening that Nick had invited me to. During the event, Nick screened a film that he had co-produced with a young man he called Dee, a twenty-something year old who was currently serving a long prison sentence for drug dealing. Dee used to 'exploit children', according to Nick, but having recently had a baby daughter while in prison, 'he had decided to turn his life around' and had agreed to collaborate with the police to raise awareness around county lines. Shot inside a prison, the film featured the blurred-out figure of a young Black man sitting in a small, sparsely furnished room with a barred window. Dee's voice had been digitally altered to hide his identity, making him sound sinister. He began: 'If you are running away from authority, you run into a different sort of authority. A worse authority. It's gonna control your life. It's a game that has been set up. Everyone ends up dead or in jail. It's a game designed for us to lose'. Over the course of fifteen minutes, Dee relayed the horrors of county lines, using street language occasionally translated with subtitles. 'Youngers' [the young 'runners'] were recruited by 'elders' to do small favours, like 'being asked to buy clingfilm' [used to wrap up the drugs]. They might be asked to 'hold' things as well—'a stash down the road', some 'hard food' [Class A drugs]. Things would then typically take a more serious turn: 'youngers' would find themselves set up by their own 'elders', who would rob them of their drugs, thereby keeping the young runners chained to them through debt, and exposing them to violence. Dee concluded: 'It's always your best friend who becomes your worst enemy. It is a ticking time bomb. You're definitely gonna end up dead or in jail'.

It was precisely this idea that drug dealers might be criminally exploited that, in Nick's eyes, necessitated a protective stance where they had committed drugs offences. 'They need protection from themselves', is how Nick put it at the parents' evening, 'and our job is to make sure that we safeguard them'. Nick explained that as an institution, safeguarding did not come naturally to the police. 'Traditional police culture; the macho police culture that looks towards a scumbag is a scumbag is a criminal is a slag is a shit; so, anyone who commits an offence is automatically a toe-rag'. At the same time, Nick was also insistent that the 'cultural shift' he was advocating for was not one grounded in what he dismissively called 'liberal-leftie thinking'. Rather, if there was now a different mindset that recognized young drug dealers 'almost as a default position as a victim, not a criminal' who should be safeguarded, then this also, by the same breath, implied that their perpetrators, typically from within the same communities, could and should be punished severely for their unfathomable crimes. 'And those people', he said, 'we should prosecute now under the *Modern Slavery Act* because they have literally trafficked someone according to the letter of the law'.

'Trafficking someone according to the letter of the law'

Let me conclude by returning to Glodi, introduced in the last chapter, whose legal case answered Nick's plea to use modern slavery legislation to prosecute drug dealers who are seen to stand behind the 'trafficking' and 'criminal exploitation' for more than just a drugs crime. In 2019, Glodi, alongside two co-defendants, was the first county lines dealer to be convicted in a jury-led trial for human-trafficking charges. His case made precedent in English law, proving that it was indeed possible to prosecute drug dealers for modern slavery offences, elevating 'exploitation' and 'trafficking' over and above any drugs charges. I first met Glodi, then aged twenty-nine, in January 2023, a few months after he had been released from prison, having served half of his sentence. He was in some ways no stranger to me: I had followed the entirety of his trial in 2019 (Chapter 7), when the lead prosecutor invited me to the proceedings after a mutual colleague had put us in touch. Yet, until 2023, we had never spoken. During the trial, court rules prevented me from reaching out to him. After his conviction, my efforts to speak to him in prison had remained unsuccessful. Eventually, Selam Gebrekidan, a friend and investigative journalist who I had told about Glodi, managed to reach him after much effort. Her story, published in the *New York Times* (2022), and shortly after Glodi came out of prison, would become Glodi's first positive press coverage. Glodi and I met a couple of months later.

The day Glodi and I met on a January afternoon in 2023 marked the beginning of a friendship, facilitated by Glodi's easy way of being and his sense of humour. As we got to know each other better, Glodi would share details about his life that were not put before the court during his human-trafficking trial. From the age of fifteen, when he was arrested with drugs the first time, he had spent the majority of his life in confined institutions. His first experience in Cookham Wood, a youth detention facility notorious for its high levels of inmate and staff violence and multiple failings, was rough. One time, he had his head smashed into a wall by a prison officer, a blow that knocked him unconscious. There was no CCTV on the landing where the incident had taken place, and no one was ever held accountable. When Glodi came out of prison aged eighteen, he was desperate to move on. Yet, as we saw in the last chapter, his old boss, for whom he used to deal, told him that he had a sizeable debt to pay off for the drugs and money that the police had seized off him during his arrest. His boss, who appreciated Glodi for never having 'snitched on him', offered him a deal: this time Glodi would not be the one running drugs on the street; he would hold the main phone deal line for a drugs line called the 'Fly line' that was delivering to Portsmouth, a seaside town south of London.

Now, as the main line holder, Glodi would keep his phone on, take calls from drug users, and pass on the requests to the runners and direct them where to go for the hand-to-hand deals with users. While this was his main responsibility, like many other young men in his position (see Chapter 3), Glodi would occasionally do other jobs. On one occasion, when his boss was short of runners, he was asked to take drugs down to Portsmouth himself. Glodi stayed for the night. While guarding the drugs in a user's flat, rivals overpowered him, attacked him with knives, and left him bleeding on the floor. Glodi did not dare call the ambulance for fear of police attention; he could not afford to lose the drugs again. He managed to call his boss before passing out; his boss would send someone from London, an hour and a half drive's away, to attend to give him medical treatment and to attend to his wounds. On another occasion, his boss asked Glodi to meet M.W., an individual who had expressed interest in working for him. Glodi remembered how confident M.W. had appeared the day they met up on a South London estate, not far from where Glodi had grown up: M.W. had come with two friends and was bantering with them the entire time. The first time M.W. was sent to Portsmouth, Glodi went with him to show him around. Glodi then went back to taking calls from drug users, telling M.W. how much of the drugs to bring, how much to charge, and where to take the drugs.

Around 5am on a September morning in 2014, when Glodi was at home in bed, armed police broke through his door. The house was full of drug paraphernalia, including a hydraulic press, scales, and mixing bowls, as well as the mobile phone advertising drugs to users. He was handcuffed, and informed that he would be arrested for drugs and human trafficking, and

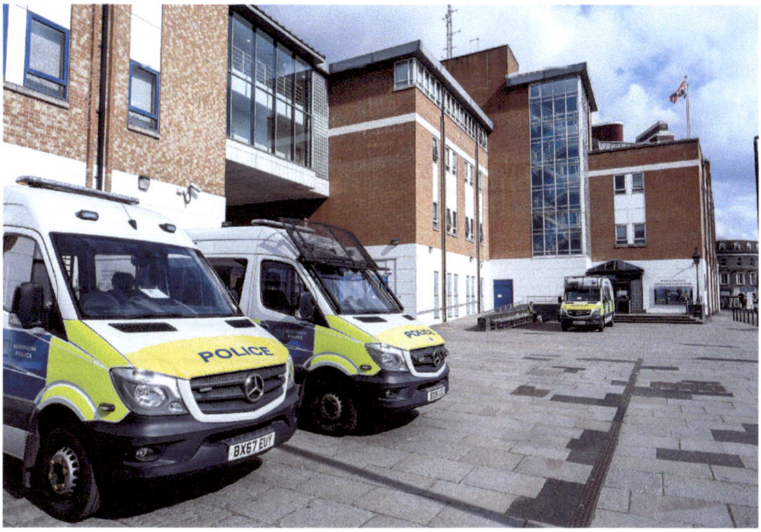

Figure 2.2. Lewisham Police Station, Europe's largest police station and the place where Glodi was taken into custody after being arrested.
Source: © Reece Grant 2025.

taken to Lewisham Police station, Europe's largest police station, as featured in figures 2.2 and 2.3. below. Initially, only the drugs trial went ahead. Glodi was one of fifteen co-defendants to be charged for conspiracy to supply Class A drugs. He pleaded guilty at the outset and was sentenced to five years. In 2016, while he was in prison, Glodi was charged with human trafficking. In 2017 (and while still waiting for his human trafficking trial), he was allowed out of prison on bail. Reflecting on this period of his life, Glodi remembered how low he felt upon his release. 'I had decided to change my life when I was back in prison again. But when I came out, I had to move back to my mum's house, she had downsized, there was no room for me, and reality sat in quick. I was still signing on at the police station twice a week, had very strict license conditions, couldn't get a legitimate job, and I just felt like "what's the point of it all"'. While on bail for human trafficking, Glodi went back to dealing drugs. In 2018, barely a year after being released on bail, he was seen by police exiting a drugs property in Aberdeen, Scotland, and was arrested. Glodi pleaded guilty in front of a judge in Edinburgh, and was given eight years. This was his third time in prison.

In 2019, Glodi was in court for the trial of his final and outstanding human trafficking charge, alongside two co-defendants, Michael Karamera and Dean Alford. The prosecution told the court that together, between

Figure 2.3. Glodi calling the custody line inside Lewisham Police Station.
Source: © Reece Grant 2025.

2013 and 2014, the three defendants had trafficked six teenagers and one vulnerable adult from London to Portsmouth with a view to exploiting them. Glodi was accused of having trafficked one of the youths in question: M.W., the same youth that Glodi had met years earlier at his bosses' request, accompanying him to Portsmouth before supervising his street deals and directing him to customers from a distance. Until now, Glodi had always pleaded guilty to every charge. But this time, he was adamant that he would be pleading not guilty. And he would not change his mind, even when his co-defendants, halfway through the trial, entered a late guilty plea. Much later, in 2025, he would tell me why he had not pleaded guilty: 'I put my hands up when I know I have done something wrong', he said. 'But with this charge, I felt that the government, they built this picture of me, and it wasn't right, and I wanted to tell my own story. Yes, I am not a saint, yes, I went to jail, yes, I am a criminal, but there's a reason for these actions'.

The trial took place in Inner London Crown Court, after several collapsed trials that I describe further in Chapter 7. Glodi soon learned what, on the prosecution's account, had turned him from an ordinary drugs dealer into a human trafficker: the step had happened when he became the line operator for the 'Fly line', taking phone orders from drug users and dispatching them to runners to carry out the street deals, rather than being the person running the drugs on the streets himself. M.W., the youth that he was accused by prosecution of having trafficked with a view of exploiting him, refused to act as a prosecution witness. The court was shown phone traffic involving hundreds of phone messages exchanged between the phone attributed to Glodi and that of M.W., all of which was evidence of Glodi's coercive and controlling behaviour, according to the prosecution. The fact that M.W. had agreed to sell the drugs; that he had travelled to Portsmouth on his own accord; and that, in his own statement to the police, he 'knew exactly what he was doing' did not matter: consent is no defence to the offence of modern slavery, and the legislation, as prosecution reminded the court, had been designed 'to protect vulnerable people from themselves'. The prosecution's perspective was that there was no 'boss' that Glodi had been indebted to and was working for; Glodi himself *was* the boss. He was convicted.

As I describe in Chapter 7, the conviction was celebrated in the media as a precedent-setting case, one proving that county lines drug dealers could indeed be prosecuted successfully for modern slavery charges (BBC, 2019; Guardian, 2019). It was only in the years to come that Glodi was able to tell a different story in the news (Gebrekidan, 2022; Garcia, 2024) and on social media.[7] In the hours we have spent talking about his trial history, Glodi has never wanted sympathy. But he does not see how his own story is all that different from that of M. W., who the police had readily identified as his victim, indeed as his own trafficked slave. As he once said to me:

> M. W. was transporting drugs on my behalf and that of others, I don't deny that. But they said I trafficked him. *I wasn't just a drug dealer*

[7] See for example https://www.youtube.com/watch?v=E0OXBcrIu1s [accessed 3 March 2025].

> *anymore, I was a human trafficker in their eyes.* It's still difficult for me to get my head around the fact. I went to prison when I was fifteen for selling drugs and no one ever said that I was trafficked or a victim. So I didn't understand that what I had done [with respect to M.W.] was wrong, I wasn't sitting there thinking 'oh my god this is terrible, he was 17, I was 20', I was thinking 'I done this when I was younger, when I was a kid, no one ever said I was vulnerable'. My dad used to report me missing all the time before I went to jail, no one cared, no one even came looking for me, so why should I have the mindset of thinking I have done something wrong? [my emphasis]

It may be possible to put the differences in the police's treatment of a young teenage Glodi down to timing. When Glodi was dealing drugs as a fifteen-year-old runner, this was still years before the government would discover county lines, and even longer before they would connect county lines drug dealing to modern slavery. And yet, we can argue that even twenty-one-year-old Glodi who was charged with human trafficking was still not all that different from sixteen-year-old M.W.: Glodi, on his own account, was still at the bottom rung of a multibillion-pounds drugs industry (holding the phone line as opposed to running the drugs); he had a boss to answer to; and he was doing the work that he was directed to do. Perhaps more so, and again on his own account, he had a drug debt to pay off and that was the reason why he had gone back into drug dealing in the first place. Like Harun Jama, then, the sixteen-year-old boy from Birmingham who was murdered in 2018 before being identified as a modern slave, Glodi had not been free to walk away. Glodi, M.W., and Harun were all working-class and racialized youth or young men who, at different points in time, were involved in the street-level economy of heroin and crack cocaine, performing a number of roles on behalf of others: holding the phone, delivering drugs, and guarding drugs from rivals, with lethal and near lethal consequences.

The difficulty of upholding a clear binary of victims and perpetrators in county lines cases has been pointed out in the literature (e.g. Carvalho et al., 2025; McLean et al., 2020; Moyle, 2019; Marshall, 2024; Wroe, 2021). When I pushed them, law enforcement too were willing to admit that the line between victims and perpetrators could be vanishingly thin. 'The trouble is that it's not black and white', is how Nick, the police officer, put it. 'It's different shades of grey. And you can go back from being an offender back to being a victim to being an offender, too'. Indeed, we have seen this ambiguity in the case of Harun who, on some accounts, appeared as a victim of criminal exploitation, and on others signified a harbinger of evil as he had come from the big city to bring drugs to Oxford, imagined as innocent and law abiding. But if officials were willing to acknowledge the complexities of these cases, then we have also seen that modern slavery trainers—whose remit now also includes victims of criminal exploitation in county lines cases—insisted that with the right amount of professional training and 'vigilance', it was possible to determine with accuracy on which side of the coin an individual fell. Indeed, this vigilance implied that drug dealers like Glodi, Harun, or M.W. should not be believed: their own words and depictions of the complicated circumstances and dynamics including those of friendship, debt bondage, and social hierarchies that defined their role and status in the drugs business, were deemed immaterial in a situation where vulnerable victims were believed to 'need protection from themselves'.

For virtually all professionals I spoke to, this overarching emphasis on protection indicated a move away from the government's 'war on gangs' and its harsh drugs policing and prosecution towards safeguarding and care. My suggestion, however, is a different one. I would argue that the difficulties of distinguishing victims from perpetrators, or slaves from traffickers, reflect the inherently fraught nature of neo-abolitionist efforts that have constructed modern slavery as an interpersonal wrong, removed from structural conditions and disconnected from Britain's imperial past. Thus, today, the discovery of slaves in the bodies of exploited drugs runners who would have previously been caught under anti-gangs policing has gone hand-in-hand with the discovery of their exploiters and traffickers, who typically emanate from within the same communities, are often their friends or acquaintances and only a few years older than the so-called slaves. Here, enemy logics that have long targeted Black, minoritized, and racialized youth as the law's constitutive 'other' have been amplified and more deeply entrenched, as the expansion of victimhood has gone hand-in-hand with the doubling-down of the punishment of their perpetrators as slave masters. If, in Bhattacharyya et al.'s words, the fear in dominant constructions of county lines policing is 'that black criminality is migrating out of black urban enclaves and spreading, virus-like, into unsuspecting parts of the country' (2021, p. 33), then the same communities become further dangerized by constructing them as vulnerable to exploitation from 'within'.

Judged from this perspective, the discovery of 'modern slavery' in the figure of the exploited drugs runner and their trafficker loses its neutral, benevolent fold. Rather, it revives a colonial logic of saviourism already central to earlier neo-abolitionist efforts (Kempadoo, Sanghera, and

Pattanaik, 2005; O'Connell Davidson, 2022) and that has repeatedly justified the use of state violence against racialized and working-class communities in the name of protecting them from their own kind (Abu-Lughod, 2002; Day and McBean, 2022; Kempadoo and Shih, 2022) 'Take up the White Man's burden', Rudyard Kipling exhorted in 1899, 'to serve your captives' needs'. We can see this narrative of redemption at work, when government bodies declare that modern slavery is a unique moral wrong and locate it within racialized and working-class communities; when an industry of professionals professes to protect the most vulnerable (even against the latter's own wishes); and when law enforcement promises to 'go tough' on those believed to stand behind these crimes in the name of doing good. And yet, as Glodi's perspective has shown, this narrative is not uncontested. In the next two chapters, I will discuss how the voices of young people and their families challenge the official story of redemption by bringing into focus the social suffering that they experience at the hands of multiple structural forces across the state's victim/perpetrator divide. Taken together, these chapters reveal the workings of a deeply disjunctive democracy that has extended a colour-blind narrative of care while allowing substantive and racial injustices to flourish in its midst.

3
'Hood Economics': Drug Dealing, State Failures, and Social Suffering

Introduction

When I returned to Park End, a post-industrial council estate on the edges of the town that I introduced in the last chapter, my intention had not been to study 'modern slavery' or 'county lines'. On the contrary, I had come back to my long-term fieldsite because I wanted to better understand how daily life on the estate had changed under the weight of austerity politics implemented by a Conservative-led government after its election into power in 2010. I had been away for three years, having last visited the estate in 2015, when many of the government's far-reaching public-sector cuts and welfare reforms had only just started hitting home. People were still expecting the worst to come from these reforms, implemented in the name of remedying a public deficit. In the first few days of being back on the estate, Lindsey, a white working-class woman, mother of three, and a long-standing community organizer on the estate, offered to take me on a walking tour of the neighbourhood, including to the informal community centre where I had volunteered back in 2009. 'Things have gotten really bad here since you left', Lindsey said when we set out that sunny July morning. 'We are struggling to keep things going'.

I quickly got a sense of what she meant. The community centre was located in the middle of the estate, a concrete block built in the 1960s that residents had often proudly described to me as the 'heart' of their estate. Once a place hosting a range of public services, from free cups of tea to a credit union offering low-interest loans to those deemed credit unworthy by the bigger banks (often because they were benefit recipients), the building was largely empty now. Lindsey explained that cuts in services meant there was not enough money left to run the drop-in centre anymore. The credit union was still open a couple of days a week, but faced a major crisis because residents were defaulting on their community loan payments, with more

Drugs, Race, and the Politics of Modern Slavery Law. Insa Lee Koch, Oxford University Press.
 DOI: 10.1093/9780198899631.003.0003

people than ever facing unemployment and economic hardship. Many of the community groups that had once made use of the centre's large hall for their meetings were also gone; they simply could not afford the subsidized rent for the hall that was owned by the local authority anymore. This included a self-help group for recovering drug users; a networking group for parents with little children; and a group of elderly residents who met once a week for a cup of tea and a game of bingo.

Next, Lindsey took me across the road to where the youth centre stood. Where once the voices, laughter, and play fighting of children of all ages could be heard, there was now an eerie silence. This formerly free-for-all service had been turned into a 'watered down needs-based service', as Lindsey put it, for the selected few. Now, to access local authority-run youth services, one usually had to be deemed difficult: 'But who wants to attend the centre if you are outed as a problem family?' she asked me, bitterly. 'Our young people have nowhere to go, and the government wonders why [they] get sucked into crime'. Our next stop, about twenty meters up from the old youth club, was the local church, built in the 1960s and used by the Caribbean, African, and white communities for worshipping, christenings, weddings, and funerals. That day, however, the main door to the building was barricaded. 'We can no longer use the hall for worshipping', Lindsey said. 'The roof is leaking, and it has been deemed structurally unsafe. Nobody can give money for it, so it remains shut'. Our last stop for the day was the local library, a concrete block built opposite the church that many residents used to access computer facilities. Lindsey thought they were lucky that, unlike many other libraries that had shut down as part of the government's austerity politics, this one was still operating at a reduced service level. 'But they can still take it away anytime', she added.

Lindsey's walking tour through the heart of the estate—its community centre, youth club, church, and library—was marked by the visceral effects of austerity coined so powerfully by Robinson and Sheldon as a spectre of abandonment (2019). Here, vital spaces of social reproduction have been virtually abandoned by the state as resources have been cut, previously universal and free services been degraded into means-tested forms of assistance, and community buildings left to face infrastructural neglect. In the years that followed, things would only get worse. The community centre would first shut down and then be demolished altogether in favour of new accommodations in the name of regeneration. For the residents of Park End, the reduction in community and welfare services alongside the closing down of vital infrastructure was, though painful, not altogether new: it made sense to them as part of a much longer trajectory of state-led dispossession that, over the past few decades, has systematically turned Britain's increasingly post-industrial neighbourhoods into places of disinvestment, welfare withdrawal, and, at times, displacement by gentrification (Dench, Gavron, and Young, 2006; Hanley, 2007; Rogaly and Taylor, 2009; Koch, 2018; Willis, 2023).

Here, I take these experiences of state-induced loss and withdrawal of provisions and services as my point of departure to ask: What are the effects of austerity and neo-liberal dispossession on the lives of working-class families like Lindsey's and, in particular, on their teenage children and young adults? How do the structural exclusions faced by young people cut across the rigid boundaries of victim and perpetrator, slave and trafficker, invoked by state policies and the law? What do state efforts to lift young people out of the illicit economy accomplish in a context where resources are limited and funding for welfare has been cut? And what does this tell us about the logic of redemption that professes to care for the most vulnerable? In the last chapter, I critically unpacked the government's narrative of county lines as modern slavery, and the alleged benevolence that it implies in policy thinking. I argued that the 'making' of county lines dealers as slaves and exploiters hinges on an idea of suffering 'from within'—central to the idea of 'criminal exploitation'—that portrays Black, minoritized, and working-class communities as in need of saving both for their own good and from their own kind. And yet, we also saw that the tale of redemption breaks down in the face of stories like Glodi's; he was the first county lines dealer to have been found guilty in a jury-led trial of human trafficking offences. On his account, his experiences growing up in one of Britain's deindustrialized neighbourhoods and becoming implicated in the street-level economy were not all that different from those whom the state has classed as victims.

Building on such experiences, this chapter moves from examining the state's narrative of redemption to centring those now identified as both victims and perpetrators. To do so, I begin with a fact, so forcefully illustrated in Lindsey's walking tour, that has not featured in public debate: that the same government that discovered street-level drug dealers as potential slaves in need of state protection has also driven inequality to 'peak levels' (Dorling, 2018) through its public sector cuts on top of decades of neo-liberal welfare withdrawal and industrial decline. I share the stories of several young people who became involved at the lowest rung of the street-level drugs economy. While motivated by their hopes for access to money and social rewards, they also have had to reckon with dangerous, unpredictable, and harsh conditions. And yet, state interventions designed to lift drug dealers out of the illicit economy were also experienced by their families as attempts to 'set them up to fail'. I argue that these experiences bring into sharp relief the 'social suffering' confronted by those at the margins (Kleinman, 1997; Das et al., 2000, 2001), a situation that needs to be understood as part of a colonial continuum that also includes a history of racial extractivism and welfare exclusion, and its imperial roots. As such, social suffering illuminates the workings of a deeply disjunctive democracy that has formally extended a narrative of care while allowing substantive inequalities to flourish.

Ethnographically, I focus on the voices and experiences of young people and their family members. I draw upon my long-term relationships with families on Park End estate (Koch, 2018), a neighbourhood on the edges of a town that the authorities have discovered as a primary target for county lines activity and that is situated about five miles from the police station where many of the officers introduced in the last chapter worked. Over the years, I have seen young people in this community come to age, and listened to the worries of close friends as they have seen their children become involved in the illicit economy of Class A drugs. It is precisely my long-term involvement in the community that allows me to analyse county lines through the lens of structural inequalities. In addition, I draw upon fieldwork, mostly conducted between 2018 and 2022 while attending public events and conferences with 'reformed' dealers who typically work as youth workers, community organizers, or public speakers. While I have no doubt that narratives of their past involvement in the street economy have been carefully curated for the largely professional audiences that they face in these moments, I believe that my more informal knowledge of the social biographies of these young men and their family members helps me place former dealers' stories in context. Before I get to their stories, however, let me first situate the debate.

Racial extraction, welfare withdrawal, and social suffering on Britain's estates

Lindsey's walking tour of Park End was a small window into the realities of the dispossession and neglect experienced by those living in Britain's multiracial and working-class low-income neighbourhoods. These neighbourhoods, dotted around the country in areas where manufacturing bases once stood, constitute spaces of what Loic Wacquant has called 'advanced marginality', defined as 'the novel regime of socio-spatial relegation and exclusionary closure . . . that has crystallised in the post-Fordist city as a result of the uneven development of the capitalist economies and the recoiling of welfare states' (2008, pp. 2–3). In Britain, chief among these spaces are its post-industrial council estates ('estates'), found often in inner cities but also in urban peripheries and rural areas across the country. Built largely in the post-war decades as housing for the then-Fordist working classes, estates were once seen as an emblem of an inclusive welfare state that cared for its citizens 'from the cradle to the grave' (Timmins, 2017). This was always a grossly oversimplified depiction (Koch, 2018), for it not only failed to acknowledge how the consolidation of the British welfare state coincided with the systematic dismantling of the British empire but was also shaped in significant ways by the racial structures of empire that preceded it (Bhambra, 2022; Danewid, 2023).

Bhambra has provided a comprehensive analysis of these dynamics and their enduring legacy on social structures in the post-war welfare state. Focusing on the case of nineteenth century colonial India, she has shown how relations of racial extraction that bound India to the British polity—chiefly through taxation—did not translate into redistribution for colonized people, but were channelled back into the British nation. This 'imperial dividend' further continued after the formal end of empire. Thus, with respect to the newly independent countries, Britain wrote down the debt it owed to them, appropriated the dollar-earnings of its remaining colonies, and subordinated the economic development requirements of those colonies to its own national needs. But on the domestic front too, the 'national project' at the heart of Britain's post-war welfare state was realized through differential access to social citizenship. As I have shown elsewhere (Koch, 2018), the post-war British welfare state was premised on the model of the white male British breadwinner. Many of the most vulnerable communities were hence prevented from accessing public welfare, including homeless people, traveller communities, as well as migrants from former colonies who had come to Britain to help build its post-war economy,[1] performing the labour that the indigenous population were often unwilling to do. This situation directly reproduced the differentiated structure of class interests between the British and colonial working classes within the domestic economy (Gilroy, 1987).

[1] This was aided by the *British Nationality Act* 1948, which gave people from the colonies the right to work and live in Britain (though the *Commonwealth Immigrants Act* 1962 would impose much stricter controls on immigration again).

From the late 1970s onwards, Britain entered an economic recession following a global oil crisis. With the election of Margaret Thatcher in the 1980s, Britain became the forerunner for an aggressive laissez faire politics that went hand-in-hand with deregulation, large-scale privatization, and outsourcing, including to the countries it had formerly colonized. Britain's post-war estates were directly implicated in these processes. Here, housing policies, including the 'right to buy' policy introduced with the *Housing Act 1980*, allowed sitting council tenants to buy their homes at a much-reduced rate. This soon resulted in polarization: the more desirable estates became owner-occupied, whereas those with high numbers of social tenancies became the dumping ground for society's most marginalized. It was on the latter estates (depicted in figures 3.1. and 3.2.), often located in inner-city areas, that colonial practices of state-sanctioned racial segregation were replicated (El-Enany 2017); families with histories of migration, homeless populations, and the unemployed (exactly the same demographics that had previously been excluded from accessing social housing) were moved to these communities. As members of the country's growing surplus population, many remain trapped in low paid jobs, experiencing periods of under-or-unemployment and indebtedness (Rogaly, 2021), subjected to a punitive welfare state and, as the next chapter shows, 'law and order' policing. These people therefore not only face both extreme precarity and a penal state but, as the tragedy over the lethal fire in the Grenfell tower showed, remain situated within 'a much wider cartography of imperial and racial violence' (Danewid 2019; Bulley, Edkins, and El-Enany, 2019).

Life on the inside of these multiracial working-class estates has become more difficult over the generations. Let us return for a moment to Lindsey's own family, whose history over the past three generations shows the downward mobility that many have had to face, though it also reveals the white privilege of the male breadwinner in the post-war generation. Lindsey's father, a white English factory worker, was offered housing in the late 1960s on Park End. When the factory faltered in the 1980s, he was given a redundancy pay out that allowed him to buy his council house, only to sell it at a profit a few years later and to retire by the coast. The next generation lacked many of these benefits: Lindsey and her sister Sue still lived on the same estate, but they were renting their house now from private landlords, albeit with state rental subsidies. While Lindsey was working for the local church as a community organizer, her sister could only find work as a care giver, paid minimum wage on a zero-hour contract. She was employed by a

Figure 3.1. Glodi and a friend on the council estate Glodi grew up in.
Source: © Reece Grant 2025.

private company that sent her long distances to visit patients in their homes, only paying her for visit (not travel) time and requiring her to work shifts of up to twelve hours. Some of the male members in Lindsey's family experienced long periods of unemployment and low-wage precarious employment, including the father of two of her mixed heritage white and South Asian children. Others were 'lucky' to still be employed in the car factory, but on an 'agency contract'. This meant that wages were lower, there was no sickness or holiday pay, and they were made to compete with migrants, increasingly from Eastern Europe, for their jobs.

Figure 3.2. A council estate in South London.
Source: © Reece Grant 2025.

Lindsey's own children, nephews, and nieces were coming of age when the government, in 2010, introduced its politics of austerity, following the global economic crisis of 2008/2009. In a process coined by commentators as 'austerity localism' (Lowndes, 2012; Clayton, Donovan, and Merchand, 2015; Dagdeviren, Donoghue, and Wearmouth, 2019), the government pushed the responsibility for the fiscal crisis onto local authority bodies, which, in turn, implemented harsh cuts to local spending. Lee, Lindsey's fifteen-year-old nephew, who I introduced in Chapter 1, illustrates how estate children too were made to bear the brunt. Lee was deemed a 'problem kid' by his teachers and excluded from school. Now, aged fifteen, he faced yet another hurdle: the labour market that had still been open to his parents, albeit in limited ways, had little to offer boys like him. Lee dreaded going to the 'Job-centre', the agency administering welfare payments. The same government that implemented austerity had also created a new system of benefits called 'Universal Credit' under the *Welfare Reform Act 2012*. This act introduces a highly coercive and commodified logic, one that requires welfare recipients to sign up to individualized 'contracts' that come with duties to perform and the threat of 'sanctions' in case of non-compliance (Koch and Reeves 2021) and to update online work diaries on a weekly basis. The following extract from a claimant's commitment form, signed by a nineteen-year-old unemployed young man from Park End, illustrates the coerciveness that comes with this new system:

> *My commitments*
> Accepted on 9 August 2018.
> *I'll do everything that I can to find work or earn more.*
>
> *Work I can do*
> I'll look for and take any work that I'm able to do, including:
> - Seasonal Work
> - Retail
> - Hospitality
>
> I'll also apply for any jobs recommended by my work coach.
> I'll look for full-time work for the minimum wage or more.
>
> *My availability*
> I'm available for job interviews immediately and will participate fully.
> I'm available to start work immediately.
>
> *Travel to work*
> I can travel up to 90 minutes to work.
>
> *What I'll do*
> I'll normally spend 35 hours a week looking and preparing for work.
> I've agreed with my work coach that I'll:
> - Using online job sites—CV Library, indeed, daily info and applying directly on employers
> - Handing my CV out to employers
> - Sign up to 5 agencies
>
> *Meetings with my work coach*
> I'll attend and take part fully in all meetings with my work coach. I'll tell my work coach immediately if I can't do this.
>
> *Using my online account*
> I'll sign in to my online account often to:
> - complete all activities in my to-do list
> - report changes to my circumstances promptly, including changes to work. If I can't get online, I'll report any changes by calling [the Jobcentre's number]

The ethnographic literature has analysed the intimate effects of welfare reforms and austerity in Britain and beyond (Bear, 2015; Loopstra, 2015; Bear and Knight, 2017; Forbess and James, 2017; Knight and Stuart, 2017; Cohen, Fuhr, and Bock, 2018; Powers and Rakopoulos, 2019; Robinson and Sheldon, 2019; James, 2022), paying attention to their human costs as well as their disproportionately harsh impact on migrants and people of colour (Bassell, 2018; Rogaly, 2021). This literature also directs the analytical gaze to what anthropologists have called 'social suffering': the assemblage of human problems that have their origins and consequences in the injuries that social forces inflict on human experience (Kleinman, 1997; Das et al., 2000, 2001), chiefly those involving structural violence. The concept of social suffering is illuminating where suffering involves forms of criminality that are all too frequently seen as the outcome of individualized pathologies. In their ethnography of heroin users in the San Francisco Bay area, Bourgeois and Schonberg argue that abusive phenomena—from domestic violence to drug use—have to be examined 'in their relationship to political-economic, cultural-ideological, and institutional forces, such as the restructuring of the labour market, the "War on Drugs", the gentrification of San Francisco's housing market, the gutting of social services, the administration of bureaucracies, racism, sexuality, gender power relations and stigma' (2009 p. 32).

When I first returned to Park End in 2018, I heard stories about 'criminal exploitation' and 'modern slavery' from both frontline officials and local residents (although the latter did not tend to use the official terminology at the time). Here, I turn towards social suffering as an analytical lens through which to deepen my critique of the government's narrative of county lines as a situation in which individualized suffering—or 'criminal exploitation'—emanates from 'within'. This is not to romanticize the illicit street-level economy: As with the government's own language of suffering, young people spoke of the control, violence, and even death that they faced at the hands of others involved in the drugs trade. And yet, to limit ourselves to such a view would mean to ignore the structural context in which young people's decisions to join the illicit economy were made, as well as the limited, if not counter-productive, effects of state interventions in the name of redemption that reflect a longer history of welfare failures and their colonial logics. I argue that the mismatch between the state's *de jure* construction of individualized exploitation and the *de facto* structural exploitation that is central to young people's experiences of social suffering brings into sharp relief the workings of a deeply 'disjunctive democracy' (Caldeira and

Holston, 1999; Holston, 2007) that has extended a narrative of care while allowing substantive inequalities to flourish.

'County lines as a job centre for the young'

Standing at the front of a large conference room, the young man looked the part. He was dressed smartly in a tight white shirt and clean jeans and wore his black hair in a neatly cropped fashion, alongside a carefully trimmed goatee beard and black thick-rimmed glasses. He had the distinct look of a businessman in casual wear, though his gold front tooth and large tattoos peeking out on his brown skin from under neatly rolled-up sleeves also spoke of a different life. Later, he would tell his audience of mostly police officers and other frontline workers that he was in the habit of 'dressing up' for public events because he wanted to be taken seriously as a professional—not just as 'someone from the hood'. He started: 'My name is Tee, short for Tyrese. I am here today to tell you about my life as a drug dealer and the time I have served in prison and what I have done with it'. His face opened into a larger smile as he took in the audience in front of him.

Tee then shared some brief personal history with us. Now in his late twenties, Tee was born and raised on one of East London's inner-city housing estates, where, in his own words, 'crime was ripe'. He described himself as 'Black', being the son of a South Asian mother. He grew up in the shadows of abandoned docks and warehouses where previous generations had laboured—first white English working-class people, before they were joined by migrant labourers from Britain's former colonies and beyond. Unlike some other young men, whose experiences in the street-level drugs economy I only became privy to through their mothers' pained retellings (Chapter 4), Tee was a redeemed drug dealer who had turned his criminal biography into a basis for an entrepreneurial career. Having served time in prison and come out 'the other end', he was the founder of a successful youth charity working with 'at-risk' young people. Today, on a rainy morning in September 2019, Tee was delivering a half-day training session on 'gangs' and 'county lines' to a group of professionals in the local authority's townhall, about five miles away from Park End estate. I had been invited by Nick, the police officer introduced in the last chapter, who heard about Tee's workshops through an officer colleague in London and had secured funding for Tee to speak to us.

Tee said he wanted to share his story by going back to the beginning. His mother, a first-generation immigrant from Bangladesh, had raised him and his three siblings. A working-class woman with no formal qualifications, she struggled to make ends meet for her family in a country whose own wealth had in part been accumulated through the colonial pillage of her home country. Tee recalled the different jobs she had: working on a factory line, cleaning, and cooking meals for the estate community, which Tee himself described as 'mixed, Asian, Black, all sorts'. While Tee did not say so, I wondered, listening to him speak, if his mother too would have confronted the bitter racism expressed against South Asian migrants by the white British majority when she arrived in Britain. His father, who Tee described as 'a bit of a gangster', was absent much of the time, coming in and out of prison for robberies and other offences. Tee and his siblings were often left to their own devices, playing on the estate's streets and going to the youth clubs when they were a bit older. 'Now that is also gone', Tee said, referencing the government's public sector cuts from 2010. 'So many young people don't even have whatever basic provisions I had when I was a kid'.

Tee was keen to emphasize that he had not had a 'bad' childhood, for the strength of his mother had carried him through his early years. Money was tight, but his mother always made sure there was enough at the table for all the children. She would do what she could to keep them 'on the straight and narrow', and Tee grew up in a community where he knew most of his neighbours and their children. But this is not how the outside viewed him and his family. Police officers, social workers, and council officials would regularly come into the family's life, offering their remedies for what they considered to be a 'problem family' with a father who was in prison and a mother who was working and raising her children much on her own. Tee remembered negative involvement on the part of the authorities going back to when he was 'three years old', as well as being taught coping strategies for 'disengaging' from them in order to be left alone:

> When I was growing up, every service would come in, and they would try to walk alongside me. 'You carry knives, your dad did that to your mum . . .' I had services in my life from the age of three, I knew the questions they were going to ask, I knew what they wanted to hear, I could dig it, my mum told me what to say when social services came around and next-door neighbour would give us a can of beans to put in the cupboard. I knew if I disengaged then they will leave me alone . . . [they say

to me]: 'you don't care!' Yes, I do, I just don't care about you! You just ask me twenty-five questions, write a report, and send me home.

Tee's early childhood experiences of having professionals visit his home, quick to intrude into private spaces with their forms and questionnaires—making him answer questions, significantly, that revealed professionals' lack of care—were a premonition for his own dealings with authorities in years to come. Thus, punctuated in his narrative of how he became a drug dealer in his early teenage years were moments of neglect, confrontation, and punishment on the part of institutions that should have exercised a duty of care. From the age of eleven, he recalled being constantly stopped and searched by police, who would profile him on the streets because of the colour of his skin and a postcode that spoke of his working-class roots.

In school, teachers had no time for 'the likes of us, kids from the estate'. Like many estate schools in London in the 2000s, Tee's was already seriously underfunded well before the Conservative-led government would introduce its politics of austerity after coming into power in 2010. Tee recalled the teachers just being busy managing crowded classrooms. He would regularly be punished for breaching the school's behavioural codes ('just for acting like a kid'), being taken out of class and put in a separate area where he was made to work in complete isolation, in silence, away from his peers. When he was fourteen years old, Tee was expelled from school for carrying a knife in his rucksack. He recalled: 'Nobody asked any questions about why a young person aged fourteen was carrying a knife, they just assumed that I was at fault, that I should be punished for it'. He was permanently excluded from school and made to attend weekly appointments with his youth offending worker. But this came with its own risks: In order to get to his youth offending worker's office, Tee had to cross another estate, where some of his enemies lived. 'They didn't care if I would get stabbed on my way there, they just said if I didn't turn up, I would be punished'.

The truth was that Tee was carrying a knife in school because he felt he needed it for protection. He had started dealing weed initially to drug users on his estate and in the school yard, and was in the habit of protecting himself from anyone who might want to rob him of the drugs or otherwise had some 'beef' with him. Asked how he first got into drug dealing, he said, 'It was just what we were doing, everyone was hustling'. 'Hustling' was a term that several people—including Glodi—used when speaking to me about their experiences surviving in and through the informal, and sometimes illicit, economy. It referred to various means of generating money, profit, or even just a warm meal in a context where opportunities for more formalized forms of accessing cash and economic rewards were limited or outright absent. Hustling could include anything from selling stolen or bought goods at higher prices to doing odd jobs for neighbours or friends. But it could also mean being involved in low-level drug dealing, and many of his peers were doing just that. 'Drugs were part of our world', Tee continued. 'Growing up on the estate we knew about drugs, you would see the drugs getting imported in barrels, and people were cooking them, cutting them up. Drugs were never far away from us'.

At the time, Tee was only selling 'a bit of weed'. But following his permanent expulsion from school, he made the acquaintance of some older youths he knew from 'seeing about'. They were dressed expensively, had a reputation for violence, and were known in the area for 'getting all the girls'. When they offered him work, he accepted eagerly. This was his introduction to street-level dealing of crack cocaine and heroin, or in his words, 'white and dark'. By the time Tee was sixteen, he had stopped going to school altogether, working instead for 'elders' on his estate. Soon, he would be sent 'out of town', taking drugs that he was given by the elders to places all over the country, typically by travelling on the train or bus, sleeping in the flats of drug users whom he had never met, and staying in these places until he had sold all his drugs. He would then go back to the city 'for a reload'. He would not see the elders much: mostly only to drop off the money and pick up new drugs, and sometimes, they might turn up in the places where Tee was working. His peers were the other runners with whom he spent much of his time during the long weeks away from home; they were his friends and support network and the people he turned to when he needed help.

This life continued for some time. Tee would be spending days, sometimes weeks away from home, coming back to London for intermittent periods only to leave again for a new drugs job. It was easy enough to do; none of the authorities were interested in what was happening to him. One day, while out in the counties dealing drugs, Tee recalled getting a phone call from an unknown number: he picked up and it was an officer from the London Metropolitan police, back in London. His mother had reported him as missing, and the police were reaching out. 'The officer asked me if I was doing okay, and I said yes, and he hung up, and that was it'. Nobody came to safeguard him at the time, it being a few years before the government would 'discover' county lines, and the language of exploitation had not been popularized yet. During this time, Tee was moved into care because relations with his mother—who had begged him to not follow his father's footsteps—had become strained. When Tee started absconding from the care homes he was placed in, aged seventeen, it would often take days for his mother to be notified of his disappearance. Nobody from youth services tried to track him down in those days, leaving Tee much to his own devices.

The official neglect worked to Tee's advantage at this point. He could abscond more easily and take drugs to different places in the country. Then, he realized he wanted more: he was not happy simply as a 'runner'; he described himself as 'ambitious' and 'streetwise'. Hard-working and quick to think on his feet, Tee was soon entrusted by his superiors with more responsibility, being promoted to a middle-level 'worker'. As a worker, he would still be sent out of town occasionally, but typically stayed behind in drug users' flats and sometimes hotels and rented apartments, where he would guard the drugs and supervise the street runners. His pay went up, from 50 to 200 pounds a week. Tee recalled being able to buy himself trainers and other goods he desired. But even that was not enough for him. 'The elders made it sound like it's hard to run your own line', he said, 'but it soon clicked that I could do it myself'. With money he had saved from street selling weed, and working for the 'elders' on the line, he bought himself a larger stash of Class A drugs and decided to set up his own deal line. Tee recalled: 'I was able to save 80 pounds from thefts and from selling weed and stuff, and with that I bought crack—one eighth of crack at the time. I started my own business, cutting out my rocks of 0.2, 0.4. The drug users always asked for brown [heroin], so I started saving and then I started buying heroin'.

Bourgeois et al., drawing from long-term research on one of Philadelphia's notorious narcotics blocks (located in a socially abandoned urban zone inhabited mostly by Puerto Ricans), investigated how youths who were unable to find legal jobs wound up 'selling high-quality, inexpensive opiates and cocaine to primarily white customers in the shadows of the factories that used to employ their grandparents' (2021, p. 264). In Britain's post-industrial neighbourhoods, blighted by poverty and structural decline, the situation is not dissimilar (Coomber and Moyle 2018). For young people like Tee and many others, becoming involved in drug dealing was 'the only game in town', as one former dealer put it, in a situation where virtually every circumstance militated against them from early on in life. One former drug dealer I spoke with described county lines as a 'jobcentre for the young', referring to it via the name of the government agency administering welfare benefits. How, then, is this street economy part of a broader, pyramid-shaped illicit economy that exposes those at the bottom to the highest risks? And how do the young people employed at the lowest rung of this 'jobcentre' experience constant threats to their personal safety and well-being?

The lowest rung

For young people like Tee, the introduction to street-level drug dealing often happened through friends and personal networks—at school, within their own families, and around the estate. Indeed, young people often had an intimate knowledge of where drugs were sold: particular corners of the estate were known as dealing spots, particular houses were known as 'trap houses', and particular individuals were known to be dealers. 'You knew where to get drugs', recalled Monique, a former drug dealer and a thirty-year-old Black woman from Brixton, a South London neighbourhood historically dominated by Caribbean populations. 'They were everywhere. The police knew too, they weren't interested to stop the problem'. Older drug dealers—those that Tee called 'elders' and others 'yardies'—were not only known to young people growing up in the community, but could also be treated with great respect, if also fear. Monique, for example, did not think of the 'yardies' as apart from the community. On the contrary, they were part of local life, not only hiring young people and other members of the community to run drugs, but also offering loans and gifts to local families, such as paying for funerals and birthdays. Nick, the police officer from the last chapter, dismissively described this as a patron-type role.

Though a young Tee or Monique may have been acquainted with the sights and goings on of the 'yardies' and 'elders', as novices to the drugs world, they started off at the bottom rung of the trade. While there is huge variation within and across different drugs lines (Coomber and Moyle, 2018; Spicer, Moyle, and Coomber, 2020), with county lines being described as a hyper-flexible and neo-liberal model of drugs distribution (Spicer, 2021), there is typically a division of labour in place. Each person receives commands from the person directly above them. At the lowest rung are the 'runners' (or 'couriers', as lawyers call them in court), individuals who transport the drugs and sell them directly on the streets. The runner is in possession of a 'burner phone' (typically a pre-paid temporary phone) through which they communicate with the next person up. This person is in charge of running the drugs phone line, sending out advertising messages and passing orders on to runners. He or she may or may not be the owner of the county lines drugs line, someone who is not only in possession of the drugs phone—the most valuable commodity, as it gives access to buyers—but responsible for buying the goods. The owner would have either taken the line from others or established it themselves by building a client base, a process described in the last chapter. There might be 'workers' or 'middle managers' in between the different levels. Workers may also be needed for other jobs, including (depending on the state of the drugs when bought) processing pure cocaine paste into cocaine and crack cocaine; cutting the crack into 'rocks'; adulterating the heroin; 'bagging up' the drugs in clingfilm for street distribution; recruiting other runners; and overseeing their work of selling drugs.

While there are clear hierarchies in place, the same person can also occupy multiple roles and/or shift in and out of different roles; for example, a person can go from being a worker to being a runner to holding the line, depending on the staffing needs of their boss. We saw in the last chapter that Glodi, the first young man to be convicted of human trafficking charges in a jury-led trial on county lines, had been working as a runner for a drugs line when he was arrested and convicted at the age of sixteen. After having spent time in one of the country's most notorious youth facilities, he came out determined to turn his life around. Yet, upon release, he ran into the man that he used to work for, who in turn told him that Glodi had a debt of several thousand pounds to pay off: the value of which was the money and amount of drugs that had been taken off him by the police when he was arrested a few years back (a common story among young people who wind up with such debt). His boss offered him a deal: Glodi would go back to work for him. But this time, he would be promoted one level up, typically staying in London with the deal line number on him while sending out runners do the riskier work of delivering and selling the drugs. Yet, even while Glodi was holding the line, he would occasionally run drugs himself, such as when his boss was short of workers and needed the 'odd job' done.

When first entering the drugs trade as runners, the young people I spoke with were not necessarily familiar with this structure; however, they learned fast, coming to understand expectations and hierarchies. Compliance with strict rules could be rewarded with promotions to the next level, whereas failure to perform would often be harshly punished, including with corporal punishment. Daily life was hard as a drug dealer, and few succeeded as Tee had in climbing the social hierarchy, with threats, dangers, and death lurking around the corner at every level. Common to young people's stories were long work hours, being sent to undisclosed locations, being made to sleep on the bare floor in drug users' homes while facing unpredictable and sometimes violent customers. Work conditions were unsafe and physically demanding, with runners typically being expected to store the drugs inside their bottoms (called 'plugging'), in condoms with 1,000 pounds worth of drugs stuffed into a sausage-like shape (called a 'G pack'). Not all 'elders' were good bosses either, as some took advantage of the young to get cheap or even free labour. Young people spoke of not being paid their promised wages, with elders insisting that they had come up short in proceeds, and of having their every movement controlled through phone-tracking devices and other apps. They were expected to be available to work at all times.

Worst of all were stories of young people being set up by their bosses to be 'robbed' of their drugs, thus putting them in a position of perpetual debt bondage that required them to work for free, often performing the most dangerous and menial jobs. Here, young people's accounts often mirrored the stories told by professionals in the last chapter; but importantly, their stories placed them within a broader context of structural exclusion, racism, and state failings that has not featured in the official policy narratives. Let me turn to Samson, who I met while shadowing a youth charity in which he had become a mentor after leaving the illicit economy. A young Black man from a North London housing estate, Samson got involved in drug dealing at age fifteen, when he found himself expelled from school. A group of older boys offered him work, and he eagerly accepted. His only condition was that he insisted on working together with his best friend, someone he called Frankenstein, with whom he made 'a pact' to protect one another. Soon, Samson and Frankenstein were sent on their first trip 'out of town'. He was sent to a town he had never been to in his life, with nothing on him but the drugs and the clothes he was wearing, a phone, and a train ticket. Samson remembered 'sticking out like a sore thumb', his dark skin setting him apart from the majority-white town population, and leaving him worried that he would become the target of both police attention and drug rivals. On this and subsequent occasions, Samson slept in a drug user's flat on the bare floorboards, often living in squalor, with used needles, drugs, and weapons lying around.

Samson ate only intermittently, having to ask the next person up the hierarchy if he was allowed to use some of the proceeds he had made from drugs sales on food. He was never paid; his boss always had a new excuse for why he did not deserve his pay. But it was the physical affront to his body, including having to 'plug' the drugs (insert them into his anus wrapped in condoms and clingfilm), that stood out in Samson's description. At a presentation he delivered to a group of law enforcement and frontline professionals on the topic of county lines (he had been invited to speak as someone with 'lived experience'), he recalled the first time he was sent 'out of town' with Frankenstein:

> I had earlier referred to the term plugging. That's how we concealed drugs earlier that day, that whole process—you get your parcel, crack and heroin wrapped, you insert it into yourself. I had never inserted anything in me before, it was a very, very uncomfortable experience but as I said, the mentality was you are just doing anything to get money. I got to the house [of a drug user] with Frankenstein, and the knittie [drug user] started asking for his bee—I am referring to heroin, that he was owed from the older. I had to go into the toilet, in the house. The living conditions were shocking, black, grey, brown colours, candles around. At this point I called the older, the knittie is asking for his brown. I went into the bathroom, had to bend down, actually squeeze this pack that I had plugged, squeeze it out of me. What I didn't like is that once I had to poo it out of me, the whole pack itself was covered in my faeces, you have to unwrap that, make whatever changes you have to make and then put that back in me [...]

Even worse, however, was the ever-present risk of being attacked or set up by a rival. Precisely because those sent to deal 'out of town' were operating in unknown territory, knowing who one's enemy was and who to trust was often a tricky game. Young people described how they would never put down their knives or weapon when sent to a new destination or when staying at a 'knittie's house' (a drug user's house)—they could never be sure who would walk around the next corner or through the door. Yet, even with the best precautions taken, dangers were not always predictable. One particular risk was that of drug users setting them up. Drug users were considered unpredictable and easy to manipulate, so runners worried about users being bought off by rival drugs lines. When this happened, a drug user was typically promised free or cheap drugs in return for giving up the location of a runner who, in turn, would be hunted down and possibly robbed of their drugs and mobile phone, which contained access to the runner's customer base.

Samson experienced what it was like to be set up vicariously through his friend, Frankenstein. Initially unbeknownst to Samson, Frankenstein broke the pact they had made to only go out-of-town together, agreeing to deal drugs alone in another town and, as usual, stay in a drug user's home. One night, when Frankenstein was trying to catch up on sleep, his host let two men dressed in balaclavas and armed with zombie knives into the flat. The men threatened Frankenstein, demanding his drugs and money, and when he refused to hand them over, stabbed him multiple times. While Frankenstein tried to fight them off, determined to protect the drugs and money that he carried in a pouch, he was eventually overpowered, robbed, and left bleeding on the floor. It later emerged that Frankenstein had been set up by his host, a former runner for a rival line who had a drug debt to pay off. Like Glodi, whose experience of being attacked when holding drugs I discussed in the last chapter, Frankenstein did not want to call the ambulance for fear of drawing unwanted police attention to him. He also did not trust the police to do him any good, knowing, as he said, that 'they would just look at him like they do at all Black guys and treat him like a criminal'. Miraculously, Frankenstein survived, though he had a permanent limp from the stabbing wounds on one of his legs.

Both Frankenstein's and Glodi's refusal to call for help was not unusual. Police arrest, and the potential repercussions one could face with one's boss, were ever-present dangers in the lives of young runners working at the lowest level of the drugs trade. Being arrested, more often than not with drugs on them, carried the risk of being channelled into a deeply punitive and racist criminal justice system, a point that I will come back to in the next chapter. Especially when young people refused to give up the names of those they were working for, they could receive steep sentences—as we saw in the case of Glodi, who received three years for his first drugs offence as a young drugs runner. Often, prison also did not mark the end of a young person's involvement with crime, as they incurred debts from losing drugs and money at the point of arrest that had to be paid back to their drugs bosses as soon as they came out. 'This is the logic of hood economics', Tee said to a room of police officers during his training. 'Do you wanna die or do you wanna go to jail? Which one? That is the choice that young people face'. Tee himself had learned the hard way. He had stayed in the game for a long time. Each time he went to prison, he saw it as further education in the making of a drug dealer (since drugs and dealer information freely circulated in prison); and each time he came out, he went back into drug dealing. Eventually, he was able to set up his own drugs line: 'I wasn't the champagne kind of guy', he recalled, 'but I was doing alright'.

One day, while Tee was driving a car in his neighbourhood with his baby daughter in the backseat, a bullet went through the windscreen. It narrowly missed him, but his daughter was crying hysterically in the back. This was his turning point: he decided that if he did not want to end up dead, he had to find a way out. Yet it would take another stint of prison for him to be able to extricate himself. After he came out, he moved to the other side of the city, cutting ties with many of his friends and family members, some of whom were involved with drugs. He never went back to the estate where he had grown up, knowing that at least among certain circles, he would no longer be welcome. Tee's voice went quiet, his face betraying pain as he retold this phase of his life to audience members. 'Next week I am turning thirty', he said. 'It hurts to know that I will not be able to go back to my family, that I will not be receiving phone calls from my family that day. But at least I know that me and my kids are safe'. And yet, safety may also be a precarious good. As the next section will show, particularly when the authorities intervene in the name of 'safeguarding' those found to be victims of criminal exploitation, such interventions can be experienced as setting families up to fail, leaving one mother to say that the 'state is guilty of grooming, too'.

'The state is guilty of grooming, too'

Let me illustrate this point by returning to Lee, the teenager from Park End and nephew of Lindsey introduced in Chapter 1—the first 'modern slave' I encountered. There, I had described how Lee, a low-level drug dealer who had been asked to guard drugs for older men on the estate, had confided this experience in his mother. His mother Sue, in a desperate attempt to save her son from what she feared would end up as a lethal game, had gone to the police. Sue had told me that she would rather have Lee go to prison than for him to be found dead on the street. Yet, contrary to Sue's and her sister Lindsey's fears, the disclosure did not result in Lee being channelled into the criminal justice system—at least not yet. In the weeks that followed, we learned that the police were treating the fifteen-year-old boy, a school dropout who had repeated run-ins with the authorities, as a victim of 'criminal exploitation'. This assessment was confirmed a few weeks later when the National Referral Mechanism (the official system for recording and identifying victims of modern slavery and human trafficking) determined that Lee was a victim of human trafficking. This finding set in motion a number of processes. Rather than being prosecuted for the offences that Lee had knowingly committed, he was 'safeguarded' at the hands of a 'multi-agency' team. Police officers would regularly drop by to have a chat with Lee in the hope that he would open up about the identity of his exploiters; social workers would pay the family regular visits; and above all, the family were offered a socially rented tenancy by the authorities outside the area where Lee had allegedly been groomed.

When reflecting on these responses, the professionals involved were enthusiastic about the 'holistic solution' that they had developed in response to the situation. Indeed, Lee's case became a 'flagship' that was repeatedly cited anonymously at training sessions and professional events, including at the parents' evening described in the last chapter and during which the chief inspector of the local police force cited Lee's case as an example of 'best practice'. He told the thirty or so parents present:

> Do we treat [young drug dealers] as victims or as offenders? My thing is that we don't wanna criminalise children. My job here is not to put children in prison. So how can we help children? A mother was worried about how serious her son's involvement with drugs was getting and she was panicking about it. She phoned us. We went round to her house and supported the mum and the child. Our problem-solving team spent a long time working with the child and he disclosed what had been going on. A lot of [multi-agency] work has been going into this and that work still continues. That whole family got moved because we got them on top of the housing list. We understand the problem now. We got a lot of partners involved and we help them with agencies. We might go through steps of looking like [the victim] is getting arrested in case he is being watched by others but then we will safeguard them. They will leave the child alone if they really think it's getting too hot.

And yet, if Lee's case was cited by law enforcement as an example of a broader cultural shift that recognized the need to care for and safeguard vulnerable children (see the last Chapter), I soon came to understand that the picture looked very different from the perspective of the families concerned. Not only did the narrative provided by the chief inspector silence how some of the 'successes' attributed by him to the authorities' efforts had in fact been the outcome of long fights led by desperate family members, it also failed to acknowledge how professional interventions were often experienced as evidence on the part of families of being 'set up to fail'.

I became privy to these more complicated, and ultimately, much more painful stories, in the months following Sue's disclosure to the police. It started from the day Sue had gone to the police. The police sent the family away to an undisclosed location, supposedly for their own protection, while they were 'investigating' the case. Sue was told that they could not come home for two weeks. She would later tell me how worried she had been while they were passing time in the undisclosed location, not knowing what would wait for them upon their return. When they were finally allowed back into their house, the police informed them that they were still investigating. Now, Sue and her family were consistently sworn to secrecy: 'The police told me that I was not allowed to speak to nobody, not even a lawyer', Sue would remember later. Her sister Lindsey called me one night, sounding upset. Would I be in a position to contact a lawyer to find out what Sue's rights were? Sue had been told that her son would be moved into one of the country's underfunded children's homes. This, the social worker had told Sue, would ostensibly be for Lee's own safety. Sue could not think of anything worse: the prospect of her son being placed in care, potentially hundreds of miles away from his family, where he would be at a higher risk of being sucked into drug dealing.

Sue never let me contact a lawyer, having retracted her consent the next morning again for fear of aggravating the situation. She did, however, continue the fight by herself, insisting with the social worker that she would not let her son be moved into care. Eventually, the authorities conceded to an alternative with Sue: the entire family would be moved, under a so-called 'management transfer'. A successful management transfer awards priority status to a social housing transfer application if the applicant's circumstances require them to move as a matter of urgency. This sets into motion a long, drawn-out competitive process. Sue now had to 'bid' for properties online, trying to outdo other social housing bidders who had similarly been accorded priority status. She knew she would not be able to reject the offer of a house, otherwise she would risk being thrown off the housing transfer list altogether. But finding a suitable house was not easy. Apart from the fact that it had to be within commuting distance to her husband's work at the factory, there were legal requirements about the size she could not ignore. Having three more children apart from Lee, she needed at least a three-bedroom property, lest she would fall foul of regulations that made it unlawful to 'overcrowd' a social housing tenancy. At the same time, she was not allowed to go for too big of a house, or she would be hit by the 'bedroom tax', the name colloquially given to another austerity measure that penalizes social housing tenants who under-occupy a property by cutting their access to benefits (Koch, 2014).

For months, Sue and her family were left in limbo, not knowing when or whether they would be offered a home. Meanwhile, it felt like their old family home had been invaded by the authorities, turning intimate spaces and everyday relations into arenas for both state surveillance and informal threat (see also Chapter 5). CCTV cameras were installed outside their house, ostensibly for the family's safety, but this made Sue feel like she was under watch in her own home. The visits on the part of police and social workers also continued, but they had started taking a more threatening underdone, as Lee was told that he could still be prosecuted if he continued to give up the name of his 'exploiters'. The police's ban on talking to anyone about the case, including close family members, reinforced Sue's feelings of isolation and fear. Sue started resenting her son for having brought this upon her family and his other siblings. She felt exhausted, and eventually she had to sign off from her work as a carer because her anxiety got to be too much. Meanwhile Lee saw his biggest fears come true: his 'exploiters' had issued death threats against him, including by putting eggs and foul meat through the letterbox. Expelled from school and afraid of running into his previous bosses, Lee refused to leave the house. Sue worried that her son would become suicidal, especially when in the heat of the summer, temperatures hit nearly forty degrees in his bedroom.

When reflecting on this period later, both Sue and Lindsey felt bitter. Lindsey could not rid herself of the feeling that the offer of a management transfer had been a calculated move, undertaken by the authorities not because they cared for her sister but because they had turned Lee into a 'poster child' for their emerging modern slavery responses. Sue, too, would reflect on how the process of being safeguarded made her feel abandoned and alone:

> This nearly broke us; it nearly broke our family, and I had to be signed off work. I am on [benefits] because of the mental health problems it's caused us, and the anxieties and everything. I had to quit my job. I just want it to stop and to move on. But how can I do it? Who is going to help us? Nobody talks to us. Nobody keeps us informed. Nobody is there to help [Lee]. The schools didn't help at all, they didn't see the problem, they just saw him as a problem kid and that's it. There are no provisions, no facilities available to help young people, we are told that there is a lot in London to help these young people, but up here there is nothing for them. The police don't tell us what's going on, they said that this could take years before they can tell us more, we don't know what's going on. He was put on this NRM thing [which certified that he is a modern slave]

> but again what difference did it make? . . . What do we do now? How do we get out of this mess?

As I got to know more mothers and other female carers who were fighting for their children's welfare (see Chapter 4), a pattern emerged where interventions on the part of professionals ended up compounding the stresses that the families were already under. To illustrate these points, let me turn to the story of K.S. which I will return to in more depth in the next chapter. I came across K.S., a sixteen-year-old Black boy from South London, during his trial for murder, and became close to his sister Tami, who was seventeen years his senior and acting as his legal guardian during the trial. Much of K.S.'s life leading up to the murder trial had been marked by the authorities' failures to 'safeguard' him properly. K.S. was born in prison while his mother was serving a sentence, his earliest days already being marked by the carceral violence that would haunt him as a teenager. Tami would visit K.S. in prison and take him home whenever she could for short stints of time. When their mother was released, things did not improve. K.S. was, on Tami's admission, their mum's favourite, being the youngest of five, but she struggled to offer him a stable home. Coming out of prison, she was homeless, and K.S. and his mother spent the first few years sofa-surfing, sleeping on family members' couches, and moving around. 'No local authority helped my mum get housing', Tami remembered. 'They just passed the blame from one to the other'.

Like Lee, K.S. was a young teenager when he first became involved in drug dealing. At that point, he was living with his grandmother on a north London housing estate, and had started missing school on a regular basis. K.S. had been struggling academically for some time; his sister suspected that in addition to coping with early childhood traumas that had resulted in attachment difficulties, he was also neurodivergent. However, her pleas with the school to have her brother assessed for autism were ignored. Aged fourteen, K.S. was shot in the leg while out in a park one night. It turned out to be a stray bullet; he had become an accidental target in a fight between two groups. Yet, this did not matter to the police, who still classified him as a 'gang member' on account of his being shot. They entered this information in a shared professional database, where it was kept until, as we will see in the next chapter, it would be used as evidence by prosecution against him in his murder trial. A few months after being shot, K.S. disappeared from home, and was subsequently found in Slough, a town miles away from his home city, London, in a drug user's flat. K.S. too had drugs on him. His youth worker entered him into the National Referral Mechanism which, as in Lee's case, found K.S. to be a victim of human trafficking.

In K.S.'s case, however, this finding made no difference to how his case was treated by the professionals around him: Tami was desperate for K.S. to be given a house together with his mother outside of the area where he had been dealing drugs. Yet once more, her pleas with the local authorities only met deaf ears. Rather, when K.S. continued dealing drugs, he was eventually placed on a child protection plan, a term used to refer to the host of interventions that become authorized by law when a child is deemed at significant risk of harm to themselves. Only this time, K.S.'s sister found that this plan was being used not to support, but to judge. 'When you go to social services, and you make a referral, they kind of shun you off and, get on with it like this: "We're restricted in resources and stuff like that", she said. 'And then when things go really bad, they spin into action and put your child straightaway on child protection, where there's so many measures they could have put in place before it got that way'. Tami felt stigmatized by the fact that her brother was put on a 'child protection plan', telling me that these measures were normally reserved for children who had suffered from domestic abuse or problems within their own family household—when in this instance, the problems lay outside his home, for his family had no knowledge of the drug dealers for whom K.S. was working. K.S. was now moved into the care of the state, being placed from 'foster place, to foster place, to foster place, to foster place'.

During that time, K.S. would repeatedly go missing after absconding from the places he was put. Worse even for his family, however, were the failures on the part of the local authorities to keep them informed. On one occasion, and unbeknown to his immediate family, K.S. had been missing from his foster home for over six months. This only came to light when he was run over by a motorcyclist and the hospital called his mother to inform her. His sister Tami recalled: 'We could not believe it, it turned out he had not spent a single night in his foster home for six, seven months, and nobody had bothered reporting it'. Tami's pleas for support were becoming increasingly more desperate; she wanted proper support structures in place for her brother, including a secure home, schooling, and a psychological assessment. Eventually, some of her pleas were heard, although not in the way she had expected: K.S. was offered a place in a secure care home in Manchester, over 200 miles from his home and nearly a five-hour drive away. This made it impossible for his family, who struggled to pay the expensive train fares, to see him on a regular basis, causing them to slowly lose even more control over his life. All of these events lead to the tragic summer when, aged sixteen, K.S. would go missing and become embroiled in a dubious murder charge (see next chapter).

Unlike Glodi, whose story we considered in the last chapter, K.S. and Lee had been drawn to the attention of professional authorities at a time when the language of modern slavery and of safeguarding victims of criminal exploitation was becoming popularized. And yet, what stands out in their stories is how counterproductive attempts were on the part of the authorities to 'lift' these young men out of county lines and their said state of exploitation. Not only was the state's tight grip over their daily lives extended, but ultimately, both Lee and K.S. became more deeply entrenched in criminality. Perhaps unsurprisingly, these young people and their families found that the treatment they received began to display the same insecurities that their sons confronted as part of the illicit economy. Just as the 'elders' sent runners to unknown locations, removing young people from their families and support networks and exposing them to huge risks, so now, at the hands of the state, youth could find themselves moved into care against their own or their families' wishes. They could be sent to foster homes, often far away from their home communities; be drawn back into drug dealing; and placed in the care of authorities that ostensibly neglected their welfare and safety. And just as the young people had been found to be 'enslaved' at the hands of their exploiters, so they experienced the process of being rescued by police and social workers as one of fundamental unfreedom, for they now had to reckon with intruding visits, requests for information, and co-operation at all times. It was precisely this sense of a repeat experience that was captured in the words of one mother, who said, 'The state is guilty of grooming, too'.

Britain's disjunctive democracy

In June 2019, more than a year after Lindsey and I heard that her sister Sue had gone to the police to 'disclose' her son's involvement in drug-dealing activities, I decided to pay the family a visit in their new home, located about an hour and a half's drive away from their old estate. On a sunny morning, I took the train from London, where I was living at the time, to the closest train station. From there, it would be another forty-minute bus ride to the village where their new home was based. The bus took me through winding roads into the green countryside, past small hamlets with churches and whitewashed cottage houses with thatched roofs. The house that Lee's family had been moved to was on the edge of a hamlet, on a new estate consisting of a combination of privately rented and government-owned housing built in the same style as the older cottages surrounding it. Looking out the bus window, I could not help but be reminded of the walking tour of Park End that Lindsey had taken me on a year earlier. The contrast between the two sites could not be any more extreme: the concrete jungle of Park End, a post-war, low-income social housing estate with its cramped and high-rise housing had given way to leafy fields and cottage houses. The ghost-like feeling of Park End's old youth club and community centre, abandoned under the weight of public sector cuts, had been replaced by the calming emptiness of the open countryside. Moreover, Lindsey's desperate plea to make researchers like me see and understand the visceral effects of austerity had been silenced by the chattering of the cheerful voices around me on the bus.

And yet, these images of a bucolic countryside life wore thin as soon as Sue opened the door to her new house. She looked worn, with rings under her eyes and having lost some weight, and was soon fighting back tears. As we sat in her backyard, smoking the cigarettes I had brought along, she told me what it felt like to be moved away from Park End. She had found the move extremely isolating, having been separated from her local networks of care, including from close family members like her sister, Lindsey. Her younger children had struggled to settle into school. Sue could not rid herself of the feeling that this was because they were 'working class' in what she described as 'a very wealthy and middle-class area'. Having to give up her job due to stress when things got tense with Lee and the police a few months back, Sue had further struggled to find work. Sue soon found herself at the mercy of Universal Credit, the demeaning means-tested benefit system described earlier that made her feel like she was now, in her words, 'enslaved' to the state by requiring her to regularly sign onto her online journal, see a job coach, and endure their humiliating questions—and illustrating yet another way in which people drew parallels between the state and the alleged slavery pertaining to the drugs economy.

Things got even worse when an unexpected tax payment hit the family, and they found that they could no longer pay their bills (the social rent being much higher in their new home because of the area's general affluence). Sue started going to the local food bank, taking a bus for over half an hour to get there. Queuing outside just to get a bag containing tins, a loaf of bread, and some essentials, she felt ashamed of the stigma, like people walking past judged her. After a while, she was told to not come back anymore; the food bank had a policy of only accepting customers for a limited time. There were too many people in need and just not enough resources to keep giving to everyone. Worst of all, however, was what happened to Lee. Nobody helped him find a job or a way back into education after the move; 'It feels like we've just been plonked here and left to our own devices', Sue said. Bored and not knowing what to do with himself, he soon found himself getting back into street dealing and had recently been arrested carrying Class A drugs. 'And now the police are saying that they can still prosecute him'. The situation had come full circle: Lee had changed from a drug dealer into a modern slave worthy of saving, to a suspected criminal once more.

Law enforcement had a name for young people like Lee: they were called 'alpha victims', individuals who had gone from being genuinely exploited in the eyes of the authorities to having mastered the game of victimhood too well (Chapter 5). From the police's point of view, alpha victims were the worst kind. Not only had they failed to better themselves, having received the support of professionals who had lifted them out of what they saw as their exploitation and experiences of being trafficked, but they had *lied*—pretended to be vulnerable when they knew full well what they were doing. From the point of view of many frontline professionals, Lee had failed to act like a proper victim by refusing to be grateful and allowing himself to get 'sucked' back into drug dealing after he had officially been safeguarded and law enforcement had extended their trust and support to him—making him, once more, a suspect and perpetrator. In the years that followed, Lee would still be visited by law enforcement for 'chats', but the tone of the conversations changed. Lee was told again that unless he gave up names of those higher in the chain, he would be prosecuted for drugs charges. Sue meanwhile was informed that she faced a parenting order[2] for her alleged failures to keep her son off the streets. In 2023, when I paid his family a visit, Lee was awaiting trial for a number of different charges.

If, from the point of view of many frontline professionals, Lee had failed to act like a proper victim by failing to allow himself to be saved, the situation looked very different from the perspective of his family and many others I have worked with. 'They are setting our children up to fail', said one mother, whose child had also been called an 'alpha victim' by police

[2] A parenting order is a court order that comes with obligations for better parenting set out by the judge and failure to comply can result in prosecution.

for having returned to drug dealing after he had been arrested. Saying that 'they'—government bodies, frontline organizations, law enforcement, and others tasked with the role of helping young people exit the illicit economy—were 'setting children up to fail' was not to imply some singular masterminding behind the failure to help vulnerable people thrive. As we saw above, just like with the constituencies that they serve, local government bodies have had to bear the brunt of austerity politics, making do with little by way of funding and resources from central government institutions. And yet, by taking seriously the accusation that the state is failing the very people it claims to be saving, we can bring into focus a fundamental disjuncture between the government's story of redeeming individualized suffering—which centres on the harm suffered by a victim at the hands of their perpetrator—and its failures to see, let alone mitigate, the social suffering that cuts across the state's binary of victim and perpetrator, and that includes, but is not limited to, the interpersonal violence so central to government narratives.

In the context of democratization processes in Brazil, Caldeira and Holston (Caldeira and Holston, 1999; see also Holston, 2007) coined the term 'disjunctive democracy' to describe a situation where citizens have been granted the kinds of procedural rights usually associated with political democracy—such as free elections—but where a majority of citizens still cannot rely on the institutions of the state to respect their full citizenship. Their case study concerns the routine and mundane ways in which executive and judicial bodies violate civil liberties of citizens, particularly those of poor and racialized citizens. Disjunctive democracy is not limited to countries outside of Europe, nor is the state's violation of citizenship exhausted by a focus on civil liberties alone. When it comes to the inhabitants of Britain's multiracial and working-class post-industrial neighbourhoods who are now discovered as potential victims and perpetrators of county lines activity, the government's discovery of 'modern slavery' has happened alongside successive waves of austerity politics implemented on top of decades of neo-liberal welfare withdrawal. But this affront to people's livelihoods and their communities is not necessarily new. Rather, the most recent period of welfare restructuring and cuts needs to be understood in the context of colonial histories that have long enforced differential social citizenship, delegating racialized and working-class subjects to the periphery of welfare (Bhambra, 2022) and rendering them utterly dispensable, while at the same time exploiting their labour for profit accumulation.

From this perspective, the social suffering at the heart of this chapter identifies the workings of a deeply disjunctive democracy that has formally extended a narrative of care to those now deemed vulnerable to modern slavery, while allowing substantive inequalities to flourish in its midst. This is a disjunctive democracy whose politics of austerity and neo-liberal reforms have not only created the conditions in which young people become implicated in the illicit economy, but where the state's piecemeal, inadequate, and conditional solutions should be understood as part of an on-going history of state failures to extend welfare to some of its most disenfranchised and racialized communities. But it is not only at the hands of the welfare state that the communities now considered in need of 'saving' continue to experience social suffering. As the next chapter will show, they also remain the subjects of a deeply punitive criminal justice system that continues to charge, prosecute, and convict young boys and men for drugs and other offences. Once more, we will be able to see disjunctive democracy at work—this time in the contrast between the state's claim to deliver neutral and colour-blind justice and the lived realities of racist state justice meted out against racialized and working-class populations.

4
‘Enslaved by the Criminal Justice System’: Law, Racial Injustice, and Modern Slavery Failures

Introduction

I met Valerie in the spring of 2019, during a conference on county lines and safeguarding organized by a London-based local authority for a professional audience. Nearly fifty years old, a Londoner of Caribbean descent, and a mother of a twenty-one-year-old young man she called M. to protect his identity (I would only learn his full name months later), Valerie was someone who had what professionals call ‘lived experience’ of county lines: her son had been involved in drug dealing from the age of fourteen, having worked for several drugs lines over the years. He had gone missing repeatedly, and been arrested by the police in different parts of the country. He had never been treated as a victim. His story, as Valerie told the audience, was not unique. ‘There is so many of us’, she said. ‘We are all being failed by the system’. After listening to Valerie share her story, I introduced my research to her and asked if she would be willing to talk to me more. ‘I am very busy’, she told me. ‘I am still in the midst of fighting for my son’. I left my contact details with her, not expecting to hear from her again. Three days later, however, an email landed in my inbox: it was from Valerie. Some time had unexpectedly opened up, and would I like to meet her?

Valerie and I arranged to meet one morning under the huge billboards in Waterloo station, one of London’s busiest train stations, located on the Southbank of the River Thames. I spotted her from afar amongst the crowds of people making their way in and out of the trains and underground passages. Immaculately dressed in a black leather jacket, wearing bright orange

Drugs, Race, and the Politics of Modern Slavery Law. Insa Lee Koch, Oxford University Press.
 DOI: 10.1093/9780198899631.003.0004

earrings and a matching orange top, her dreadlocks held back by a colourful hair band, Valerie put my own informal outfit to shame. We walked to a nearby café. As soon as Valerie and I sat down, with our coffees laid out in front of us, she got her smart phone out. 'Before we start our meeting, I want to show you a picture of my son', she said, 'so you can put a face to him'. She didn't have any recent pictures of him, she added, because he had been in and out of prison over the past few years. The first picture she showed me was from a summer holiday she had spent with M. in France: there she was, in a white linen jumpsuit with her long dreads tied up, her face beaming with a mother's pride. She was standing next to a young dark-skinned man with cornrows. He too was dressed in a smart white shirt and long linen trousers. The young man had his arm casually around his mother, looking relaxed and at ease. 'We had such good times together', Valerie laughed. 'We used to go on holiday together, like a normal family'.

The next picture was a close-up shot of her son. This time he was sitting on the steps outside what looked like a holiday home, topless, his muscular body exposed. His eyes were squinting as he looked up into the sun, facing the invisible photographer. I noticed a number of huge, fleshy scars on one of his arms, and drew in my breath. 'Yes, look at them', Valerie said, noticing my reaction. 'This is from when he was stabbed, they stabbed him many times, in the arm, in the chest. It was premediated, they followed him in a car, and they got him on the motorway and stabbed him there and then left him'. Valerie went silent, going through pictures on her phone before showing me a final picture, this time of a little girl with pigtails and a bright, beaming smile that exposed her little white teeth. This was Nola, M.'s baby girl and Valerie's first-born granddaughter. Nola's mother was Chinese and Caribbean, Valerie said with pride in her voice, hence her granddaughter's stunning beauty. Nola was born the day M. was recalled to prison; to this day, her son had never met her. Now she was over a year old, and Valerie was taking care of her granddaughter several days a week. 'She's a sunshine', Valerie said, smiling again. 'She is my son's spitting image'.

I do not know why Valerie showed me these pictures the first time we met. Perhaps it was an unspoken plea on the part of a mother to recognize M. as a family member—as a son and as a father—rather than merely as an abstract 'case study' for research or, worse, as a criminal, a 'gang member' who deserved to be punished. From hearing Valerie speak at the conference,

I knew that this was a label he carried: M. had been charged, convicted, and sentenced several times for drugs and other offences. He was someone who the authorities would describe as an 'alpha victim' (Chapter 3)—someone who, having been steeply implicated in county lines, had long gone from being a 'victim of criminal exploitation' to becoming a 'perpetrator'. But if this was a seemingly straightforward case from the perspective of professionals, then from the point of view of his mother, the story looked very different. As Valerie said at the conference, her son had 'never been treated as a victim by the system', not even when he first began dealing drugs aged as a young teenager. In fact, he had never even been entered into the government's mechanism for recording victims of human trafficking and modern slavery, the National Referral Mechanism (NRM), despite his mother's desperate pleas. At this very moment, Valerie said, her son was back in prison on remand, awaiting trial for new drugs charges: 'It would have never come to this, if the system had not failed us'.

Valerie's words brought home the realities of a criminal justice system that refuses to accord victimhood status to the very same young people that it purports to save under the government's 'modern slavery' agenda. In this chapter, I take this double bind as my point of departure to ask a series of questions: how do boys and young men involved in the street-level economy of class A drugs continue to be criminalized despite or perhaps even because of the government's impetus to 'save' county lines victims? How do such processes become evident at different levels of the criminal justice system, including through policing and the courts? What do their mothers and other family members' fights on their children's behalf reveal about the embedded racism, and its intersection with classed inequalities, at the heart of the justice machinery? And what does all of this tell us about the logic of redemption at the heart of dominant government narratives today? In the last chapter, I explored the mismatch between the state's narrative of modern slavery that sees suffering as the outcome of a harm inflicted by a perpetrator upon their victim, and the social suffering at the hands of multiple structural forces and confronted by young people across the state's binary of victims and perpetrators. I argued that this mismatch brings into relief the workings of a 'disjunctive democracy' (Caldeira and Holston, 1999; Holston, 2007) that is purporting to 'save' the most vulnerable, while allowing substantive inequalities to flourish in its midst.

In this chapter, I take this analysis a step further by linking young drug dealers' and their families' encounters with the welfare state to their experiences with the criminal justice system. Thus, the same racialized and working-class constituencies considered in the last chapter who have been hit most harshly by austerity politics also count among those targeted by a punitive criminal justice system (El-Enany and Bruce-Jones, 2015; Williams and Clarke, 2016; Bhattacharyya et al., 2021; Day and Bean, 2022). Here, my starting point are the boys and young men who ostensibly meet the government's own criteria for who counts as a modern slave, but who still find themselves prosecuted, with their involvement in county lines often acting as an aggravating factor in sentencing strategies. Moreover, as my ethnography with their mothers and other female carers shows, anyone who dares to speak on defendants' behalf can potentially find themselves attacked and criminalized by the system. Young men's encounters with the criminal justice system and their family members' struggles are then another example of the 'social suffering' confronted by those at the margins, defined in the last chapter as the assemblage of human problems that structural forces inflict upon human experiences. They further reveal the workings of a disjunctive democracy whose claims to provide colour-neutral justice are betrayed by the lived realities of racial injustice.

I draw upon ethnographic work conducted mostly with the mothers, and sometimes older sisters, aunts, and other female family members, of the boys and young men caught up in the criminal justice system. I met these women in different places. Some I encountered during my first fieldwork on Park End (Chapter 3), and I have known since 2008 (Koch, 2018). Others I met more recently, by attending a 'modern day slavery' conference, turning up at their son's and male kin's trials, or through snowballing effects. My ethnographic focus on these women is first and foremost a testimony to the marginalization that defines their loved ones' lives. Once their sons, brothers, and other male family members are caught up in the criminal justice system as defendants, the latter become literally bereft of the ability to speak for themselves as police take them away, lawyers silence their voices (Cunningham, 1992), and, as we will see in Chapter 8, prison authorities refuse access to researchers but also to family members. To understand what happened to those the system refused to recognize as victims, I therefore had to speak to people who continued to bear the burden of care, typically their mothers and other female relatives. In the process of getting close to them, I also ended up taking on advocacy roles of various kinds, joining their own struggles to make alternative stories heard—a point I shall return to in the concluding chapter of this book.

Racial neo-liberalism, drugs policing, and the criminal justice system

When mothers like Valerie told me that their sons were never recognized as modern slaves, this did not, in some ways, come as a surprise. It reflects the realities of a criminal justice system that over-polices, under-protects, and selectively criminalizes its Black British citizens and other minoritized groups (Shiner et al., 2018, p. 60). The 'war on gangs' that we looked at in Chapter 2 provides a forceful illustration. There we saw that following the 2011 civic uprisings after the Metropolitan police killing of a young Black man named Mark Duggan, the government blamed what it saw as a pathological 'gang culture' for the ensuing unrest. It saw these 'gangs' as rooted across the country's urban housing estates, which are home to many of the young people involved in 'county lines' today. Policing quickly intensified with the introduction of a database by the Metropolitan police, the 'gangs matrix', which increased surveillance via multi-agency work in the lives of suspected 'gang' members and their families.[1] Patrick Williams and colleagues have repeatedly pointed at the flaws in the internal logic of the government's anti-gangs agenda, with its lack of a clear, evidence-based, operational definition of a 'gang' (Williams, 2015; Williams and Clarke, 2016; Nijjar, 2018; Waller, 2024). Now, predominantly Black and minoritized working-class boys and young men became the subject of heightened stop-and-search tactics, civil injunction orders, and so-called 'joint enterprise' prosecutions that allow for the collective punishment of groups believed to be in 'gangs', as explained below.

Such openly authoritarian state measures need to be understood in relation to the coiling back of welfare measures that we looked at in the last chapter. There, I argued that systemic disinvestment in, and welfare withdrawal from, Britain's urban housing estates have created widespread social suffering that is disproportionately born by their multiracial working-class residents. Against this backdrop, the punitive policing of Black, minoritized, and working-class communities has been theorized as an example of 'racial neoliberalism', a concept which Fatsis uses to highlight 'how neoliberal economics encourages state practices that destroy the conditions required to sustain welfare, but also censure and punish those who need it the most due

[1] The 'gangs matrix' has now been overhauled, following a successful legal challenge raised by the civil liberties charity Liberty on behalf of Awate Suleiman and UNJUST UK. UNJUST UK is a community interest company that challenges injustice in the criminal justice system.

to racialized patterns of urban social inequality and exclusion' (2019). As a state ideology, he argues, racial neoliberalism denies responsibility for the disorder that its anti-welfare policies create—of which drug dealing is an example—and instead accuses individuals of the deterioration of their surroundings, 'often attributing such decline to a lack of civility and a cultural propensity for gang violence, instead of the state's reckless disregard for the safety of its citizens' (2019). His study was concerned with the British state's criminalization of drill music, as this rap style has been identified by the police as a public threat, and been used for intelligence and evidence gathering in criminal investigations of urban Black youth (see also Chapter 6).

To highlight the intimate connection between neo-liberal welfare and racist policing is of course not to say that policing was ever benevolent. Rather, as Laub has put it, government interventions such as the war on 'gangs' are 'contingent upon a history of policing and social control embedded in imperialism, colonialism, patriarchy and class struggle . . . and, in the short run, the crisis of Fordist capitalism in the 1970s' (2024). As once the world's largest empire, Britain has always employed its police in the interest of the ruling classes and against working classes and racialized minorities both in the colonies and within the metropolis itself (Nijjar, 2018; Elliot-Cooper, 2021; Laub, 2021, 2024; Fekete, 2022). Indeed, even during the supposedly 'golden decades' of post-war social democracy, an idea critiqued in the last chapter, the policing of both working-class and minoritized communities was an entrenched feature of British democracy (Davey and Koch, 2021). Immigrants, many of whom had come from Britain's former colonies to help build Britain's post-war economy, were not only excluded from many forms of welfare, but subject to extensive racist policing, such as via the sus law, and openly racist violence by white mobs that police at best ignored or played down, including in Notting Hill in August 1958 (Elliot-Cooper, 2021).

It was from the late 1970s onwards that Britain ushered in a self-conscious 'law and order' state that brought these racial logics more blatantly to the fore. Stuart Hall spoke of incipient Thatcherism as the 'great moving right show' (1979) that aimed to create consent in times of crisis. In *Policing the Crisis* (Hall et al., 2013), Hall and colleagues showed how this was contingent on the production of a moral panic around 'street mugging' that placed blame with urban Black youth for wider social, political, and economic upheavals that Britain was experiencing at a time when the post-war welfare consensus had come under open attack. The early years of Thatcher's tenure witnessed the militarization of the police, the violent breaking up of trade union movements, and miners' strikes; violent clashes between police and civilians during the 1981 'race riots' across major cities; and an expansion of police budgets (Koch, 2018). In the 1990s and 2000s, tough 'law and order' policies were carried forward and became further entrenched under the New Labour government's 'third way policies' whose mantra promised to 'go tough on crime and tough on the causes of crime'. It was during these years that Britain saw the expansion of policing, a proliferation of an unprecedented number of new criminal laws, and a steep rise in prison numbers and sentences, as well as a host of measures implemented in the name of 'public safety' and 'national security' (Newburn, 2007; Koch, 2018; Bhattacharyya et al., 2021).

From 2010 onwards, Britain ushered in its period of austerity politics. Thus, the same logic of cuts that was applied to vast amounts of welfare (considered in the last chapter) also came to govern its justice institutions, with the criminal justice system and the police becoming subject to strict oversight and severe cuts to personnel, pay, and budgets (Laub, 2024). And yet, Laub has argued that cuts did not so much result in the displacement of the police as in a process of 'austerity-driven policification' (2024), namely the police's repurposing: the police came to take on key roles in welfare, social policy, and education institutions that had otherwise been defunded, thus rendering those institutions more coercive while 'normalising and instilling in them a police view of the world' (2024). It was this blurring of the 'left' and the 'right' hands of the state (Wacquant, 2008) that was also evident in the reworking of the government's 'war on gangs' as part of an emerging government response to 'county lines': the drive to turn Black and minoritized working-class communities into hyper-policed communities on account of their being 'gang' members went hand-in-hand with an ideological emphasis on safeguarding through multi-agency work those who had been exploited 'from within' (Chapter 2).

The result is that today, in an era often claimed to be post-racial (Commission on Race and Ethnic Disparities, 2021), racial disparities remain extremely high, not just in policing but across the entire criminal justice system. In Chapter 1, I showed that this is nowhere more clearly evidenced than when it comes to drugs policing (Eastwood, Shiner, and Bear, 2013; Shiner et al., 2018; Williams and Clarke, 2018; Koram, 2019; Woolley, 2021). Analysis undertaken by Release (Eastwood, Shiner, and Bear, 2013) found that even though Black people were less likely to use drugs than white people, they were six times more likely to be stopped and searched for drugs. Furthermore, throughout 2019–20, all racially minoritized groups were over-represented in police-recorded searches for drugs (33.8 per cent) when compared to their proportion in the general population (an estimated 15.6 per cent). Comparatively, white people were underrepresented in police searches for drugs, accounting for 50.4 per cent of searches for drugs against their proportion in the population (84.4 per cent) (Allen, 2021), and notwithstanding the fact that drug use remains most prevalent among white people who often acquire drugs from within their personal networks. The discrepancy in the application of drugs laws has helped create a situation in which the proportion of Black people imprisoned, in relation to the proportion of the total population of the country, is higher in the UK than in the US—with the latter often held up as a case of extreme punitivism (Koram, 2019, p. 6).

Critical commentators have started to link these figures to broader debates around racial (in)justice and its deeper historical roots. Indeed, going against the idea that the 'colour line' was a colonial construct that was abolished with the formal ending of colonies and empires, Koram has argued that the international 'war on drugs' acts as a contemporary arena in which differences in racialized subjectivity and experiences continue to be produced through enforcement practice and policy (2019). Far from constituting neutral policies, less even positive interventions that improve the conditions of life for all peoples in the world, laws that prohibit the production, sale, and possession of drugs further large-scale displacement, death, and incarceration (Arias and Grisaffi, 2021). Moreover, this suffering is not distributed evenly but instead is disproportionately borne by specific groups of people—in particular those who have already been historically oppressed through preceding colonial-racial projects (Koram, 2019, pp. 2–5). Similarly in a UK context, Williams and Clarke have argued that state articulations of Black criminality, central to drugs policing, serve to produce and justify the implementation of punishing penal apparatuses and strategies that assuage the (white) public's concerns about the perennially transmogrifying and racist stereotypes of young Black men as 'dangerous, violent and volatile' (2018, p. 2).

It is against the backdrop of these critical perspectives that I revisit, and further unpack in this chapter, the government's narrative of redemption central to its discovery of county lines. When, in 2018, I first started working with the mothers, aunts, and sisters of the boys and young men who find themselves at the receiving end of drugs policing and criminal justice interventions, I noticed how the official story of saving the vulnerable did not match up with the social suffering I was witnessing on the ground. On the contrary, a disjunctive reality shifted into focus: this time, between the state's claims to neutral and colour-blind justice and the lived realities of brutal racial injustice. Not only did the boys and young men racialized as 'other' (on account of either their skin colour or class or both) persistently find themselves constructed as a threat, but their family members were silenced for their attempts to make counter perspectives heard. What is more, as I became privy to the mothers' engagement with various agents of the criminal justice system, I began to realize how systemic these attacks were. If the last chapter argued that families' experiences of failure at the hands of welfare interventions exemplify the workings of a deeply disjunctive democracy, then this chapter highlights democracy's disjunctive workings through the criminal justice system's mundane enactments of 'state racial terror' (El-Enany, 2020) in the lives of defendants and their primary carers.

'Never recognized a slave': A mother's tale

The day Valerie and I met in the café at Waterloo station in 2019 would be the start of a close relationship. As we became friends and colleagues speaking together in front of policy audiences about our respective work and experiences, I became privy to a painful family story that had been unfolding over the previous five years. Valerie would 'never in a million years have dreamt' that she would have to face the challenges that life had thrown at her. A second-generation migrant in Britain, she had grown up in a strict religious household in South London together with her sister, her Jamaican father, and her Trinidadian mother. Her parents had come to Britain as part of the Windrush generation from the West Indies, to help build Britain's post-war economy. They had worked hard to make England their new home. Her father first worked in the factories before becoming, in his late age, a taxi driver; her mother worked in the local authority where, Valerie proudly recalled, she made a successful career in local governance despite the bitter racism that she faced in those days. Valerie herself had always tried to teach her son to be a respectful young man. She was proud of the opportunities that she had been able to afford him: a stable and loving family home, summer holidays in France, and even international sports competitions that he took part in through his local school.

Losing her son to the 'underworld' had been a huge shock to Valerie. She sometimes struggled to see her son for who he 'really' was after all he had put her through, at times feeling overpowering anger and resentment towards him. She had not slept a proper night in five years, being constantly worried for her son's safety, always half expecting the police to call to say that her son had been killed. 'I literally didn't know if he would come home alive in the evening or if the police would call and tell me that they found his dead body', she shared. Over the years, his involvement in criminal activities had put her and her family at risk. After her son's most recent arrest, his daughter's mum had received death threats through the door, leaving her acutely worried for Nola's safety. M. had also made her liable for his own financial misgivings. Once, several months after he had been taken in for an offence, Valerie started receiving letters from a bailiff, stating that she was liable to pay a debt of 2,000 pounds. It turned out that her son had given her name as a warrant when renting cars on credit—she did not know at the time why he would need a car, but now she understood it was to deliver runners and drugs. Valerie had no idea how to pay off the debt. She started worrying that the bailiffs would come knocking on her door, and that her elderly father who lived in the same house would find out: as an upright Caribbean man, he would never be able to forgive his grandson. Valerie was going through acute stress that eventually resulted in her experiencing a mental breakdown.

In hindsight, Valerie knew that much of M.'s behaviour could be explained as a consequence of his being coerced by others. He had drug debts to pay, and was acting under the control of others higher up the drugs chain. Like many mothers I met, Valerie had trained herself in the language of 'criminal exploitation', 'modern slavery', and 'trafficking'. To her, her son's behaviour matched the precise pattern of what the government called a victim of 'criminal exploitation': from his disappearing episodes to his cagey body language, lies, aggressive behaviour, and implication in violent incidents, he displayed what Valerie called 'all the classical signs'. But her views were not shared by any of the professionals she turned to for support. 'They just see him as someone who made lifestyle choices, a gang member', Valerie said to me once. 'He has been arrested countless times. I have a stack of letters at home, for each and every time he had been arrested, there is a pattern, you can see it in the letters: nobody ever came to help him, nobody ever tried to get him out of this'. When she turned to her son's school, M.'s teachers insisted that he had brought it upon himself. Then, when her son turned eighteen, the authorities told her that her son was an adult now and that they had no duty of care towards him. In a write-up initially produced as part of testimony she was hoping to share with politicians in a desperate attempt to make the story heard, Valerie repeated and further revealed additional failures on the part of professionals. I produce the write-up verbatim here:

- There were growing concerns for his [M.'s] safety and his hygiene
- He would go missing for days, weeks and then months to the point of me having to agree to publish an appeal in the Metro Newspaper via the Missing People Charity (major support emotionally also 24-hour service helpline).
- I had begged for help for the best part of 5 years from the start of my son becoming exploited
- To prevent my son from becoming embedded in what I called an 'Outside Influence' I told every agency [. . .] that unless my son was seen as a victim then things will escalate as they were seeing him as making a life style choice at the age of 14.
- I was constantly told by all authorities that unfortunately for me to get support my son would have to be convicted.
- When I asked the police if there was anything they could do as he was constantly going missing, they said their hands were tied as they do not have the power to do anything
- Up against constant barriers of needing consent, no agency registered my son on NRM
- From 2012 to date my son has been in care to keep him safe at the time, on a tag, arrested many times, spent time in youth prison, arrested once again, on remand, released without a fix abode, stabbed 3 times in the foot, palm of his hand, chest and biceps which was almost fatal, arrested again, on remand and now sentenced as an adult (aged 22) for being a victim of exploitation.
- In 2021 due to be released soon [. . .]. Trying to prevent him from being released without any shoes on his feet and clothes on his back as this happened in 2018 when released from Belmarsh [a high security prison].

The refusal on the part of the authorities to recognize her son as an individual who fitted the government's own depiction of a county lines slave was highlighted by Valerie's failures to get her son entered into the NRM. The NRM is a bureaucratic mechanism set up by the Home Office for purposes of recording and identifying victims of modern slavery and human trafficking. While the decision is not legally binding, a finding that an individual is a victim of human trafficking and modern slavery (called a 'positive conclusive grounds decision') can weigh strongly in not bringing drugs (or other) charges against that individual; or, where charges are brought, it can be used to support the use of the modern slavery defence, and act as a mitigating factor in sentencing (see Chapter 6). Valerie desperately wanted her son to be entered into the NRM, partly because she wanted it confirmed 'by the system' that M. had indeed been a victim, and partly because she was hopeful that this could help with his pending case; perhaps even result in his being acquitted.

In the months after Valerie and I met, I became involved in helping her with a range of issues involving her son's case, including in her ongoing attempts to get him entered into the NRM. The basic problem we faced was that a family member is not allowed to make a submission to the NRM. Submissions work via so-called 'first responders', designated bodies—such as the police or a local authority—that have been given statutory powers to make such submissions. They must prepare a portfolio of relevant documents that are then assessed by a bureaucrat before a decision is reached in a two-stage process on the basis of balance of probabilities, the civil standard of proof. For Valerie, putting pressure on the police to have M.'s files submitted to the NRM was not an option given that the police had only ever treated him as a perpetrator. Our only hope was her son's so-called 'personal advisor', the name given to an appointed local official responsible for supporting M.'s transition from living in care to independent living (M. had been living in care for a while before his most recent arrest). We wrote several emails to M.'s personal advisor, but never received any reply. It was only when we managed to get hold of her supervisor on the phone several weeks later that the personal advisor responded: in an email, she expressed being willing to try to initiate the process, adding, however, that she was not confident M. would be found to be a victim given his 'history'.

In any case, the advisor specified in her email, Valerie's son had to give his consent to be entered into the NRM. Because he was over the age of eighteen, the submission could not be made without it. Yet, gaining M.'s consent while he was held in prison was not as straightforward as it may sound. Prisons are notoriously closed spaces, and to get any form to M., it would have to go through the prison's own channels of communication, be approved, and then be forwarded. Once more, our emails to the prison management to get the process rolling did not elicit any reply. When Valerie asked M.'s personal advisor if the advisor could book herself for a visit and hand deliver the form to her son, the advisor told her that she was too busy, and that the prison where M. was held was far outside of London (where the advisor was based). Discouraged by these hurdles, Valerie hoped to implement a plan B ahead of M.'s court case: she wanted to ask his probation officer to write a report about M.'s history of exploitation that could be submitted to the judge as mitigation at the sentencing stage. Once more, however, we did not know how to contact M.'s probation officer as these details had not been shared with Valerie, since her son had turned eighteen. Valerie was feeling stressed. 'Time is running out now', she said, so 'obviously I need to make sure that I am covering [my son's case] from all possible angles because I don't know what will happen'.

In the end, this was all to no avail. In August 2019, a few months after we had met, an email landed in my inbox. It was from Valerie. Her son had pleaded guilty, before we had been able to make any progress with either the NRM submission or a letter from his probation officer. Her email bears spelling out in full:

Morning Insa

I hope this email finds you well and that you had a good weekend. Sadly my son is another victim of exploitation to do time.
See as follows:

- Sentenced to 5 years
- To serve halve of the time above
- Which means he has 2 years left as he's been on remand for 6 months
- The trial took place Friday 1st August

It's heart breaking, soul destroying, devastating—but I'm keeping it moving after breaking down.

I don't know where he will be yet (as in which prison) but he called me on Saturday. He said it's not the end of the world (I said it is for a parent). He's completely desensitized so this response isn't surprising at all. He seems and sounds ok. [. . .]

Have a good day.
Take care.
Valerie.

Valerie's story, 'soul destroying, heart breaking, and devastating' as it was, was not unique. What stood out in the stories shared with me were the persistent ways that mothers, and sometimes other family members of the young men and boys, continued to encounter the brunt of a punitive system that was claiming to protect and save those involved in drug dealing and county lines. For mothers like Valerie, this came as no surprise: it spoke of, and reflected back, the realities of a justice system that, despite its claims to the contrary, continues to treat young minoritized men as 'criminal collectives' (Nijjar, 2022). Some of the mothers I spoke with felt that exposure to such a system had rubbed off on their children in a negative way, making them believe the system's characterization of them. When I called Valerie after receiving her news in that email, she repeated that her son had sounded 'totally desensitized' over the prison phone: he did not think that he was a victim, after all, she said, and hence did not expect any better. Lisa, a white English mother who will be introduced shortly in more detail, once said that she had come to think of the system as having an 'abusive' hold over her son. Mirroring the language of 'exploitation' and 'enslavement' that we already encountered in relation to the mothers who spoke of their own and their children's encounters with safeguarding agencies and the welfare state, she said:

> It's not only the exploitation and the modern slavery of drugs but *people are also exploited and enslaved by the criminal justice system now*. If they were to safeguard the victims, they would recover much more quickly [from the trauma and experiences suffered] . . . What is the point of the NRM? They are not using it. He has picked up a certain mentality just from being through the criminal justice system, he believes himself to be an offender. The system is just as guilty as the people who exploit him: it's a kind of abuse [my emphasis].

In the next sections, I turn more closely to the advocacy work of these women, showing how their attempt to call out the 'abuse' of the system was not only an emotionally exhausting and all-consuming task, but also made them vulnerable to attack.

On angry and overbearing mothers

I met Lisa through Valerie, having been introduced to her after explaining to Valerie that I was interested in speaking with other parents whose children had experiences with 'criminal exploitation'. Valerie had been pleased about this request, telling me that 'there are so many of us, and we have all had to suffer in silence', but also warning me that the issue would have to be handled delicately: the traumas that families experienced at the hands of the threats from drug dealing and the criminal justice system ran deep, she said, and care had to be taken not to 're-traumatize' when researching with them. Still, she said, she would be happy to pass on a written invitation to speak to me to her contacts, as it would be important for their stories to be heard. A few weeks later, an email landed in my inbox, coming from a woman called Lisa: she would like to share her son's story with me, the email said, and asked if I would be free to meet her together with her father at a café in the Southbank Centre, the UK's largest arts centre located on the south bank of the river Thames. I knew exactly which café she meant, having spent many hours in it too. Located in the large entrance area of the theatre, the expansive venue offers visitors and passersby an anonymous and calm space in what is otherwise a buzzing and busy area of London. I immediately agreed to meet with her.

Lisa was a white English woman in her late thirties who self-identified as 'working class', having grown up as the daughter of a factory worker and a trade unionist in Peckham, an increasingly gentrified, but still with a large working class and African population. She was the mother of T. (once more I would only learn his full name months after we had met), a nineteen-year-old mixed heritage white and Black Caribbean young man. Lisa used to work as a teaching assistant in a local school, before 'it all started', but she had not been able to keep the job when 'things started going badly with her son'. Now, she told me, she was surviving on Universal Credit, the meagre social benefit payments that required her to turn up to the Jobcentre, the agency administering welfare payments, every other week and undergo what she experienced as a humiliating ritual (Chapter 3). Lisa's nervous disposition, and the enduring anxieties she freely admitted she still had, were palpable. She had come with her father for extra support. A quiet but confident presence next to her, he would frequently touch his daughter as if to offer reassurance, or help her finish her sentences, when she became visibly too anxious to do so.

During the afternoon we spent together at the Southbank Centre, Lisa told me her story, emphasizing many of the same struggles that Valerie had faced. It all started when T. was fourteen, and he started dealing drugs for older teenagers in his neighbourhood. Lisa struggled to get him away from it, the school that he was attending at the time refused to take the problem seriously, instead expelling him when he was found with drugs on him. Gradually, things took a more serious turn. Aged fifteen, T. went missing. It was not the first time that he disappeared for inexplicable reasons, but it was the longest—he was gone for over two weeks, leaving his mother acutely anxious and convinced that he would be found dead. One day, Lisa received a phone call from police in Northampton, some eighty miles away from his London home. Her son had been found in a drug user's home, with drugs and weapons on him. Lisa recalled travelling to the police station in Northampton on a long bus ride. She was shocked to find her son looking almost unrecognizable when he was brought out of the cell by the duty officer: 'He was almost feral', she said, 'he was like a wild animal. I don't know what they had been doing to him, he wouldn't talk, he looked like he had not been eating in days, he was so dirty'.

Following the incident, T. was entered into the NRM mechanism by the authorities and shortly after received a 'conclusive grounds decision' that he had been criminally exploited. Yet, this did not stop Northampton police from pressing charges for drugs. This was not the first time T. had been arrested and convicted, and the police now cited his previous convictions as a reason why it would be in the public interest to prosecute this case. By then, however, Lisa had heard about the *Modern Slavery Act*, having done her own research into it on the many lonely evenings that she spent waiting for T. to return home. She had learned on social media that there were many children like her son involved in county lines, and that specific policies had been put in place to safeguard and to protect, rather than to criminalize and punish them. Yet, when she mentioned all of this to her son's duty solicitor—someone she described as a white English woman—the solicitor simply laughed in her face: 'She said that the modern slavery policies have nothing to do with my son, that they were not meant to be for drug dealers like him'. Lisa could not help but feel it was 'racism': 'They just don't think that Black boys can be victims'.

On the day of the trial, Lisa chose her outfit carefully. She liked to dress in gothic outfits and black net-tights, prominently displaying her tattoos of black skulls and red roses along her arms and legs. That day, however, she said she wanted to look as professional as she could. She covered up her tattoos and wore a simple black outfit. She also asked her daughter, T.'s twenty-three-year-old half-sister, to join her. Unlike T., his half-sister was not mixed heritage but white, and Lisa felt that this would be to T.'s advantage. Together they travelled to court, back on a long bus ride to Northampton, and watched the trial from the public gallery. T. was given a suspended sentence and some hours of community service. To this day, T. is convinced that had his mother and sister not been there, the outcome could have been very different:

> T. thinks that it is only because me and my daughter were both there in court that they didn't send him to a young offenders' institution but that he was allowed to come home with us. My son thinks that the only reason he didn't go to prison is because I am white, and maybe he is right. We were in court, and they were really nice to me and my daughter, I put on a posh accent [laughs] . . .

T. might well have been right. As we will see later, those racialized as non-white can find that their court experiences are very different, as their presence in the public gallery during a family member's trial is often seen with suspicion, if not outright criticism. For Lisa, the outcome of the case was a small victory. After the trial, she brought T. back home. She was hopeful that things would be different this time. However, she soon realized that T. was getting 'sucked back in': he would steal money from her, be abusive, and repeatedly abscond again. At the time, she did not understand why he would do this; now, however, in hindsight, she suspected that her son had incurred a drug debt when he was arrested, and that he had been asked to work off his debt. Lisa was desperate to get the support in place that would help her son exit his life as a drug dealer, a process that was ongoing and had become all-consuming, leaving her utterly drained and exhausted.

On a sunny day in June 2019, a few months after we met, Lisa invited me to her two-bedroom socially rented flat in Denmark Hill, an urban neighbourhood in South London not far from Peckham, where she had grown up. Lisa had a modest home, located on the top floor of an old Victorian building that had been cheaply converted into separate flats. As she led me into the kitchen to boil some water for tea and handed me some chocolate biscuits, she commented on all the things that were broken: the drainage did not work properly, there was a crack in the kitchen window, and the heating was dysfunctional. 'The council don't care', she said. Today, however, she wanted to talk about her son. As I sat down on the worn leather sofa that stood in the middle of an otherwise almost empty room, Lisa passed me a heavy A4 folder in a three-ring binder. As I opened the folder, letters, envelopes, and printed emails started spilling out, falling onto my lap, the sofa, and the floor. 'I tried to organize what I have done', Lisa said somewhat apologetically, 'but it's too much, it's been years of doing this'. The letters were proof of the work that Lisa had undertaken, in vain, as she had contacted just about every single authority, professional, frontline worker, and agency to support her son. That afternoon, as we went through a fraction of the documents in the folder, she recalled various moments of confrontation, at times reducing her to tears, at others causing her to laugh out loud in disbelief.

Women like Lisa felt deeply judged by professionals for their attempts to advocate on their children's behalf. 'People see you as an overbearing parent', 'they think that you are over the top or too emotional', 'they tell you that you shouldn't tell them how to do their job', were some of the things that mothers had been told. During the afternoon I spent with Lisa going through her folder of communication with professionals, she picked out a printed letter. Several pages long, written by her son's previous social worker and sent to her on behalf of the local authority's multi-agency group (composed of a social worker, police officer, and other local officials), the letter concerned a 'risk assessment' that the authorities had carried out on her son. The risk assessment had found that T. was at high risk of 'desisting' (ironically while being at low risk of being 'regroomed'). By court order, he would be placed on an electronic curfew tag, where an electronic device could check if T. was at home on his specified curfew orders, with a monitoring centre being notified in case of failure. In the letter Lisa passed to me, T.'s previous social worker explained that the tag was to prevent T. from desisting. The letter also stated that T.'s family support, in particular from his mother, was an issue of concern. The relevant section, entitled 'Parenting Capacity of Lisa Grey' reads as follows:

> Mother Lisa presents as a parent who appears to be concerned for the well being of her son. On the surface her concerns are well founded and I believe they are coming from a good place. However, throughout the course of this and previous assessments, she has struggled to keep cordial relationships with professionals involved in her son's life. She has made a number of formal complaints, including one against her son's previous social worker who compiled the previous assessment as well as members of the [Youth Offending] team. As well as this, I have been informed that she is very protective of her son, and in the past has been excluded from school meetings as she was unable to contain herself and responds negatively to any criticisms of [T]. At a recent court hearing she again had to be excluded from the Court because she was unable to contain herself.

The letter continued to state that 'T. does not have a positive relationship with his mother: Mother Lisa continues to escalate her concerns about T., and this causes him distress to the point where he has stopped communicating with her and has requested that she is not involved with his case'. While Lisa laughed about the use of the term 'Mother Lisa'—an ironic twist she felt on 'Mother Theresa', a nun remembered for her selfless dedication to the poor—the letter just summed it all up: the institutionalized mistrust, suspicion, and attacks that parents like her had to endure for wanting to speak up for their children. She was well aware that relations between her and her son had not always been good: how could they be, given that he had repeatedly been absconding, lied to her, been abusive and secretive? And yet, she also knew that even in their most strained moments, she had been his only advocate. It was precisely this determination to fight for him that was now called into question, as she was presented as irrational and overly emotional, as being 'unable to contain herself', as 'struggling to keep cordial relationships with professionals' and as being too 'protective' of her son. Indeed, the assessment continued to state, under a section entitled 'what needs to change', that 'the relationship between T. and his mother needs to improve in order that mother can feel involved and in turn will be able to build positive relationships with professionals involved with her son'.

Here, then, a mother's efforts to achieve what she considered to be best for her son became the very reason for pathologizing her labour of love. More so, it served as a justification for ignoring any concerns that she expressed about her son's well-being and safety, as the latter were presented as misplaced or, worse even, ill intentioned. In Lisa's case, the failures on the part of the authorities to take her concerns seriously had almost lethal consequences. Let us consider for a moment Lisa's request that she and her son be offered a managed housing transfer that would allow them to move outside of the area where T. had met the drug dealers he was working for. For Lisa, a managed housing transfer was the only hope to get out of the area: as in Sue's case that we considered in Chapter 3, Lisa did not have the means to rent a flat in the private rental market where rents were more expensive than what she paid for her socially rented flat, and having her son be moved into care was unfathomable for her. But the local authorities had repeatedly rebutted her request, insisting that her case was not 'high enough priority', including one time in my presence when I had gone with her to the housing office to support her case. Yet, trapped in her flat, Lisa was beside herself with worries that the people T. used to work for would come after him. Eventually, Lisa saw her biggest fears come true:

> T. got stabbed outside his home. There is two of them that did it. T. came back from Argos [a store] and they were following him and cornered him from opposite sites like a trapped animal, and he tried to run away and

> tripped over and then they stabbed him in the buttocks. I asked if it had been a warning, and police said, 'no, they wanted to kill him'. They only stopped because a neighbour saw it and they ran away. Then they sent threats on social media. The police's attitude is appalling. They said to him, 'either you give us names, or we won't move you', because that's what he had asked, to be moved because he is not safe. This is not on—they wanted to use him just to get information! If he had given them names, they would have washed their hands off him. They just wanted the information . . . If he had gotten killed, the state would have been guilty of murder.

Drawing on historical work, Adam Elliot-Cooper (2019) has argued that poor women in Britain and those living under colonial rule in geographically and temporally specific ways fell outside the gendered norms of respectability and the nation. Imperial constructs in eighteenth and nineteenth century Europe framed colonized subjects as essentially violent, hypersexual, and criminal, while the domestic working classes were considered morally underdeveloped. While we have seen how the popular image of the criminalized Black folk devil has been projected onto Black male youth, Black British feminists have discussed how these traits can also be inscribed onto women (Phoenix, 1997; Reynolds, 1997), making Black women among the most marginalized in British society (Mirza, 1997). Working-class white and minoritized mothers fighting on behalf of their children face a similar stigma: as Lisa's story has shown, in their attempts to push back against the authorities' refusal to recognize their children as anything other than criminals who have made bad 'lifestyle' choices, they found themselves ridiculed, belittled, and stigmatized as angry and overbearing. These labels, however, were not just a symbolic affront. Negative labelling could be used as a justification to exclude women from any professional interaction, sometimes even under the threat of punishment, and with further negative consequences on their children's lives. Let me turn to Tami now, and to her advocacy during her brother's trial.

'The slave who became a murderer'

In the spring of 2019, I received an email: 'Come to Snaresbrook, Monday 10am, co-defendant is running the modern slavery defence'. The message came from a criminal defence barrister who had heard about my research through a mutual colleague. Revealing no further details about the trial,

I assumed that this would be another drugs case like others I had attended (Chapter 6), where a group of defendants had been charged with possession with intent to supply Class A drugs or, alternatively, with drugs conspiracy. These tended to be the type of cases where defence lawyers might try the 'modern slavery defence' under s.45 of the *Modern Slavery Act 2015*. On the day of the trial, I arrived early in Snaresbrook, one of London's Crown Courts and a Victorian courthouse located in the heart of East London, an area historically home to London's dock workers and successive waves of immigrants. More recently, like many other post-industrial neighbourhoods, it had also become the seat of heightened gentrification. Having gone through stringent security and taken a seat outside the designated courtroom, I noticed a woman roughly my age sitting across from me, looking at her phone. This was Tami, a Londoner of African-Caribbean descent. Dressed in black, with glasses and long plaits that she wore tied back, Tami looked like she had dressed for court. Assuming that she was a professional, I decided to introduce myself and ask her for more details about the upcoming hearing.

Tami was visibly taken aback by my questions about what had brought her to trial. She was here as the appointed guardian of K.S., one of the defendants, she said after a moment's hesitation, and added that she was a trained social worker. We chatted awkwardly for a while, and both of us were relieved when the usher called to let us into the public gallery, interrupting our conversation. Tami had failed to tell me that morning that she was not only K.S.'s guardian but also his sister, being seventeen years his senior, and his de facto primary carer, having been his most stable point of reference and family member from a young age. I can only suspect that her failure to tell me this information was deliberate, once more an expression of the stigma that family members of young Black men experience for being their advocates. But more so, she had said nothing about the actual charges brought in this case. Contrary to my assumption that this was a drugs trial only, I learnt through the prosecution's opening that K.S., a fifteen-year-old Black boy from London, had been charged on three counts with drugs, affray, and, crucially, alongside his co-defendant, with murder. His defence lawyer was only running the modern slavery defence in relation to the drugs charges.[2] K.S.' co-defendant was A.B., a twenty-one-year-old white man from Chelmsford.

[2] The s.45 defence under the Modern Slavery Act 2015 does not apply to murder charges.

The background circumstances of the killing had been established as 'agreed facts' by the legal parties. Both K.S. and A.B. had been out dealing Class A drugs for a drugs line called the 'Top line'—which went from London to Chelmsford, a town in Essex about an hour's drive from London—around midnight in late June 2018. There was no question about the fact that they had sold heroin and crack cocaine to the victim, himself a fifty-something year old white man from Essex and a long-standing drug user, and a runner for a rival drugs line, the 'Amani line'. Nor did the co-defendants deny that shortly after the drug sale, an altercation had occurred between them and the victim, during which punches had been thrown. It is what happened thereafter that was in the dark. At around 12.40 that same night, a friend of the victim (who was also a drug user and a runner for the Amani line) called the ambulance to inform them that the victim had been stabbed. By the time rescue services arrived, police had already attended to the scene, having been called out by a neighbour who had heard the victim screaming for help. They were performing resuscitation, but to no avail: the victim died shortly after from a traumatic cardiac arrest, nobody claimed that they had seen the stabbing, no murder weapon had been recovered, and no DNA was found on the victim's body that could point to the identity of his killer(s).

None of this, however, mattered. K.S. and A.B. had been charged with murder under the doctrine of joint enterprise. Although a broad, imprecise, and non-legal term generally used to refer to cases in which two or more people are accused of having engaged in criminal activity together, joint enterprise, or secondary liability, emerged as a prosecution tool for the collective punishment of groups where it can be proven that the suspects were 'in it together', often relying on stereotypical depictions of individuals as 'gang members' (Williams and Clarke, 2016). Each participant in a crime is tried, sentenced, and labelled as if they committed the crime themselves, even when there are stark differences in the contribution each made. The law distinguishes different types of joint enterprise, including situations of joint perpetration where two or more people carried out the crime together (here, the prosecutor must prove the elements of the crime alleged were committed by the defendants acting together), or situations of 'accessorial liability', where there are persons who did not carry out the crime but were complicit in it (here, the prosecutor must prove that the defendant assisted or encouraged the crime, not that they actually committed it and that they intended to help the principal to commit the crime). While these are distinct situations, prosecutors do not have to distinguish between principals and secondary parties, and in many cases, the evidence does not reveal for sure who committed the conduct that led to the offence (Waller, 2024, pp. 8–9).

Although with a much longer history, joint enterprise prosecution strategies became notorious in the aftermath of the London uprisings that followed the police's killing of Mark Duggan, and were used to convict people of serious offences, usually murder, in the course of committing a prior offence (Williams and Clarke, 2016). Critics of the doctrine have long pointed out that this has created situations in which it would be easier to convict several defendants than a single defendant for murder, especially when it comes to assessorial liability (Carvalho, 2020; Waller, 2024). We can see this problem at work in the trial of K.S. The prosecution in this case never specified the precise role that each defendant had played in the crime alleged. This was a situation, they simply told the court, where two drug dealers had been running a successful 'drugs empire', willing to use any violence to protect their profit margins against a rival drugs line, the Amani line. Granted, one of the defendants—A.B.—was older, had a long history of criminal involvement, and was the one who was known in Chelmsford as a successful drug dealer. But K.S. (the defendant who the defence claimed had been 'exploited' by A.B.) was on the prosecution's account a well-versed criminal too. The prosecution told the court that it did not matter which of the two defendants had committed the stabbing that resulted in the victim's death, or whether both had. As long as the jury were satisfied that at least one of them had done it and that there was a joint venture, they could find them both guilty of murder.

In the weeks that followed, I would witness the prosecution build their case around a narrative that heavily tapped into 'gang' imagery, intended to establish not only a parity between the defendants but also to highlight the idea of a joint undertaking. The defendants' criminal histories of drug dealing, and in A.B.'s case of violent offending, were highlighted. Further 'bad character' evidence was introduced, including photos retrieved from K.S.'s phone of him holding a machete and internet searches with the tag line 'prayers for forgiveness'. The prosecution's cross-examination of K.S. was further aimed at discrediting him, as was that of his co-defendant's lawyer. Both argued that K.S. was a known 'gang' member, that he had come into the crossfire of 'gang warfare' between two well-known London gangs, the 'Stokeys' and the 'Pagans', and wound up getting shot in the leg as a result. Numerous aspects of his appearance, including his nickname, were held up as evidence of K.S.'s own steep involvement with these gangs. The following is an example of dialogue from the hours' long cross-examination that the prosecution (P.) subjected K.S. to about his other nickname, 'Y.L.':

P.: Did you get to Chelmsford through D. [an older male who introduced K.S. to A.B.] and ended up drug dealing?
K.S.: Yes.
P.: Calling yourself Y.L.?
K.S.: Yes.
P.: Why?
K.S.: No specific reason. It doesn't stand for anything. I can't remember the reason.
P.: I suggest to you that some young people that deal drugs try to associate themselves with established and successful drug dealers, by calling themselves young [name of the dealer]. Does Y stand for young?
K.S.: It stands for what you want.
P.: Were you trying to look gangster?
K.S.: No.
P.: Did you call yourself Y.L. because you were young, and you used the initial of someone's name [who was a well-known gangster]?
K.S.: No. No specific reason.

There was nothing surprising about this portrayal. As Williams and Clarke have pointed out (2016), nebulous concepts of 'the gang' are frequently invoked by prosecution in joint enterprise cases to depict young Black men as a criminal group, reflecting the longer colonial legacies of treating minoritized communities as criminal collectives (Nijjar, 2018). And yet, this portrayal failed to account for a very different view of K.S.'s life, one that I became privy to via Tami. Having initially been suspicious of my role, we grew close over the coming months. As we would sit next to each other in the public gallery every day for the following six weeks, taking our lunch breaks together and travelling back from court every day, I learnt what K.S. had been through in his young life. From being born in a prison while his mother was serving a sentence, to spending much of his childhood homeless, to being subjected to racist slurs in school ('they called him monkey and threw bananas at him'), Tami's brother's upbringing had been far from protected. Aged fourteen, he had been shot in the leg, not because he was in a 'gang' but because a stray bullet hit him in the park. Shortly after, K.S. started working as a low-level runner for various lines. While the NRM found him to be a trafficked victim, none of the authorities made attempts to safeguard him. A.B. had hired K.S. a couple of weeks before the killing to work on the 'Top line'. Once in Chelmsford, he received little pay for his long work shifts, was made to sleep in drug users' homes, and, a week into working for A.B., was robbed of drugs and money by members of the 'Amani line'. Told by A.B. that he had to recover his losses, K.S. was given a machete and tried to face his robbers, resulting in the affray charge he was facing.

While this alternative story at the very least questioned the idea of joint venture central to the prosecution's 'story telling' (Waller, 2024), for Tami this was not the only doubtful part of the prosecution's narrative. Worse, even, was the way the murder investigation was conducted, something she told me about only months after the trial's conclusion. One day in late summer 2018, a few months after the killing, K.S. was at his sister's house when the police broke through the door without any warning. They dragged him out in his underwear, handcuffed him, and took him to the police station, where he was held for seventy-two hours and interrogated at all times of the day and night. As the appointed guardian of a minor, Tami was present during the interrogations. She saw the police 'play dirty games': K.S. was told that 'his own mother had set him up' and 'handed him in' because 'she did not love him'. K.S. was repeatedly shown pictures of the blood-stained victim and asked to confess to the murder. The officers were taunting and mocking him, and K.S. was getting increasingly stressed and agitated. Meanwhile, Tami felt that alternative routes for investigation were never taken seriously: No attempts, for example, were made to recover the murder weapon, which on A.B.'s own girlfriend's account she had gotten rid of that same night. Nor was she produced as a witness for the prosecution's case, less even as a co-defendant to the joint enterprise murder charge. Tami could not help but feel that the investigations had been biased from the get-go against the 'one Black boy from London'; all the other actors—victim, co-defendant, and his girlfriend—were from Essex, much older, 'English and white'.

Determined to make sure that her brother had a fair trial, Tami had come to court to be a watchful presence in the courtroom. She promised him at the outset that she would fight until the bitter end, and that at the end of the trial, he would 'come home again'. K.S. had been on remand for nearly the last year, and Tami had only been able to see her brother intermittently when visiting him in prison. It was therefore important to her that he could see her every day in the public gallery, from the secure enclosure of his glass-panelled dock. While Tami knew that much of her brother's story would never be heard by the court, she did her best to advocate for him. After the prosecution's cross-examination, she asked the court to rectify their portrayal of K.S. as a 'gang member' by acknowledging that they had quoted an erroneous finding by social services following the shooting he had become a victim of a few years prior. This did not happen. Her insistence that a proper psychological assessment be carried out in light of K.S.'s traumatic childhood experiences and her long-held suspicion that her brother had a neurodivergent condition was rejected (her suspicion would much later be confirmed, but not until after his conviction). Perhaps most importantly, Tami felt strongly that the NRM decision, which found that K.S. was an exploited victim shortly before becoming involved as a runner in the 'Top line', should be made admissible to the jury to mitigate the prosecution's portrayal of K.S. as a 'gangster'. Yet, once more, the judge refused, arguing that this would be unduly prejudicial information for the jury.

On a Tuesday morning, 2 April 2018, more than two months into the trial, the jury found both defendants guilty of manslaughter by a majority verdict of 11:1, manslaughter being by law an alternative route to a verdict of murder. They also found K.S. guilty of both the affray and the drugs charge, rejecting the 'modern slavery' defence. In his sentencing, the judge further rejected K.S.'s plea for mitigation on the grounds that he had been exploited, telling the court that he was 'entirely satisfied' that K.S. 'had made a conscious choice aged fourteen to extricate himself from support' and that he was 'voluntarily involved in drug dealing'. Mirroring the imagery of 'gang' violence used by the prosecution, the judge spoke of the 'horrendous violence', 'absolute disregard for others', and the desire for 'revenge, compensation, recompense' that had motivated the killing. So vicious indeed were the acts of both defendants, the judge ruled, that they met the criteria of being dangerous individuals, a special category in sentencing law that allows judges to pass an extended sentence without the prospect of early release after half time. K.S. was sentenced to fifteen years in prison, with a minimum custodial term of nine years, with years on license after his release. On 24 September 2021, the Court of Appeal reduced K.S.'s sentence to twelve years, comprising a seven-year custodial sentence and a five-year extended license, on grounds that the judge had miscalculated K.S.'s age (he assumed that K.S. was older than he in fact was). K.S.'s fate was sealed. He had gone from being a victim of modern slavery according to the NRM to becoming a 'hard core gangster' during his prosecution to, finally, becoming a killer in a joint enterprise with his co-defendant.

From neutral state justice to racial injustice: Disjunctive democracy revisited

Tami strongly felt that the trial had been prejudicial against K.S. from the get-go, from the way the investigations had been carried out to the joint enterprise charge to the trial process itself. 'It feels like you're feeding your kids to the wolves', she once said to me. But this was not all: equally shocking and painful to her was how she, as her brother's guardian and closest support, found herself targeted by the courts as a suspect (and to a lesser extent me, too). One day, after the prosecution had closed their case and without any warning, the court's usher approached Tami and me to tell us that, at the judge's request, we would not be allowed to sit next to each other in the public gallery anymore. Until that point, we had been sitting close together throughout the trial, not least because I would share some of my handwritten notes on the proceedings and occasionally explain to Tami some of the more complicated legal terminology or happenings. We were further told that an anonymous complaint had been made against us, that we were 'disrupting the public proceedings' (a serious offence which comes with imprisonment) and that we would be banned from court if this happened again. Our insistence that we had not done anything wrong met deaf ears, as the usher insisted that neither she nor the judge would be willing to discuss the matter 'in any more depth'. For Tami, the fact that we were targeted—allegedly as related family members, despite us looking ostensibly different (I am mixed heritage Asian and white; she is Black)—was proof of the fact that 'they target everyone who has colour in them, because everyone else in the trial is white'.

Serious as the usher's allegation was, it paled in comparison to the complaint that was sprung upon Tami one day at the close of the case, just before the jury retired for deliberation. I was running late for court that day and Tami called me when I was on my way to the station: 'Don't come in', she warned me, her usually calm and measured voice sounding upset, 'or else you might be arrested'. Tami had received a phone call from the police at court: a juror alleged that Tami and a male family friend who accompanied her to court that day had intimidated him outside the court setting, and both had now been banned from court under the threat of arrest. While no mention had been made of me, Tami was worried that given our run-ins with the usher a few weeks prior, I might become a target, too. Now, a formal investigation for juror intimidation would be launched, and she asked me to be prepared to give a witness statement. Over the following days, as Tami was asked to give several statements to the police, she also learnt more details about the allegation. The head juror, a middle-aged white man, claimed that she had followed him out to the platform on the underground station located near the court, and muttered threats in his direction under her breath. Tami vehemently denied that this had ever taken place, but this could not change a crucial fact: until the investigation was concluded, she would not be able to set a foot in the courthouse. Tami was distraught. 'I came to this trial as an advocate', she said to me, 'and I am leaving it as a criminal'.

In the end, CCTV evidence provided by the underground train station proved that the juror's allegations had been entirely unfounded, and the investigation for juror intimidation was dropped. But in the meantime, the juror's 'lie', as Tami referred to it, meant that she had failed to deliver on the one thing she had promised her brother to do: namely, to be with him until the end, a watchful presence in the courtroom. On the day of his verdict, Tami called me again, this time in tears. Her brother had been all alone when the jury announced their verdict, silently crying, she had been told, into his hands. 'This is my autistic brother', she said, 'who never cries'. For Tami, there was only one thing she wanted to do: to get the judgment overturned on grounds that the conviction had not been 'safe', a legal term used to refer to the fact that the verdict was not based on reliable evidence and likely to constitute a miscarriage of justice. This was a case of K.S. being confronted with a biased and racist criminal justice system. More so, she felt that her being targeted in public by court staff and the jury member had further contaminated the justice process, as 'K.S. was made to look like he is from a family of gangsters'. Tami wrote a long email to K.S.'s defence team, pleading with them to appeal the conviction. K.S.'s defence, however, rejected the allegation that racism could have been at play and that the conviction was unsafe, going so far as to say that Tami was 'paranoid'. For Tami, this was the straw that broke the camel's back, the final proof of how all professional actors had failed her and her family. A year later, during a recorded interview, her anger still came through:

> The system is not working and it is clear that corruption is taking place to conceal the impact that the juror lying has had on the verdict outcome and parties, who have been targeted, which is not fair for K.S. or me but I am an adult, and I will fight this tooth and nail like I have been. It's not fair at all and in fact, it is law enforcers acting illegally which is extremely concerning but I tell you one thing, this judge will be held to task as he

> has power of that court room but not over my life. God alone has that power and what he is doing until I take my last breath, he will pay for it, he's forgetting even he has someone to answer to.

I would like to conclude with Tami's words—her talk of 'corruption', of 'law enforcers acting illegal', and of judicial actors 'lying'—because they turn on its head the state's description of both these women and their loved ones as criminals, gangsters, and outlaws who deserve to be punished, excluded, and silenced. Just like the women in the last chapter who talked about experiencing the safeguarding interventions of the welfare state as 'setting their children up to fail', so here, Tami's words betray the workings of a criminal justice system whose claims to protect, safeguard, or even to simply be even-handed break down in the face of the social suffering confronted by defendants and their families. Tami was not alone in her assessment that the law failed to provide justice for families like hers. When Lisa calls out the state for being guilty of 'murder' or talks about how young people are also 'enslaved and exploited by the criminal justice system', or when Valerie speaks of how the system 'failed her son', these women are not only giving expression to righteous anger, but revealing the racism and inequality written into the fabric of the official machinery of justice.

El-Enany, drawing on the work of Razack (2020), has defined state racial power as that which 'evicts from the circle of law and humanity those persons deemed unable to progress into civilisation' (El-Enany, 2020, p. 5). While her own analysis is concerned with bordering practices as artefacts of ongoing coloniality that exclude formerly colonized populations as non-national 'others', an analogy can be drawn with British nationals on 'home ground' who the system refuses to treat as victims deserving of state protection. Thus, young minoritized men like T.M. and K.S. find that they are never accorded the victimhood status that they should have been on the government's own logic. On the contrary, their involvement in county lines becomes a conduit for ever more punitive responses, as police and other certified professionals refuse to respect the decision of, or even to enter them into, the NRM; as prosecution see young people's involvement in drug dealing as evidence of 'gang' activity; and as judges use this as an aggravating factor to impose extended life sentences. But racial state terror also extends to those who love the young men. As this chapter has shown, their mothers' and sisters' refusal to accept the state's construction of criminality not only results in the women being labelled angry and irrational, but their pushback becomes a reason for excluding and criminalizing them and for separating them further from their loved ones.

To take the analogy with state racial power further, the experiences of the young men and their family members in this chapter are no mere happenstance or historical accident. As critical scholars have reminded us time and again, the workings of the contemporary criminal justice system need to be understood as on a carceral continuum with historical experiences of enslavement and colonial subjugation (Bhattacharyya et al., 2021; Elliot-Cooper, 2021; Nijjar, 2022; Elliott-Cooper, 2023). We saw above how drugs policing under racial neoliberalism cannot be understood outside a colonial history that deployed the police in the interest of the ruling elite in both the metropolis and the colonies. The judiciary, too, is not separate from this racial order. In 2022, a high-profile study found that 'institutional racism' is ripe in the higher echelons of the judiciary (Monteith et al., 2022). 'Judicial racism is as much about history as it is about law', Leslie Thomas, a professor and barrister, wrote in his preface to the report. Referencing the period of the British plantation system during the transatlantic slave trade, when it was customary for the planters to become magistrates, Thomas points out that entrenched racism did not disappear post-emancipation: 'They [the magistrates] were the people responsible for constant whipping and other forms of torture of enslaved Africans, in addition to performing their roles as justices. After emancipation, the planters continued to act as magistrates and dispensed justice, sometimes very harshly' (2022, pp. 4–5).

In the last chapter, I argued that the government's politics of austerity, on top of decades of structural dispossession, reveals the workings of a disjunctive democracy that has extended a narrative of care while allowing substantive inequalities to flourish in its midst—a situation that caused great suffering in the lives of the families profiled. Here, the social suffering at the hands of a punitive criminal justice system reveals yet another disjunctive feature of Britain's democracy: namely, the contrast between the state's claim to deliver neutral and colour-blind justice and the actual realities of racist injustice (and their intersections with class and gender). State racism within the criminal justice system then targets those it considers 'criminals' while silencing anyone who fights for them. And yet, what does that mean for those who argue over and dispense official justice today? And what does this disjunctive democracy tell us about modern slavery laws not just as a juridical development but as a political project in times of deep hegemonic crisis? In the next three chapters, I will turn my attention to how law enforcement and other frontline professionals, lawyers, and judges enforce, defend, and prosecute modern slavery issues by engaging in various forms of 'techno-moral governance'. I show how their practices reproduce and cement enemy logics at the heart of the law, giving rise to murky and contradictory results. The final chapter will place the current conjuncture within a deeper crisis of racial reckoning before returning, one last time, to the young men, their female family members, and the ethnographer herself.

5

‘Cuckooing’, ‘Mate Crime’, and ‘Remote Mothering’: Securitizing Vulnerability at the Front Line

Introduction

When I arrived in the large conference room at the mayor’s office on a cold November morning in 2018, the room was already filling up with professionals seated at the groups of tables arranged in a large circle. I had come back to the town introduced in Chapter 2, my long-term fieldsite, to do more research with frontline professionals on their understanding of modern slavery policies. Today’s meeting, held in the town mayor’s hall but hosted by the local police force, had been long in the planning, and was attended by more than a dozen professionals. Later, during a round of group introductions, I would learn who the individuals in attendance were: a couple of neighbourhood police officers, a detective sergeant, a homelessness officer working for the local authority’s outreach housing project, two probation officers, two social workers, a representative from the local national health trust, an ‘anti-social behavior’ manager working for a local housing organization managing socially rented properties, a mental health worker, and a representative of the local adult safeguarding board.

The purpose of this ‘inter-agency meeting’, as our host referred to it, was to develop a strategic response to what the police and local authorities had identified as a growing number of ‘vulnerable’ individuals being drawn by incoming dealers into county lines (Chapter 2). It was jointly chaired by Mandy, a stocky, white British police officer perhaps in her forties, and by Chris, a white, British, recent university graduate perhaps in his late twenties. Chris was working as a ‘civilian analyst’ for the same police force, a new role created to collect and analyse crime data on alleged criminal exploitation that would feed into operational responses at the frontline. Mandy welcomed us. ‘Thank you so much for making the time to come’, she said.

Drugs, Race, and the Politics of Modern Slavery Law. Insa Lee Koch, Oxford University Press.
 DOI: 10.1093/9780198899631.003.0005

'Today's meeting is about defining what makes a victim, why some people are targeted, and ultimately, about figuring out how we can work best together as agencies to support those who are targeted'. She added, with a self-conscious smile, that it was a 'funny thing' for the police to host a meeting of this nature: 'We are better known for locking people up than for safeguarding them'.

Mandy wanted to spend a bit of time setting 'the context for today's meeting', to make sure that we were all singing from the same hymn sheet. 'Let's start at the top. We are here today because of the UN conventions on organized crime and the trafficking of persons'. She explained that offenders who fall into this category of 'traffickers' are persons who use 'power or coercion as a tool to exploit another person'. She then cited the definition of coercion from the *Oxford English Dictionary*: 'Coercion is the action of making somebody do something they do not want to do, using force or threatening to use force'. This definition, Mandy continued, was insufficient for what we were dealing with today: it failed to consider the 'bigger picture' of what coercion might feel like to a vulnerable person. Someone might be suffering from a drug addiction, and if that person was approached by a drug dealer with the promise of food and free drugs, this meant that they were being subjected to coercion. It was the same with *The Modern Slavery Act*, Mandy added, which 'was the government's response to how we [can respond to] coercion'. Once more, the government had not defined every single detail of what coercion looked like. 'It now falls on us to develop the right responses. For us, it's about how we can support people as victims rather than as perpetrators'.

Mandy continued to explain that there were many forms of coercion in county lines, but today's session was specifically about exploring the meaning of coercion as it relates to 'cuckooing', a term that has recently come out of government and police practice (cf. Spicer et al., 2020; 2021). Similar to the practices of a cuckoo who hides their eggs—their own children—in another bird's nest to use the latter for hatching, in the case of county lines cuckooing, drug dealers are believed to take over the property of a vulnerable person, using it for the storage of drugs, to house runners, and sometimes as a space to deal drugs directly. Mandy explained that the police had seen recent growth in cuckooing cases, and yet, professionals were not sure how best to identify those who had been cuckooed. What for some people seemed to be just a case of 'sofa surfing'—a person sleeping over on a friend's sofa—was evidence of slavery or exploitation for another. This ambiguity meant confronting some difficult questions. How were we to distinguish people 'crashing' at their friends' homes from, as Mandy had pointed out, evidence of modern slavery? When was the offer of a bed, a gift, or a friendship the gateway into grooming, manipulation, and coercion? Who should be 'safeguarded' from such potential abuse, and how?

These questions are representative of the challenges faced by frontline professionals all over Britain, who have been given a new mandate by the central government: the duty to identify victims of county lines, to distinguish them from perpetrators, and to extend 'safeguarding' solutions to the former. Here, I take these questions as my own point of departure to address a series of related but analytically distinct issues. How do professionals at the front line identify and respond to those considered 'at risk' of cuckooing, county lines, and modern slavery? How do multi-agency meetings and data-sharing practices become a conduit for further state monitoring and racialized policing, often in spite of professionals' intentions to do 'good'? And what does this tell us about modern slavery as a state-building project? In the last chapters, we saw that the government's narrative of individualized suffering central to 'criminal exploitation' needs to be supplemented by a different kind of story that emphasizes the social suffering confronted by young people across the state's binary of victims and perpetrators. This story not only reveals the structural dispossession suffered by these communities, but their exposure to a racist criminal justice system that continues to prosecute individuals and that silences those who fight against its workings. I suggested that these experiences bring into relief the workings of a deeply disjunctive democracy that has formally extended a colour-blind narrative of justice and care while allowing substantive inequalities and racism to flourish in its midst.

In this chapter, I take this analysis further by focusing in on the frontline professionals who are now tasked with the role of identifying and developing responses to safeguard victims of criminal exploitation and modern slavery. Against the backdrop of severe funding cuts, the professionals I met agreed on a central point: that the tools of partnership work and multi-agency thinking, central to the application of modern slavery policies at the front line, offered an opportunity to improve the lives of vulnerable people. And yet, reality was not so simple. In their efforts to identify individuals 'at risk' of county lines involvement, professionals also came to closely monitor individuals, even—or perhaps *especially*—where no crime had been committed. Such monitoring further acted as a basis for developing classificatory knowledge about 'suspect' communities that reconceived of intimate relations as a site of coercion and exploitation. I argue that frontline responses are best understood as exercises in techno-moral governance (Acosta, Bruun, and Koch, 2025) that deepen, rather than depart from, the logics of pre-emptive policing central to the government's domestic 'wars' on enemy populations (Williams, 2015; Bhattacharyya et al., 2021; Nijjar, 2022). As such, the rise of vulnerability constitutes yet another facet of liberal ordering that works through the securitization of everyday life in racialized and working-class communities.

Here, I draw upon fieldwork conducted with a wide range of professionals. This includes, first, frontline professionals in the town introduced in Chapter 2—a middle-sized town about an hour's drive from London—as well as fieldwork with professionals in London. I met these people by attending professional networking or other public-facing events, and through snowballing techniques. My role as a researcher was very different with these professionals than with the families—and in particular with the mothers—who featured in my last two chapters. The professionals were often much less wary of my presence as a researcher, insisting that research was needed in this area, including from academics; they emphasized that they would rather 'over-share' information for a good cause than not share enough. Because many of them believed in the unmitigated good that they saw their work doing, they also did not mind me using this information for my research, as long as it was anonymized. As explained in Chapter 2, I also obtained permission to shadow police officers from the local force, giving me privileged access to data-sharing practices and multi-agency work. Finally, I also draw upon fieldwork conducted with central government figures. But before discussing my data, I will first situate professionals' efforts within a national landscape that has come to speak the language of 'vulnerability' and 'safeguarding' in relation to frontline responses to county lines.

Vulnerability, safeguarding, and the front line

In her piece suitably entitled 'benevolent policing', Ana Aliverti has identified what she calls the 'rise of vulnerability' in criminal justice policy making (2020; see also Aliverti and Tawfiq, 2025). While concerns about undue suffering have of course always been expressed in relation to crime victims—providing at times a justification for punitive responses towards perpetrators—now policy and law makers have started to focus 'on the suffering and needy offender', betraying 'a conception of offending not through the lens of guilt and blame, but as a human response to disadvantage and injustice' (ibid.). This 'vulnerability zeitgeist' or 'spirit of our time', as it has been referred to by Kate Brown (2014) is not confined to the subject matter at stake (see for example Fitzgerald and Munro, 2012; Brown, Ecclestone, and Emmel, 2017; Brown, 2019; 2014; Heath-Kelly and Gruber, 2023; Boublil, 2024). And yet, its implications are most dramatic in the emerging set of institutional responses to 'criminal exploitation' or 'child criminal exploitation' in county lines cases. As we saw in earlier chapters, the government defined 'child criminal exploitation' in its *Serious Violence Strategy* as a situation 'where an individual takes advantage of an imbalance of power to coerce, control, manipulate or deceive a child or young person' (HM Government, 2018), constructing it as a form of 'child abuse' (e.g. HM Government, 2018b, 2023).

Yet, while the language of vulnerability and safeguarding has come to dominate the language around criminal exploitation and county lines, no coherent national strategy has been issued with respect to persons outside victims' own homes. This is particularly the case when such persons are adolescents (Wroe, 2021). This lack of national oversight has meant that the duty to identify and to care for vulnerable individuals in general, and vulnerable children in particular, has fallen on those at the front line. Thus, any practitioner who now suspects an individual of being the victim of criminal exploitation is instructed to get in touch with their local 'safeguarding lead' who, in turn, has a duty to liaise with their safeguarding team (Local Government Association and Independent Anti-Slavery Commissioner, 2017; Local Government Association, 2019). What is more, incorporating a language of 'multi-agency work' (or sometimes 'inter-agency work'), 'partnerships', and 'data sharing' into 'models of best practice', government documents have repeatedly called for statutory agencies to work with each other as well as with non-statutory bodies and the civil society sector (Local Government Association and Independent Anti-Slavery Commissioner, 2017; Office of the Independent Anti-Slavery Commissioner and University of Nottingham Rights Lab, 2017; Local Government Association, 2019; Office of the Independent Anti-Slavery Commissioner and University of Nottingham Rights Lab, 2022; Home Office, 2024).

Indeed, the drive for partnership work has been taken very seriously at the front line. In a report entitled *Collaborating for freedom: anti-slavery partnerships in the UK* (2017), the government found that 'most areas of the UK have some form of multi-agency partnership work in place to address modern slavery'. The report further stated that while 'newer partnerships often took the form of an informal group or network', more 'mature partnerships exhibited a mix of wider network meetings and more operationally focused sup-groups' (2017: 12), often drawing on pre-existing partnership structures. In the town where Mandy and many of the other frontline professionals I carried out my research with were based, the existing partnerships at the time of my fieldwork in 2019 included: a modern slavery networking group composed of statutory and non-statutory bodies as well as business representatives; a strategic modern slavery group for police and local authorities; a county-wide violence and vulnerability group for statutory bodies; a child criminal exploitation group chaired by the police and the council but open to other statutory bodies; a strategic group comprising multiple agencies tasked with the role of identifying signs of 'cuckooing'; and a newly designed drugs task force, comprised of members of the local council and the police, to develop what they called a holistic approach to local problems of violence and crime attributed to 'county lines'.

The benefits of 'joint up' and 'inter-agency' work are rarely called into question. According to the government, 'collaborative advantage' is one such benefit: 'by working in partnership, organisations are able to pool their expertise and resources and work together to overcome gaps in service provision and address wicked and pervasive challenges' (Office of the Independent Anti-Slavery Commissioner and University of Nottingham Rights Lab, 2022, p. 6). To the extent that partnership work and data sharing have been critically interrogated, authors have focused on the failures to implement enough partnership work rather than there being too much. For example, in its recent report on *The Modern Slavery Act*, a House of Lords' Committee officially recommended for the government to improve information and data sharing across multiple agencies through the establishment of 'a modern slavery *data warehouse*' (House of Lords Modern Slavery Act 2015 Committee, 2024, p. 45; my emphasis). This recommendation was based on a written submission made by the 'Rights Lab', a government-funded research unit at the University of Nottingham. Critiquing the tendency to 'silo' data across 'agencies and local governments, financial regulatory bodies, law enforcement agencies, NGOs, the charity sector, and other stakeholders', this submission had called for a 'requirement for inter-agency data sharing across the UK to enable a greater understanding of the nature and extent of modern slavery and trafficking in the UK' (University of Nottingham, 2024).

The tendency in government, policy, and certain scholarly circles to evaluate the workings of partnerships and information sharing merely as matters of neutral or actuarial performance is not surprising. It reflects a broader trend in criminal justice policy and scholarship to treat questions of crime control and their implementation as purely objective matters rather than as political projects in the making (Loader and Sparks, 2017; Fatsis, 2021). For example, Patrick Williams has shown in relation to police databases used for 'anti-gangs policing' how the production of intelligence around 'gangs' 'conspires in "evidence-based decision-making" reproduced by researchers who uncritically accept the police databases and list predominantly young black men as the starting point of their studies'. Here, reliance upon such sources of information serves to 'rationalise policing constructions of reality', especially 'when adopted within a "neutral social science approach to the study of gangs"' (Williams, 2015, p. 30). The same, by extension, we can argue is true when it comes to safeguarding 'vulnerability' in county lines. As critical vulnerability scholar Kate Brown has argued, we need to break with the tendency to treat 'vulnerability' as if it corresponds to 'a pre-existing reality . . . able to be identified by scientific or social measurement and indicators' (Brown, 2011, p. 319), asking instead how it operates as a mechanism for governance.

Building upon these critical perspectives, this chapter analyses the unfolding landscape of partnership agreements and data sharing practices in relation to those considered 'vulnerable' to modern slavery and criminal exploitation as an exercise in 'techno-moral governance' (Bornstein and Sharma, 2016; Acosta, Bruun, and Koch, 2025). Bornstein and Sharma use the term 'techno-moral governance' to refer to the process whereby actors come to create, transgress and navigate 'political relations . . . through techno-moral means' (Bornstein and Sharma, 2016): in 'mixing the language of law and policy with moral pronouncement, state and non-state actors posture themselves as defenders of rights and keepers of the public interest as they push their agenda and stake out distinct positions' (2016, p. 77). In so doing, they replace the political struggle between right and left with a moral struggle between right and wrong, often by displacing 'the political' into the 'legal realm' (Steur, 2018). The critical literature on human trafficking has analysed how such processes give rise to a form of 'armed love' as 'the moral imperative to act is accompanied, explicitly or implicitly, by practices of violence and containment' (2011, p. 5), including harsher border and immigration regimes and punitive approaches to sex trafficking (Fitzgerald and Munroe, 2018; Munro and Scoular, 2012; Feldman and Ticktin, 2010; Fassin, 2011, 2015; Anderson, 2013; Aliverti, 2020). Yet, it is also these regimes that speak of the continuous structural exclusion suffered by formerly colonized and enslaved peoples, as previous chapters have shown (Kempadoo, Sanghera, and Pattanaik, 2005; Kempadoo and Shieh, 2022; O'Connell Davidson, 2015, 2022).

To be clear, in analysing frontline workers' 'multi-agency' response as a case of techno-moral governance, my aim is not to attribute malicious intent on the part of professionals, nor to portray their commitment to safeguarding as simply enacting a Foucauldian logic of power. To do so would mean to ignore the complex moral reasoning that frontline officials engage in as they make difficult decisions in fraught situations (Fassin, 2015; Aliverti, 2020; James and Koch, 2020; Koch, 2021; Tawfiq, 2022; Wilde, 2022). And yet, notwithstanding the suggestion of novelty in much government rhetoric, data sharing and multi-agency work have long been key mechanisms for the profiling, surveillance, and (pre-emptive) policing of domestic 'suspect' communities, including with respect to counter-terrorism, anti-radicalization, and, as previous chapters have shown, with respect to anti-gangs policing. Here, I suggest that the kinds of techno-moral interventions that professionals come to enact in the name of safeguarding not only repurpose the far-ranging powers known as 'prevention work' in those areas, but generate new forms of classificatory knowledge—or ways of 'seeing like a state' (Scott, 1998)—that justify yet more pre-emptive policing. We can hence reconceptualize these techno-moral interventions as an exercise in enhanced state security, one that acts on the lives of some of its most disenfranchised working-class and minoritized subjects in the name of doing 'good'.

From working in 'silos' to safeguarding in 'partnership'

Matt was a 'youth drugs and exploitation' worker employed by the local authority in the same town where Mandy had organized the 'cuckooing meeting'. I met Matt in 2018, during a training session on modern slavery organized by a domestic charity for the town's various frontline professionals at the instigation of local authority staff and the police (Chapter 2). With his thinning flax blond hair, geeky classes, and loose Adidas hoodie, Matt, a white British man in his forties, had a friendly and self-depreciating demeanour about him, describing himself as the opposite of 'cool' and 'just a boring middle-aged guy'. Matt said that he had 'a tendency to overshare'; once he started talking about things he felt passionate about, he could not stop. Criminal exploitation was one of them. For me, who was keen to understand how frontline professionals navigated the landscape of county lines and modern slavery, this was a perfect match. The day we met at the multi-agency meeting I accepted Matt's invitation to accompany him back to his office on the outskirts of town 'to chat some more'.

While walking to Matt's car, I asked him to tell me more about his job. Matt told me that he had been a youth worker for fourteen years. He used to be just 'an ordinary drugs youth worker', working predominantly with substance users. Then, about four years ago, he began to notice 'a real shift', with several new cases being referred to him by the police. The first case involved a fourteen-year-old boy who had been arrested with wraps of heroin on him and been charged with drugs possession with intent to supply under the *Misuse of Drugs Act 1971*. Initially, the teenager had insisted that the drugs were for his own use. It was only when Matt wanted to send him to a drugs rehabilitation course that the boy confessed that he had been dealing them. He confided that he had started hanging out with a group of older 'lads', who on one occasion had given him crack to smoke. The next day the lads had told him that he needed to pay them back for the drugs. He was sent off to sell drugs to work off his debt. Soon this first of Matt's cases was followed by more, each following a distinct pattern: teenagers incurring debts, at times 'double bubble loans' (a loaning practice where the individual is required to pay back double the amount they borrowed) for having consumed, lost, or been robbed of drugs, and being asked to 'work it off' over a potentially indefinite period of time.

Matt stopped talking when we reached his car, a small and beaten Toyota. As he opened the door for me, he burst into profuse apologies about the state of the passenger seat—empty packs of crisps, coke bottles, and plastic bags were lying around, which Matt hastily threw into the back of the car. 'I only use this car for work', he said with an embarrassed laugh, 'I don't really care what it looks like because the young people I see don't care'. I also laughed, reassuring him that on a good day, my living room did not look different from his car, and then tried to nudge him back to the conversation at hand. Matt started speaking again once he was driving, now visibly more relaxed. 'I tried to tell the police at the time that [teenagers being forced to sell drugs] was something they needed to look into'. He had a good understanding of these issues because he had already seen something similar in relation to 'child sexual exploitation' when working on cases where underage girls had been 'groomed' by older men (cf. Brown, 2019). 'We were beginning to understand that these girls were victims and needed protection, even if it seemed like they had consented to the drugs, and relations with older men', Matt said: 'So, the language of exploitation was there; this was the language we were starting to use now for the boys [selling drugs]'.

Yet, Matt was aware that thinking of predominantly male street-level dealers as exploited victims at the hands of other drug dealers, akin to teenage girls who had been groomed by older men, would not be to everyone's liking. Some of the police officers 'scoffed' at the suggestion that this demographic could be seen as victims. Luckily, his line manager at the youth service team was on board. 'She recognized the problem for what it was—drugs exploitation, not criminality', he said. At Matt's own request, his job role and title were revised, from 'youth drugs worker' to 'youth drugs *and exploitation* worker'. Matt was lucky that this period happened to coincide with the arrival of a new detective sergeant in the local police force, a man called Conor, with decades of law enforcement experience in some of the largest metropolitan police forces, including a long stint at Trident, London's notorious 'gang unit' investigating 'black on black crime' (Chapter 2). Conor brought with him an awareness of, and appreciation for, the changing policy landscape, and introduced the language of 'modern slavery' in relation to drugs cases to his force. Within months, he had set up the first multi-agency partnership that brought together police, social care, youth work, housing, and other local authorities to develop a more 'holistic' response to county lines related offending in the town. 'It has made a massive difference', Matt said. 'Now we all talk together and act in tandem'.

For professionals like Matt or Conor, doing partnership work was attractive for a number of reasons. For one, it allowed them to develop responses to criminal exploitation in a situation where, as Matt said, 'everyone has had cuts'. Matt was referencing a situation that, in the critical literature, has been referred to as 'austerity localism'—where the state withdraws provisions from localities under the pretence of giving greater autonomy to local organizations (Lowndes, 2012; Clayton, Donovan, and Merchand, 2015; Dagdeviren, Donoghue, and Wearmouth, 2019). Thus, he explained that the local authority had struggled in recent years with resources being cut by central government. Staffing issues were putting particular pressure on those at the front line to respond to complex problems. At the same time, they were seeing more and more cases of individuals in need of help, as professionals were becoming aware of the problems of county lines. Some also reminded me of the failures of central government to make funding available for adolescents found to have been victims of modern slavery and human trafficking through the National Referral Mechanism (NRM), which is housed by a central government body, the Home Office. In practice, this meant that resource-intensive and time-consuming interventions—including the housing transfer organized for Lee, the fifteen-year-old boy introduced in Chapter 2 who was identified as a victim of modern slavery—were only possible where the local authorities acted in unison (and, precisely because this was such a hurdle, it was much more common to offer more piecemeal or ad hoc solutions, as we have seen).

Partnering with other local agencies was not just a way of activating funding and resources in a situation of limited means, however. As in the government publications cited above, it was also valued as a morally superior way of working. This was made clear to me by Conor, the detective sergeant, who I met shortly after being introduced to Matt. Conor had a quiet voice and an understated, friendly demeanour. His mantra was to share as much as possible: 'Some people might say that we share too much information. But I would rather things go wrong because there is too much sharing than someone gets murdered or dies because there wasn't enough'. Conor was proud of what he had achieved in the short time that he had worked for the local police force. Echoing Matt's words, he told me how, when he first arrived on the force and attended meetings on drugs policing where professionals from other organizations were present, 'the police would sit around the table and everyone else was sat in chairs behind them listening to what we had to say'. Conor wanted to break with this culture of working in 'silos', and of always putting the police in the driver's seat.

According to Conor, doing partnership work was therefore not just a response to limited resources and means, but a cleverer way of working: it allowed the police to 'nip problems in the bud' by giving agencies the opportunity to intervene at the earliest possible point into the lives of individuals who were considered to be 'at risk'. Conor was particularly proud of initiatives that allowed the police and partner agencies to establish a closer rapport with young men and boys who were 'on the police's radar', a rapport that he believed moved away from the historical estrangement and open hostility that had characterized the police's relations with this target group. This included a number of initiatives, like local co-operation between the police and a charity that offered recreational activities to young people; an initiative between council officials and 'cuckooed victims' that included producing a film about their experiences; and a collaboration with the Jobcentre that channelled young people exiting county lines into the welfare system of universal credit and other limited forms of welfare support while they were 'finding their feet in the job market'. Jason, the only British mixed heritage officer I met from the same force as Conor, explained that inter-agency work allowed them to approach young people 'to offer them a care package' before they became too steeply involved in criminal activity:

> So with our local drug dealers, we build relationships with them. Many of these kids have very negative views of us. They only get to see us when things go wrong—when they have committed an offence, when their parents have fallen out, when there is violence and shouting and they don't want us there. But we want to have contact with them when it's not just about enforcement. So my PCs visit these children sporadically, not because anything has happened, but just to have a chat, so it's not so negative. They speak to them on their doorstep, away from their parents so not inside the home, and they say to them, so what's going on, are you doing alright? Can we refer you to services? Because the council they offer a lot of good services—football on the weekends and in-door graffiti, but the thing is you can't just turn up to these, you need a multi-agency referral.

In short, then, for professionals like Conor, Matt, or Jason, working in partnership with other agencies and young people was almost like a labour of love. Similarly to the professionals studied by Kimbell and Bailey who saw themselves as 'prototyping welfare' (2017) or the police and asylum-screening officers with whom Aliverti and Tawfiq worked (2025), here frontline workers who were tasked with the mandate to safeguard vulnerable individuals saw multi-agency work as an opportunity to pioneer new practices for the greater good, expressing 'a need to help' which reinscribed 'an aesthetics of personal care to the workings of state processes' (Aliverti and Tawfiq, 2025). And yet, notwithstanding the language of novelty and excitement that came through in frontline professionals' own narratives, their working practices also had their own governing effects. As the next section will show, by sharing data and intelligence across different agencies and using this as a basis for deciding on further action, professionals also extended the state's hold over individuals' lives, reinforcing monitoring and surveillance purely on the basis of 'risk'—including with respect to those who had not committed any crimes.

'Grooming them back': The case of Jay

I was introduced to my first multi-agency partnership meeting by Conor shortly after meeting him in the summer of 2018. He had invited me to join the town's 'child criminal exploitation group', a group he had set up to bring professionals from across the sector together to monitor, assess, and intervene in concrete cases of criminal exploitation. The remit of this group was thus 'operational'. In a large room at the back of the police station, a dozen personnel had gathered around a table, including representatives from the police, probation service, child social care, the local council's anti-social behaviour team, the council's housing and homelessness unit, and an MA student studying criminology at the local university. Conor was evidently pleased with the turnout: 'It's great to see so many people here', he said, welcoming the room. 'For me it's a big success when partners outnumber the police'! The structure, organization, and venue of the meeting all reflected the partnership ethos that Conor wanted to institute. Each meeting was jointly chaired by a law enforcement official (typically by Conor himself) and a local authority official in order to create parity of representation; the venue would rotate between the police station, the local government offices, and the town hall; and open discussion was encouraged at all times. Each professional around the table was invited to bring in any new issues or outstanding concerns, and work allocation was decided upon collectively for the next meeting.

As I attended more operational meetings for the child criminal exploitation group, I began to understand what the daily life of partnership work was all about: it was, above all, a commitment to sharing information about individuals deemed to be 'at risk'. Names, identities, and addresses were freely passed around and entered into databases, as professionals would update one another about a person's whereabouts, associations, and occupations, their suspected involvement with 'gangs' (a concept that remained undefined), and any other issue that could be of relevance. There was, for example, sixteen-year-old Lucy, a girl who by the police's account was 'clearly a victim, not a perpetrator'. Conor told the professionals in the room that she had been initially 'exploited' by a young man a few years her senior who was a 'known gang member'. Lucy's social worker agreed with Conor's assessment, adding that the young man's name had 'popped up' in relation to other 'vulnerable girls'. Or there was Callum, a young man who had gone from being a victim to 'becoming an alpha victim', as professionals at the meeting characterized it. Various professionals listed times and places where they had seen him in the company of younger teenagers, the suspicion being that he had become an active 'recruiter'. And then there was Rico, a fifteen-year-old who had recently been found to be criminally exploited. He had been moved to a care home, and his former social worker had made contact with the new local authority to get an update on how he was doing.

Sharing data about individuals such as Lucy, Callum, and Rico served a distinct purpose: to 'risk assess' an individual and to discuss, and put in place, practical responses to ensure their safeguarding. But risk assessments were contingent upon a whole host of situationally defined factors that lend themselves to highly discretionary forms of profiling. Let us turn to the case of Jay that Conor discussed with the professionals present at a multi-agency partnership meeting. Fifteen years old, Jay had grown up on Park End, the largest council estate in the town and the same neighbourhood that Lee, introduced in Chapter 2, was from. Jay's story was 'a harrowing case of a child being exploited by a county lines gang', as Conor referred to it. Jay had been working as a runner for a number of years by the time he was fifteen, being sent by his 'elders' to places in Hampshire and other localities far from his home. One day, he had been 'robbed of his drugs' (the police suspected by his own boss) and accrued a drug debt that his boss asked him to pay back. Jay did not want to be involved anymore. But when he communicated his decision to this effect, he was kidnapped by some 'middlemen': he was taken to a flat, tied to a radiator, tortured, and nearly starved to death over the space of a week. Eventually, he was able to escape through a window and ran down the street, screaming for help, with his exploiters running after him. After initial confusion over who to arrest (as Jay's tormentors insisted that they had been exploited by Jay rather than the other way around), the police were able to establish what they called the 'true facts'.

By the time Jay came to the attention of the police following the kidnapping, he was well known to most professionals in the room: 'Multi-agency' efforts had been put into safeguarding him for some time now. Jay had built a particularly close rapport with Matt, who became his appointed youth worker. Matt told me how he had succeeding in gaining Jay's trust. Jay had first come 'into his care' after his mother had reported him to a social worker, months before the kidnapping happened. He had been spending a lot of time in the toilet; his mother was worried that he was taking drugs—it turned out that he had been plugging them rather than consuming them. Then Jay started going missing, sometimes for weeks on end. Matt knew that these were the classic warning signs of a person who was involved with county lines. He started working with Jay, initially while Jay was still involved in drug dealing. Matt described how he had built a rapport with Jay in much the same way that his exploiters might have done with him: he would invite him for food in cafes, knowing that he was hungry much of the time; take him out for rides; and made his own mannerisms and language more 'street', using words such as 'banda' to refer to a 'cuckooed property' or 'gear' to talk about 'drugs'. Matt spoke of this as a process of regrooming, echoing the language used by the mothers in Chapter 3, albeit in very different ways: 'You almost have to groom them back to get their trust', he said.

In addition to making himself more relatable to Jay by offering him, in limited ways, the kinds of perks he might have been getting from his exploiters—a free car ride, some food, a soft drink, the semblance of mentorship—Matt also tried to reason with him: 'I would tell him, you have never been officially sanctioned but your name is popping up, I know you are still involved . . . you are gonna get arrested and go to prison!' He also reassured Jay that if he did want to stop dealing drugs, 'we will do everything we can to support you, to protect you'. He would tell Jay that he had already spoken to police and social care to make sure that they could respond straightaway. He persistently tried to keep reinforcing both 'the positives and the negatives' about Jay's lifestyle. Matt told me that one time he had sat Jay down and said to him, 'Let's have a look at your day, then!' Matt showed me a document on his laptop that he had produced with Jay, detailing his daily life as a dealer:

- 8.30/9am wake up—turn the drugs line on—start receiving calls
- he would get the drugs which were often buried in bushes and places, he wouldn't keep them at home
- go into [town] city centre and make sales—this could be done by sitting up on walls, or wherever he was dealing; people would come to him, he would make four to six sales an hour on crack and heroin
- 11am—he would reload/reap—go to his boss's house—drop off money for the day before and pick up more drugs. He would hand over £1,000 pounds, which is the money he had made in twenty-four hours (since 11am the day before). He would get paid between £100-200. Sometimes he was not paid anything
- he went back work [sic]
- 11pm—work day finished

Matt tried to tell Jay that he was working 9–11 hours and only earning £100 for it, less than the legal minimum wage. Moreover, there was no sickness or holiday pay. In the two years he had worked for county lines, Jay only had three days when he didn't work. When he was sick, the 'gang' would get angry and force him to work for forty-eight hours straight to make up the money lost when he was ill.

All of this effort had born fruit. After the kidnapping incident—which professionals involved in his case described as a 'crisis moment'—Jay told his youth worker that he was ready to stop dealing drugs once and for all. A new action plan was put in place: first, Jay was moved. As Jay's parents were both deemed to be part of the 'problem' (his father being a well-known drug dealer and his mother described as 'overwhelmed'), it was decided he should leave his home. His older sister, who Conor described during the meeting as the 'only reasonable person in his family', agreed to take him into her one-bedroom flat that she was sharing with her boyfriend and their baby son. In theory, she was not allowed to accept Jay in her home: she was 'overcrowding' her home by doing so, a legal term that can constitute grounds for eviction from a social housing property. However, the authorities decided to turn a blind eye to the situation given that Jay's sister was helping them out. What is more, with the help of a social worker, Jay was able to enrol in a local college. The police reassured Jay that if he managed to stay out of 'trouble now', then he would not face any prosecution for drugs offences. For a few months, it seemed that all was going well: Jay did not abscond from his sister's place, he regularly attended college, and he came to most of his appointments with his youth worker.

Recently, however, the professionals had become concerned again. For this reason, Conor decided to bring up Jay's case at a 'child criminal exploitation group meeting' at which I was also present. Conor announced that he wanted to share some 'intel' with the professionals present: Neighbourhood police officers patrolling Park End had recently seen Jay 'hanging around' with some of the 'local boys' who were known to the police as high-risk cases. Two of the boys were also believed to be linked to a recent kidnapping on Park End; some time ago, a BMW with a non-local number plate had driven onto the estate, snatched a sixteen-year-old boy off the street, and driven him to the woods to administer a beating. The local boy was later found to be involved in drug dealing. Jay's social worker came in: Jay had also been seen going into people's homes on a neighbouring estate. A quick look into the database had revealed that these were 'known addresses', a term the social worker did not further explain. Matt now added that Jay had recently stopped responding to his phone calls, which could indicate that he was 'up to no good'. Conor and the professionals were concerned about what this 'intel' could mean. What was going on? Was Jay getting sucked back into county lines? Was it time for a preventive order? Or had Jay gone from being a victim to an active perpetrator, indicating that more forceful action was needed?

Eventually, it was decided that Matt should pay Jay an 'unannounced visit' at his college during Jay's lunch break to 'check in on him' before deciding on any further action. It just so happened that I had arranged once more to see Matt after the meeting, and now with this new plan in place, Matt asked me if I wanted to come along. I agreed, somewhat uncomfortably, and specified that I would be happy to be present as long as Jay's consent could be obtained. When we arrived at the college, we walked straight into the common room of the college where a group of young men were sitting on the sofas laughing with one another. They seemed relaxed. 'Hello Jay', Matt called out from across the room, waving at a slim mixed heritage boy with brown skin who was sitting on a sofa. The boy looked younger than fifteen, almost frail in comparison to Matt, whose own stocky built stood out. Jay's face changed when he recognized his youth worker, his smile turning into a grimace. Undeterred and with a cheerful voice, Matt asked Jay 'for a quick chat' and shepherded him towards the privacy of the kitchen, where we sat down on stools. Matt closed the door behind us. I introduced myself to Jay and explained my research to him, asking for his permission to attend the meeting. He seemed like he couldn't care less, his attention being solely on Matt.

Matt went straight to business. 'People have been talking about you, not in a bad way but you have been seen around', he started. So he was here today to 'have a chat' with Jay and to find out what was going on. He had a few questions for Jay. What had he been doing with the 'wrong crowd' the other day? Why was he going to a specific house on the neighbouring estate? Did he realize what would happen if he was arrested again? Jay readily supplied answers, in monosyllables, visibly uncomfortable: he had merely been hanging out with his friends from childhood; the house in question was his cousin's, where he went to play computer games most afternoons. And, yes, he did realize that he might well go to jail if he was to be arrested again. Jay also confirmed that the only reason he had not been picking up his youth worker's phone calls is because he had recently changed his phone number: a mobile phone company had offered him a good deal, and he had decided to go for it. At Matt's request, Jay now got his phone out and dictated his new phone number to his youth worker, who put it safely into his own mobile phone.

The entire meeting cannot have lasted more than fifteen minutes. Reminding Jay once more 'to stay out of trouble', Matt gave Jay an awkward pat on his shoulder to say goodbye. As we crossed the communal area we had entered through earlier, I was acutely aware of the group of young men staring at us, this time entirely silent. Matt remained silent too. It was only after we got back into his car that he started talking about what had just happened. Matt was satisfied that Jay was telling the truth about his recent movements and activities and that he was not 'getting sucked back in'. I asked him what it was that made him feel so sure, having myself struggled to read anything into the short interaction other than a palpable sense of tension and mutual apprehension. Matt replied that he 'knew Jay very well': what had convinced him was not down to *what* Jay had said, but to *how* he had said it. 'When he is sucked in, he's not recognizable', Matt said, explaining that Jay's whole-body language would change. He would become cagey, nervous, and unable to speak, tripping over his words. Today, however, he had seemed composed and calm, making him sure that Jay was not involved with drugs at the moment. He would report back to the police accordingly and recommend that he should be closely 'watched' but that no further action should be taken for now.

Brown (2011, 2014, 2019) has powerfully argued that attention to vulnerability opens up difficult questions about deservingness, human agency, and social control. Based upon her qualitative research with young people as well as practitioners, she has shown how the vagueness of the term allows professionals to designate an individual as 'deserving' and as in need of assistance or alternatively of control. Here, we can see a similar process at work. A professional's assessment as to an individual's involvement with criminality came down to a discretionary assessment of that person's mannerism, general demeanour, and speech. This was not the only time that I came across such discretionary exercises. Professionals would often insist that spotting or identifying 'exploitation' and 'modern slavery' was a matter of using one's 'professional instinct' or 'professional sixth sense'. Thus, as we saw in the case of Layton, what seemed to matter was not the response given (words can lie, after all), but what professionals could infer from his general ways. Likewise, I was told by professionals that individuals who seemed overly confident and who had readily embraced the language of exploitation were often the ones who were 'faking' it. At a modern slavery training session that I attended, our trainer, a domestic violence charity worker, told us that 'real victims don't even know that they are victims', and that if someone was too eager to claim that they had been exploited, this could be a sure sign that they were, in fact, in the business of exploiting others. In the next section, I will look at the call for professional vigilance in more depth, and the ways in which it enables forms of classificatory knowledge about 'suspect' communities to emerge that turn intimate relations among constituencies deemed to be 'at risk' into a site of pathos.

Seeing like a state

Let me now return to the story with which I opened this chapter, namely the 'cuckooing meeting'. As mentioned above, the meeting was organized by Mandy, a police officer, and Chris, a civilian analyst working for the police force; it was the first of a number of meetings that would take place over the following months. At this initial meeting, Mandy set the 'ground rules' for how we would work together, echoing the language used by Conor: 'The police have often assumed that we know the answers to everything', she said, 'but the point of this meeting is to make things less police-ey and more partnership-ey. Let's draw on everyone's professional knowledge and expertise to help us gain a better understanding of what cuckooing is and how we can identify it'. Unlike the multi-agency partnership meetings described in the last section, the purpose of this meeting was 'strategic': to develop a toolkit for spotting exploitation on the ground. More particularly, we would produce a 'cuckooing tool kit' consisting of a checklist of questions that frontline workers could use when visiting social tenancies. Mandy wanted this toolkit to be accessible to everyone. 'Whether it's the plumber, electrician, housing official, or police officer', she said, 'everyone should be able to sing from the same hymn sheet and spot the signs of exploitation when they visit a property'.

'Cuckooing has no legal definition but it's really central to modern slavery', Mandy told us at the start of the meeting, 'so it falls upon us to come up with a definition that we can use to help us make sense of the issues we are seeing. Cuckooing involves exploitation, but then again, what is exploitation: it doesn't have to be anything criminal, it could be anything. How then do we get at that level of vulnerability?' To engage these questions, Mandy wanted us to pull together our professional knowledge and to come up with a working definition of cuckooing that could be used by all agencies. She proceeded to split us into smaller groups for discussion. My group consisted of four people, all white and British: Chris, the civilian analysist; Mark, who had come as a representative of the local authority's adult safeguarding board; Louise, who worked in mental health for the local authority; and Linda, who had recently been appointed as the local authority's 'exploitation officer', having previously worked for their housing team managing nuisance and 'gang' problems among social housing tenants (her recently changed job spec, like in Matt's case, illustrating the shifting policy landscape). I introduced myself to my group as a researcher and academic who was interested in better understanding how professionals were developing responses to county lines.

Linda was the first to speak, announcing that she had done some 'homework' in preparation for our meeting today, researching existing definitions of cuckooing that were 'kicking about on the web'. She had been shocked to find that most web definitions used 'far too blunt of a definition of cuckooing', equating it with the use of outright force or violence. But from her own professional experience of having worked with tenants in the local authority's social housing properties, she knew that victimhood rarely looked this obvious: 'Cuckooing often involves very complex forms of exploitation', she said. There were cases where 'sex workers had taken over properties of vulnerable older men by cooking and cleaning for them but also taking them "to the hole in the wall"' to withdraw money. These women exploited the 'loneliness' of the older men for their own financial pursuits by pretending to be their companions. Then there were cases of county lines: sometimes the same women who exploited the older men would themselves be exploited by drug dealers who pretended to be in love with them, offering them free drugs in exchange for staying at their properties. You then had a case of multiple forms of exploitation. The older men were exploited by younger women; the younger women were exploited by county lines dealers; and the county lines dealers more often than not were 'runners' exploited by others higher up the chain.

Linda had prompted an animated discussion at our table about the core challenges posed by these cases: cuckooing was as much about 'befriending' as it was about anything else. Chris now interjected, reinforcing Linda's earlier message that while the media often presented cuckooing as if it was 'all about crack dens and kicking in doors', the coercion could be much less visible or overt. Louise, the mental health worker, agreed. 'What makes it even more complicated', she added, 'is that the people don't see themselves as victims, rather they are under the false impression that they are in love or that there is a genuine form of friendship going on. But we as professionals know that it is not true'. Again, there was general nodding across the table as people started discussing how loneliness and friendship needs were often linked to low self-esteem, depression, and other mental health conditions. These were cases where victims were suffering from 'Stockholm syndrome', where they did not realize that they had been exploited—a general problem with county lines, Mark interjected, where the drugs runners also did not typically want to believe that they had been 'criminally exploited'.

Our discussion, it turned out, was representative of the way the conversation in the room flowed that morning. As time was up, and we were asked to feed our discussion points back to the entire room, it became clear that all the professionals had thrown themselves into murky discussions about the appropriate remit and meaning of intimacy, love, friendship, and companionship. For all present, what might on the face of it appear to be a consensual, even altruistic, act—the giving of a gift, domestic care, physical intimacy—could constitute evidence of exploitation if judged with the supposedly neutral hat of a professional. In the minutes circulated by Mandy after the meeting, she summarized for us the various working definitions of cuckooing that the groups had come up with. What stood out in the definitions was their circularity. Cuckooing came to stand in for 'criminal exploitation', which in turn was used interchangeably with 'coercion', 'control', and 'modern slavery', often at the expense of more structural forms of disadvantage that featured in the voices of family members in Chapters 3 and 4 (being poor, low income, or on benefits were stated as problems, but not elaborated upon):

> **Definitions of cuckooing:**
> Exploitation by a group or individual by eliciting premises of . . . Moving into and take over a vulnerable person's property, using sexual favours, company, gifts, drugs, false friendship
>
> When someone's space is controlled through coercion or exploitation for gain of an external person(s). Always a vulnerability/unmet need. Manipulated/groomed to gain power over space
>
> When an individual's space is controlled through coercion or exploitation for an external person(s) gain
>
> Coercive use of someone's home, with no power or control over any of the outcomes/choices
>
> Vulnerable individual's properties taken over by means of implicit or explicit coercion and intimidation by others for some kind of gain
>
> *All groups identified a common thread of vulnerability in the 'victim'; social isolation, loneliness, mental health issues, learning disabilities, substance misuse, poor/no family support, poor/low income/ [being on] benefits etc* [emphasis in original].

And yet, the circularity of the definition of cuckooing did not seem to matter to anyone present. The point of these discussions was not necessarily to provide a singular or literary understanding of a phenomenon that everyone agreed was inherently complex and fluid but rather, as Mandy had told us, a checklist of potential indicators that authorities could use to help them reach their decision about a particular individual. Cuckooing then acted as a quasi-criminal 'proxy' or classificatory shorthand that referred to potentially any given social situation involving the presence of people other than the social housing tenants themselves at their rented property; its invocation, above all, signalled the need for heightened professional attention and vigilance. Cuckooing was also only one of several proxies that I came across in the context of professional attempts to grapple with the unfolding landscape of criminal exploitation and county lines. Others include 'mate crime' (a process whereby intimate others pretend to be friends to exploit you), 'remote mothering' (the process whereby county lines holders keep a tap on runners by controlling their mobile phones through location devices such as Google apps), and indeed, 'criminal exploitation' itself.

I was introduced to the term 'mate crime' when I accompanied Mandy to her shared office at the police station, a close walk from the local authority building where our first cuckooing meeting had been held. She had invited me back to the office to show me a presentation she had recently delivered as part of a training session for other officers, to teach them about safeguarding needs. At her office, she logged onto her computer and pulled up a basic PowerPoint presentation that rehashed some of the information she had prefaced our cuckooing meeting with, before we got to a slide with the word 'MATE CRIME' written in capital letters in the middle (see Figure 5.1. for a similar picture). I asked her to explain what that meant. Mandy now showed me a slide with a poster depicting several images of domestic life: a man washing some dishes, driving in a car, and going food shopping in a supermarket. 'Friend or fake?' she asked me: 'How do you know if a friend is fake or real?' In response to her own question, she informed me that there were 'indicators' not unlike in the case of cuckooing: a real friend would not come and occupy your house; he would not make you go shopping and buy food for him or demand to be driven around in your car without ever contributing petrol for it. 'In all of these cases', she said, 'we can speak of mate crime, it's not a legally defined term but as we are becoming more aware of the realities of exploitation, we start to see that friends are not always what they seem'.

After a couple more 'cuckooing meetings' during which we were tasked with the role of fine-tuning our understanding of 'cuckooing' and thinking about operational implications, Mandy sent around a first draft of a 'screening tool' that she had produced on the basis of our discussion, alongside some instructions for how it was to be used. Designed to 'help identify potential risks of exploitation', as she put it in her email, the screening tool included a questionnaire to be filled in by professionals visiting a social

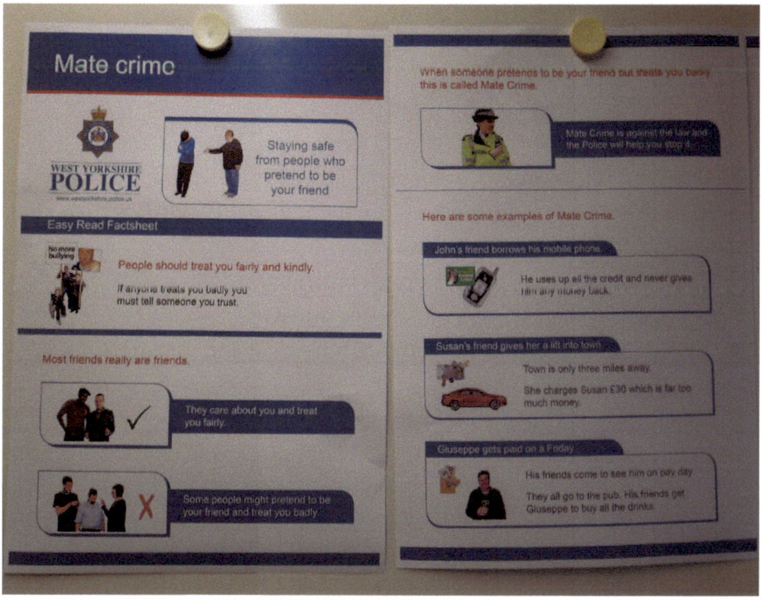

Figure 5.1. Notice board displaying an information sheet about 'mate crime', produced by West Yorkshire Police. Reproduced with permission from West Yorkshire Police.

housing tenancy that they believed to be cuckooed—with or without the consent of the individuals living there. The screening tool was to be shared with a multi-agency 'cuckooing' panel that was to make a decision on appropriate avenues for action. The questionnaire consisted of a list of indicators that professionals could check for, with space for each of them to elaborate on details, including the following:

- Persons at property claiming to be friends/carers
- Increased coming and going at property
- Unusual sleeping arrangements
- Unexplained person(s) loitering outside person's place of residence
- Increased anti-social behaviour around property
- New vehicles frequently outside property
- Person seen entering/leaving vehicles driven by unknown adults
- Evidence of unexplained use of public transport—rail/bus tickets to places where they have no known association
- Evidence of vehicle hire paperwork

- Drug paraphernalia in the property
- Increasing use of drugs/alcohol or misuse of drugs/alcohol
- Change in behaviour—being more secretive/withdrawn/isolated from peers and not mixing with usual friends
- Disengagement with support services
- Change in physical appearance—weight gain/loss, poor hygiene
- Expression of despair (depression, mental health, self-harm, suicidal thoughts/attempts, eating disorder)
- Physical/emotional abuse from a controlling adult or peer, including use of manipulation, violence and/or threats
- Unexplained marks/scars/physical injuries and attempts to conceal them
- Attendance at a hospital/surgery with a stab wound
- Involvement in offending
- Unexplained money/clothing/goods/activities
- Possessing multiple mobile phones, sim cards, or concerning use of a phone, i.e. multiple callers, frequent messages, phone answered by adult/unknown person
- Change in behaviour—being more secretive/withdrawn/isolated from peers and not mixing with usual friends

The indicators listed were vast and many. Many of them resonated with what the mothers in Chapter 4 had also described about their children, such as a change in their behaviour or the presence of odd things (such as vehicle hire paperwork). And yet, reproduced as a list without the stories of the children and thus completely taken out of context, these indicators also became reified categories devoid of any meaning. More so, what stood out in the screening tool was how a narrative harmony or fluidity was established between a vast range of behaviors—some of which were criminal in nature ('use of drugs')—others entirely legal and even considered socially desirable ('persons at property claiming to be friends/carers'). What is more, any sign of resistance or refusal on the part of the individual believed to be at 'risk' could be seen as further proof of their suspicious situation ('becoming angry/hostile if any suspicions or concerns are expressed about their activities'), thus further disabling any possibility of disagreement.

In his book 'seeing like a state' (Scott, 1998), James Scott analysed how states impose 'legibility' on their subjects by creating uniform standards of knowledge. His point was to show how the introduction of state-led metrices, such as the introduction of family names, censuses, or standard units of measurement, facilitated state control and economies of scale—not unlike the cartographic practices and processes of written documentation produced by colonial administrators (Mitchell, 1988; Anderson, 1991; Kelly, 2006). Here, we can see how the interventions on the part of frontline professionals in Britain taking on a similar governance role. By developing quasi-criminal proxies such as 'cuckooing', 'remote mothering', or 'mate crime', and giving them institutional life through 'screening tools', 'assessment trackers', and 'indicator lists' (all of which were names given to technocratic aids that I came across during my research), professionals engage in acts of techno-moral governance that render particular social groups and their relations and community structures legible. In this process, genuine relations of friendship and care that featured in the stories of young people and their family members in the last two chapters become the target of official suspicion as 'suspect' communities are being defined by their propensity to engage in pathological relations. But this is not all. Just as Scott showed how such exercises in legibility enable top-down state control, I will now argue that these forms of classificatory knowledge act as a gateway for yet more pre-emptive policing, as Britain's disenfranchised working-class and racialized subjects are drawn into the remits of an ever more extensive security apparatus for their own professed good.

Securitizing vulnerability at the front line

In the late summer of 2019, I was invited to meet Tim Champion, a high-ranking official at the National Crime Agency who was located inside the New Scotland Yard office on the banks of the River Thames. We had met a couple of times in the back office of the prosecution during the human-trafficking trial of Glodi and his co-defendants (Chapter 7); Tim would occasionally visit and have chats with the officers or prosecutors, always easing what could be a tense atmosphere in the prosecution's back office with his relaxed manner. On more than one occasion, he was described by the other officers present at the trial as the 'master brain' behind the investigation. I had been waiting to interview him for some time now, and was relieved when, shortly after the trial was over, Tim invited me to come to his office building 'for a chat'. He was already waiting for me when a security official dropped me off in an open-plan cafeteria. Having just been made to go through an elaborate security procedure at the entrance to the building ('it's exactly like at the airport', the security official had joked, as he had asked for my passport, passed my laptop and phone through a scanner, padded me down, but then also proceeded to take and print photo ID), I appreciated the informal setup and surroundings of our meeting. Tim was happy for me to get my laptop out during our meeting, and to take notes on what he was saying.

I had expected to speak to Tim about the investigation and prosecution of Glodi and his co-defendants. Yet, it turned out that this was not what was primarily on his mind. While proud of the conviction that his team had secured, he also said, laughing, 'you can't arrest yourself out of the problem even if the police will try'. Echoing language that the frontline professionals in this and previous chapters had begun to speak, he continued to explain that he was most interested in prevention, not in prosecution; or rather, that the two should go hand-in-hand. 'We recognize county lines dealing now for what it is: it's about exploitation at its heart, and we want to safeguard the children while prosecuting the real offenders, the people who do the exploiting'. Asked about where he saw the biggest potential of the *Modern Slavery Act*, Tim was quick to answer: some of the key provisions that he thought were still under-explored pertained to the civil preventive orders specified in part 2 of the Act, and which could apply both to victims and to offenders as their designated purpose was 'preventive'. Indeed, he continued, he was currently writing a manual, together with one of the defence lawyers from the human-trafficking trial. The manual was addressed to law enforcement around the country in the hope that police forces would start making greater use of these orders. Would I like to be an external consultant for the manual, he asked, to feed in my academic expertise?

Civil preventive orders—which are well-established tools in anti-gangs policing and other areas of 'public safety', such as anti-terrorism policing—are orders that may be made by a court sitting in a civil capacity at the request of relevant authorities (such as the police or local authorities). They contain prohibitions created by the court as a response to conduct by the defendant (often to do with their freedom of movement and association), the breach of which amounts to a criminal offence, usually punishable with imprisonment. They involve a hybrid civil-criminal two-step process: first, the making of the order according to the civil procedure—and hence the civil standard of proof ('on the balance of probabilities') rather than the higher standard used in criminal courts ('beyond reasonable doubt') but coupled with, second, criminal proceedings in the event of breach. Part 2 of the *Modern Slavery Act* specifies two types of orders: 'Slavery and Trafficking Prevention Orders' (STPOs) and 'Slavery and Trafficking Risk

Orders' (STROs). STPOs are aimed at those convicted of a slavery and human-trafficking offence (see Chapter 8). STROs are aimed at individuals who haven't been convicted of a slavery or human-trafficking offence; as such, they can be imposed on a person who has not committed any crimes. A court can impose any restriction on the defendant that it deems necessary to protect the public from harm. Breach of the order can result in a maximum penalty of five years' imprisonment.

For Tim, pursuing these orders made perfect sense in a situation where these interventions were designed with a purely preventive purpose in mind. In his foreword to the manual (Davies et al., 2021), he specified their twofold benefit. One, they prevent the serious harm that comes with not interrupting a county line by 'giving the police the opportunity to proactively safeguard victims of exploitation alongside key partners'. A secondary benefit, when 'the subject of the order is a child or vulnerable adult', was that their 'own criminality in exploiting others may be interrupted in their own interests, most especially when supported by a wider multi-agency intervention'. This, Tim specified, was especially the case when individuals subjected to the order 'are themselves exploited but pose a risk to others' (2021, p. 3). Tim's enthusiasm for these orders was shared by both central government[1] and those at the front line. The police force whose officers featured in this chapter, for example, regularly applied for civil injunction orders, including 'gang injunction orders' against individuals involved in county lines activity, 'parenting orders' against parents of those involved, and 'closure orders' for cuckooed individuals. The force had, at the time I worked with them, not yet applied for any STROs. Yet, Conor was excited to roll them out, arguing that they had distinct advantages over gang injunction orders:

> With gang injunctions we had a problem: once an order had been secured, people started fighting or contesting them, saying "I am not in a gang", then you have to prove they are in a gang [before a court], that's when they disappeared off social media suddenly, the pictures of the bandanas disappeared [laughs]. But with [the slavery risk orders] I can't see how they are going to contest it. All they can say is, "I am not doing it",

[1] Since the manual was published in 2021, the call for greater use of these orders has been repeated time and again. Most recently, in its response to the House of Lord's 2024 inquiry into the *Modern Slavery Act* (2024), the government suggested that further legislation be introduced to facilitate their wider use, particularly on defendants upon acquittal (HM Government, 2024, para 22).

> and we will say, "great, that's exactly where we want you to be and if you *do* end up doing it, you're going to jail for it".

Interestingly too here, Conor acknowledged the nebulous nature of the concept of 'gangs' that has been highlighted in previous chapters not as indicative of problematic policing practices, but as evidence of criminals' manipulative mindset.

I conclude with a discussion of civil preventive orders to illustrate how frontline workers' and law enforcement officials' attempts to make sense of and respond to their newly discovered mandate to safeguard vulnerable communities have come full circle. Here, an individual deemed 'at risk' of county lines activity and modern slavery (either as what police classify as a victim or as a perpetrator) can find themselves subject to draconian restrictions that severely limit their daily lives and freedoms, including being banned from associating with people (such as their own family and friends) or going to certain places (such as a neighbouring estate or particular streets within their own estate), and being required to adhere to positive obligations (such as keeping the police informed of any intimate or close relationships that they enter or their travels and movements). What is more, as breach of the order can lead to imprisonment, the person subject to an order lives a precarious freedom, a point that shall I come back to in my discussion of Glodi's situation in Chapter 8. Importantly, in assessing the necessity of such an order, any intelligence over and beyond the commission of criminal acts can be included, such as the kinds of multi-agency knowledge practices surveyed in this chapter that come down to professional 'intuition' alone.

The heightened monitoring, surveillance, classifications, and knowledge practices that are enabled in the name of protecting the 'vulnerable' and those 'at risk' should not be seen as a straightforward outcome of legislative input or, alternatively, as a matter of over-zealousness on the part of professionals. To reduce the matter to either one of legal implementation or individual behaviour alone would mean to make our analyses complicit with, and submit them to, 'the managerial, administrative or actuarial interpretations of, and responses to, law breaking' that have prevailed among practitioners and mainstream criminology (Fatsis, 2021, p. 142). Instead, I suggest that the 'excess' of state powers analysed here speaks of the inherently productive nature of vulnerability governance. As Charlotte Heath-Kelly and Barbara Gruber (2023) have argued, what makes vulnerability so potent in policy thinking is its implied futurity: 'vulnerability', they write, 'implies a pre-emptive temporality—it is used to denote the potential for something negative to occur'. Thus, the reorganization of policing and social policies in the name of protecting the vulnerable 'invents a landscape of intervention *before* a particular phenomenon manifests', justifying wide-ranging interventions in anticipation of this future threat or suffering. We have seen precisely this logic at work in the multi-agency safeguarding of county lines where professionals routinely intervene and act before a crime has been committed, and where it never might be.

From this perspective, the kinds of frontline responses discussed here appear neither as unusual nor as particularly benevolent. On the contrary, they can be reconstructed as exercises in 'techno-moral governance' (Acosta, Bruun and Koch, 2025) that deepen the logic of anticipatory temporality central to the government's wars on 'suspect' populations, including on so-called 'gang members', 'terrorists', 'illegal migrants', and 'Asian grooming gangs' (Williams, 2015; Bhattacharyya et al., 2021; Cockbain and Tufail, 2020; Nijjar, 2022). In what has been called a shift towards 'prefigurative' or 'pre-crime' (Zedner and Ashworth, 2014), we have seen the identification of all sorts of 'would-be-criminals' in situations where no crime has been committed: or, to put it slightly differently, where a new security problem is created by those enforcing it. For example, in the context of counter-terrorism policies, data sharing has allowed the family courts to extend draconian powers into the lives of individuals deemed 'at risk' of radicalization (Ahdash, 2023), while immigration policies have justified individuals' deportation allegedly because they are deemed 'more likely than not' to be 'of bad character' (de Noronha, 2020, p. 17). Closer even to the subject at stake, moral panics around 'street gangs' and 'knife crime' have justified the imposition of gang injunctions on individuals who have not committed any crimes, with dramatic effects on the civil liberties and human rights of those targeted (Williams, 2015; Nijjar, 2018).

We can hence conclude that the rise of vulnerability in contemporary policing and policy practice constitutes yet another facet of the securitization of everyday life in Black, racialized, and working-class communities. Mark Neocleous has forcefully argued that such security-building is deeply embedded in Euro-American histories of modern statecraft (Neocleous, 2011, 2025). From the early days of European colonization, liberal governments have been in the business of 'pacifying' populations in the service of imperial and capitalist interests, through what I have called techno-moral means. In both the colonies and the metropolis, governing depended not only on the exercise of raw military power but on 'softer' techniques, such as the gathering of information about 'suspect' populations, the teaching of trades, education, welfare provision, ideological indoctrination, and the construction of a market. The logic of pacifying populations then was 'not just about the violent crushing of opposition . . . [but the] shaping of the behaviour of individuals, groups, and classes, and hereby ordering of social relations of power around a particular regime of accumulation' (2011, p. 201). This, in turn, involved an army of professionals responsible for analysing, reading, and disciplining the behaviour and social relations of 'suspect' communities.

What is at stake in the safeguarding of those identified as being 'at risk' of criminal exploitation in county lines are precisely the kinds of 'pacifying' measures that, according to Neocleous, lie 'at the heart of the fabrication of social order' (2011, p. 201) and that continue to inform liberal government's wars on domestic 'enemy populations'—whether these are perceived terrorists, immigrants, gang members (2011, p. 201–204), or, we might add, those considered at risk of modern slavery. When policing these enemy populations, the identification of would-be-victims and would-be-criminals justifies wide-ranging forms of intervention in the name of security. We can see these practices of state power at work when youth workers or police officers pay 'surprise visits' to individuals considered to be suspect and offer them access to welfare, education, housing, and recreational activities. State power is also enacted through knowledge practices, such as when quasi-criminal proxies are developed that serve an actuarial purpose of 'dangerizing' entire communities (Lianos and Douglas, 2000), as we saw in the case of the 'cuckooing' meetings analysed here. And, finally, state power is exercised when individuals become the subject of civil prevention orders that stop them from engaging in otherwise legal activities, thus severely restricting their civil liberties against the threat of imprisonment, even before they have committed—or where they might never commit—any crimes (Ramsay, 2010, 2012; Zedner and Ashworth, 2014).

Let us be clear: such exercises in securitization are not racially neutral. The policing of pre-crime in contemporary Britain needs to be understood as a continuation of both colonial and martial logics; it is, in Nijjar's words, a 'mode of police warfare that calculates racial abnormality, produces racially defined future "gang" members, "terrorists", and other enemy figures, and sanctions targeted pre-emptive action to securitise Euro-modernity' (2022, p. 453). It thus expels 'racialised people from the albeit limited protection of criminal law' (Bhattacharyya et al., 2021) through the exercise of pre-emptive state powers, and by feeding into orientalist stereotypes and demonization of those thus targeted (Cockbain and Tufail, 2020). The case of 'criminal exploitation' in county lines is no different: for here, once more, the target population are urban disenfranchised and racialized youth who are reconstructed as a threat to the civil order of the nation. And yet, as Lauren Wroe reminds us, 'where previously [many of these strategies] have found themselves critiqued and scrutinised, now a liberal discourse of child safeguarding broadens the appeal of expanding police powers' (2023), and renders opposition to it difficult. In the next two chapters I will further unpack this liberal discourse of 'doing good' and its implications by turning from frontline professionals to the lawyers, judges, and jury members who now argue over modern slavery cases in Britain's Crown Courts.

6
A ‘Hot Potato’: Defending Exploitation in the Crown Courts

Introduction

In February 2020, I made the acquaintance of Chadi, a thirty-something Londoner and second-generation migrant of North African origins. Chadi was a criminal defence lawyer and a junior barrister in one of the city’s larger criminal law chambers. Having grown up on a North London council estate, Chadi had a passion for defending youth caught on the wrong side of the law, who often came from a background similar to his own. He often represented clients on charge for drugs offences, most recently in the context of county lines. After some back and forth, as we were trying to fit an initial phone call into his busy and unpredictable court schedule, Chadi finally called me one evening. ‘I am so glad you are doing research on this!’ he exclaimed into the phone. ‘I am just facing the most shambolic case right now; you should come and watch it’. This case involved conspiracy to supply Class A drugs (heroin and crack cocaine) in a drugs line going between South London and Portsmouth, a seaside town more than an hour’s train ride and about ninety miles from the capital city.

Chadi was defence counsel for a young Black man named Aidan Williams, eighteen years of age at trial but sixteen at the time of the offence. Williams had been working in the lower echelons of this particular county lines operation, sometimes as a runner, at other times guarding the drugs while others were sent out. One early morning in 2018, Williams was arrested in Portsmouth during a police raid on a ‘cuckooed flat’, or a drug user’s flat taken over by drug dealers working for the line (see Chapter 5). The police found Williams lying on a bed with drugs, a machete, and a burner phone close to him. Subsequent phone analysis was able to link the burner phone to the main deal line that had been sending mass advertising messages to drug users in Portsmouth. Williams was charged with conspiracy to supply Class A drugs alongside five co-defendants, including a

Drugs, Race, and the Politics of Modern Slavery Law. Insa Lee Koch, Oxford University Press.
 DOI: 10.1093/9780198899631.003.0006

man called Max who was described as the 'ringleader' of the drugs line; two runners from London; the drug user whose flat Williams was found in; and a young woman who the court knew as Max's girlfriend. Max was the only defendant who pleaded guilty at the outset, leaving Williams to stand trial alongside the remaining four defendants.

In the lead-up to the trial, things seemed pretty straightforward and not exactly hopeful for Williams, who, Chadi suspected, would soon be another young Black man going to prison on drugs charges (see Chapter 4). This is because Williams did not seem to have much by way of a credible defence, having refused to disclose any information about his involvement in the drugs line to his lawyer. But things took an unexpected turn two days before the scheduled trial date: Williams confided in Chadi that he had been involved in drug dealing because of a debt he needed to pay, having been held responsible for losing a bike that Max had lent to him. Max, who Williams knew 'from growing up in the neighbourhood', began sending Williams out of town on regular occasions, asking him to stay at drug users' flats. He was only allowed to return to London and his home once he had sold all of his drugs. Williams had been arrested on a number of occasions, but each time let off with a caution. Each time too, he returned to drug dealing almost immediately, being more indebted to Max than ever once the police confiscated his drugs and money. However, the police had not let him go after his most recent arrest, leading to the charges he was facing. Almost immediately after Williams's disclosure, one of his co-defendants—another runner for the drugs lines—followed suit, confiding in his respective defence lawyer that he too had incurred a drug debt with Max.

Chadi knew immediately that his client's explanation could potentially change everything: having defended county lines clients in recent months, Chadi suspected that Williams qualified as a 'victim of slavery and human trafficking' under the government's mechanism for identifying modern slaves, the National Referral Mechanism (NRM). The Single Competent Authority, as the bureaucratic body responsible for this assessment is called, makes a decision as to a suspected victim's status in two steps, an initial 'reasonable grounds' decision followed by a 'conclusive grounds' decision made on the civil standard of proof, or the balance of probabilities. While a positive conclusive grounds decision has no direct legal bearing (being a bureaucratic rather than a legal decision), the Crown Prosecution's guidelines relating to victims of human trafficking state—following the 'non-punishment principle'—that the decision should be taken into account when determining whether to bring charges against a victim of human trafficking and modern slavery. Furthermore, should the prosecution decide to continue with the case, Chadi was confident that Williams now had a defence in law: under s.45 of the *Modern Slavery Act 2015*, the 'exploitation defence' is available for defendants who have committed certain crimes—including drugs crimes—and which, if run successfully, results in a complete acquittal. Consent to the criminal activity in question is irrelevant to this defence.

Williams's situation was not all that unusual. Across Britain's criminal courts, a demographic of mostly young men and boys, typically from some of Britain's most disenfranchised neighbourhoods, are no longer treated as straightforward criminals and drug dealers, but as potential victims of 'modern slavery' entitled to special forms of legal protection. In this chapter and the next, I ask a number of questions regarding the landscape of this emerging modern slavery jurisprudence. What are the challenges that lawyers, judges, and jury members face as they are asked to deliberate, for the first time, concepts like 'exploitation', 'slavery', and 'trafficking' in domestic drugs trafficking cases? How do different legal actors, from defence lawyers like Chadi to prosecutors and judges, understand what we might call the threshold or tipping point of exploitation? And what does this tell us about the workings of state power, once more? In the last chapter, we saw how frontline professionals, often despite their good intentions, end up becoming complicit in forms of techno-moral governance that expand state monitoring, knowledge practices, and pre-emptive policing. I argued that the language of 'partnership work', 'multi agency work', and 'data sharing' central to safeguarding efforts at the front line has not only extended a wide range of discretionary state powers known to other areas of prevention work, but cemented new ways of 'seeing like a state' (Scott, 1998) that render Britain's racialized and working-class communities legible through a lens of pathos and crime.

Here, I take this argument further by shifting my ethnographic and analytical lens from frontline workers' efforts to the activities of lawyers and judges. As the most authoritative of state settings where decisions over a person's liberty are made, the Crown Courts have a duty to prevent victims of human trafficking and modern slavery from suffering undue punishment for offences that they have committed in connection with their slavery. But what this means in practice is up for grabs. Based on court watch ethnography, this chapter discusses how these issues become the subject of heated legal battles, either as part of an 'abuse of process' argument or as part of legal arguments under the s.45 defence in the *The Modern*

Slavery Act 2015. Modern slavery constitutes a 'hot potato' for the courts, as different government bodies struggle to pin down what modern slavery looks like in 'real life'. While defence lawyers like Chadi describe involvement in the drugs economy and with the authorities as evidence of their clients being exploited, prosecutors use the same facts to frame defendants as criminals who should not escape punishment. Legal contests in the courtroom over the meaning of exploitation constitute techno-moral processes that entrench, rather than alleviate, punitive logics. These battles become a conduit for state domination as the story of danger emanating from 'within' racialized and working-class communities is repeatedly enacted, contested, and confirmed through courtroom arguments.

To develop these points, I draw on court-based ethnography that I have been carrying out since 2018, both in person and, when the onset of the COVID-19 pandemic in early 2020 made courtroom attendance impossible, by attending online hearings. My 'court watch' has been based in the Crown Courts, where county lines trials are regularly heard.[1] This fieldwork was marked by many hazards. For one, there is no database that holds information about trials that raise the modern slavery defence,[2] so the only way for me to find out about upcoming trials was by word of mouth, looking for media coverage of trial stories, or even just by checking the court listings for drugs indictments (and hoping that defence lawyers would run the modern slavery defence). What is more, while in theory trials are public hearings, my conditions of access and research were completely unpredictable, wholly coloured by whoever I was associated with—whether prosecution, defence, or, as we saw in Chapter 4, family members of defendants. In total, I have attended five full trials where modern slavery concerns were raised either by defence, prosecution, or both. I spent an average of two to three months per trial in court, making for a total of over a year of intense

[1] Modern slavery issues are raised in the Crown Courts, the Magistrates' Courts, and sometimes the Juvenile Courts. Whether or not a case ends up in the Magistrates' or Crown Courts depends on how the offence is classed, whether it is a 'summary', 'either-way', or 'indictable' offence, with the most serious of these—indictable offences—appearing in the Crown Courts in front of a professional judge and an appointed lay jury. Drugs charges, which make up the bulk of offences for 'county lines' cases, are classed as either-way offences, meaning they can be trialled in either court. However, such offences are referred to the Crown Courts only when the defendant requests a Crown Court trial or when, taking into account the seriousness of the offence, the Magistrate or District Judge in a Magistrates' Court takes the view that their sentencing powers would be insufficient if the defendant was found guilty.

[2] When a defendant has been charged with an offence under the *Modern Slavery Act*, this will appear on their indictment and hence be available on court listings and in databases. However, where slavery is raised as a defence, this does not appear on the official listing (as only indictments are listed).

court-based ethnography. Through this, I also grew close to a number of barristers who would share their views with me during court breaks, on train journeys to and from court (as hearings would also take place outside of the capital city), and in the more exclusive settings of the Inns and private clubs. But before I get to the story, let me situate this chapter within the context of the Crown Courts' mandate to respond to 'modern slavery' and 'county lines'.

Modern slavery at the heart of sovereign power: Inside the Crown Courts

As the most formal and authoritative of state settings where decisions over a person's liberty are made (Scheffer, 2010), the Crown Courts have for some time now had a duty to prevent victims of human trafficking and modern slavery from suffering undue punishment for offences that they have committed in connection with their slavery. Unlike the safeguarding responses used by the frontline professionals profiled in my last chapter, this duty was legally enshrined even before the implementation of the *Modern Slavery Act 2015*. The Council of Europe's Anti-Trafficking Convention 2005, having adopted the definition of trafficking advanced in the United Nation's Palermo Protocol (Chapter 1), contains a specific non-punishment provision in art. 26 that provides for 'the possibility of not imposing penalties on victims for their involvement in unlawful activities, to the extent that they have been compelled to do so' (United Nations General Assembly, 2021). The EU's Anti-Trafficking Directive (2011/36/EU) further contains a non-punishment provision in art. 8, stating that member states shall take the necessary measures to ensure that competent national authorities are entitled not to prosecute or impose penalties on victims of trafficking in human beings for their involvement in criminal activities that they have been compelled to commit as a direct consequence of being subject to trafficking.

Partly to implement international obligations into domestic law, the UK Government's *Modern Slavery Act* 2015 provided a statutory defence under s.45 of the legislation for those who have committed certain offences as a consequence of being 'exploited'. This defence applies to victims over and under the age of eighteen who are compelled to commit certain offences because of such exploitation, though it also includes a list of offences that the defence does not apply to—offences that are deemed too serious for coverage by the statute (including the modern slavery offences covered under the same Act). It does apply to drugs offences, however. For adults, the defence can be applied when a person has been compelled to perform a criminal act; the compulsion must be attributable to slavery or relevant exploitation, and assumes that a reasonable person in the same situation and sharing the person's relevant characteristics[3] would have no realistic alternative to performing the act. 'Exploitation' is defined as including 'slavery, servitude, and forced labour as well as sexual exploitation and organ removal', and 'when a person is subjected to force, threats or deception designed to induce him or her to a) provide services, b) provide benefits to another, or c) enable another to acquire benefits'. It includes 'using or attempting to use a person for any of these purposes a)-c) having chosen a person because of their age or defined vulnerability'. For persons under the age of eighteen, no element of compulsion has to be present, nor is there a need for the child to explore 'realistic alternatives' to committing the offence.

Since the enactment of the *Modern Slavery Act*, the government has given further instructions on situations where a defendant is believed to be a victim of modern slavery and human trafficking, stating explicitly that the guidelines are also applicable to the case of county lines (Crown Prosecution Service, 2024). The policy of the Crown Prosecution Service (CPS) sets out a four-stage test that requires the prosecutor to consider: (1) whether there is reason to believe that the person is a victim of trafficking/slavery; (ii) whether there is clear evidence of a credible common-law defence of duress; (iii) whether there is clear evidence of a s.45 defence; and (iv) where there is such evidence, but the offence may have been committed as a result of compulsion arising from the trafficking, whether it is in the public interest to prosecute. The guidance further states that in answering the first question, prosecutors have a duty to 'make proper inquiries' and to refer any suspected victims into the government's mechanism for identifying victims of modern slavery and human trafficking, the NRM. While the CPS guidelines are explicit that 'a positive conclusive grounds' decision by the Single Competent Authority that presides over the NRM is not binding on the court (the decision being made by a bureaucratic body on the basis of the civil standard of proof, which is lower than the standard applied in the criminal courts), they also state that 'unless there was evidence to contradict it or significant evidence that had not been considered, it is likely that the courts will abide by the decision'.

[3] 'Relevant characteristics', in turn, refer to 'age, sex and any physical or mental illness or disability' in the law.

The extension of legal protections to those considered victims of human trafficking and modern slavery has been welcomed by government bodies and practitioners. As Kevin Hyland, the former Independent Anti-Slavery Commissioner (itself a governmental office created by the *Modern Slavery Act* 2015) put it, treating drugs traffickers as victims and not as criminals 'makes an enormous difference. You get it right, the whole process changes because you don't have that person in the dock, you start looking for someone else to put in the dock' (Cox and Forde, 2017). But what it means 'to get it right' is far from straightforward, as previous chapters have begun to show. Indeed, a wealth of reports have pointed at the failures of implementation to date. A cross-party inquiry into the *Modern Slavery Act* conducted in 2019 remarked that there is no quantitative data available with which to assess 'the scale and impact of the statutory defence', including how the defence has been 'used or potentially misused' (2019, p. 68). The same report cited law enforcement officials' 'concerns that the defence is being used as a "loophole" for offenders identifying as victims' while conversely, 'other stakeholders presented evidence that victims continue to be prosecuted for offences they were forced to commit' (2019, p. 68). Further questions have been raised about the need to simplify the very meaning of 'exploitation' as defined in the Act, the desirability of having a standalone defence for 'criminal exploitation' in county lines, and the possibility of expanding the list of offences to which the modern slavery defence applies (Home Office, 2019; Centre for Social Justice and Justice&Care, 2024; House of Lords Modern Slavery Act 2015 Committee, 2024).

Important as these interventions are, they echoe the technocratic optimism central to much criminal justice policy commentary and scholarship. Discussions of the *Modern Slavery Act* have, to date, tended to focus on its effectiveness and implementation rather than its workings as a political project (yet see Broad and Gadd, 2023; Carvalho et al., 2025; Craig et al., 2019; Fudge, 2025). This means that the dominant commentary has remained divorced from a discussion of the existing realities of institutionalized failures that mark the criminal justice system. And yet, as we have seen, the courts are not settings where neutral justice is dispensed, but act as sites of racialized (classed and gendered) state-making, with a recent report going so far as to argue that the higher echelons of the judiciary are 'institutionally racist' (Monteith et al., 2022). In Britain, young Black and minority ethnic defendants stand a much higher chance of being charged with drugs offences (Lammy, 2017). When it comes to the first prosecutions brought under the *Modern Slavery Act*, early media reporting almost exclusively focused on the conviction of young Black and minoritized ethnic men (see Gebrekidan, 2022), thus begging the question of how these prosecutions entrench deeply engrained racial disproportionalities in the law (Wroe, 2023; Koch, 2024). But even more importantly (and in the absence of any conclusive numbers), and as repeatedly argued in this book, the significance of race travels beyond questions of disproportionality as the myth of Black law breaking can attach itself to anyone on the wrong side of the law, including to drug dealers and users racialized as white.

Here, my aim is to push for a political reading of the emergent jurisprudence of modern slavery cases, one which builds and extends the analytical framing developed in the last chapter: that of modern slavery's workings as a site of 'techno-moral governance', defined here as a process whereby a range of actors come to create, transgress, and navigate political relations through a fusing of policy and law with moral pronouncements (Bornstein and Sharma, 2016; Acosta, Bruun, and Koch, 2025). Once more, it bears emphasizing that my aim is not to attribute malicious intent to the lawyers whose work I got to shadow. Like the US defence lawyers in Cheng's (2017) study who engage in processes of 'open-ended humanization' in death row mitigation cases, the UK immigration lawyers in Beyer's (2023) work who see themselves as 'expert activists' pushing the boundaries of immigration law, or the lawyers studied by Fuchs (2024) who engage in 'creative legal labour' on behalf of Dalit constituencies in India, the lawyers who appear in this chapter saw *The Modern Slavery Act* as a genuine opportunity to protect vulnerable clients. And yet, they also disagreed over what constitutes evidence of 'exploitation' as opposed to a defendant's steep involvement in criminality, often using the same facts to make a case for either position, with the outcome of the cases ultimately following a predictable punitive pattern. At precisely the moment when the law has expanded the ambit of legal victimhood, it has failed to address the racial injustices that suffuse the criminal justice system, instead re-entrenching the state's hold over its over-criminalized populations.

Pushing the remits of legal victimhood: The work of criminal defence lawyers

When I began my research with defence lawyers on their use and understanding of *The Modern Slavery Act*, I was struck by how eager they were for me to witness their cases play out in the courtroom. While I first took this sentiment to be driven by the performative zeal on which most barristers in my experience flourish, I also came to realize that they were desperate to have a researcher record what they considered a watershed moment in the criminal justice system's approach to a demographic of mostly young, often minoritized but also white working-class individuals involved in dealing Class A drugs. Let us consider these points by returning to Aidan Williams, the young man that Chadi was defending. We saw above that Williams's disclosure of his history of drugs involvement with Max marked the beginnings of a new and hopeful phase in his case: This was the information that Chadi had been waiting for, information that now opened the possibility of Williams walking free after all, as it could mean that the court would treat him as a victim of human trafficking and modern slavery. Chadi now wanted an official confirmation from the National Referral Mechanism (NRM), the government's Home Office mechanism for identifying and responding to victims of modern slavery and human trafficking, that Williams had indeed been exploited. His hope was that with the NRM decision at hand the prosecution would drop the case against his client altogether.

Together with the lawyer for Williams's co-defendant, a young man called Campbell who had also disclosed his history of drug debts with Max, Chadi submitted an application prior to the start of the trial to 'sever the indictment', that is to say, to remove the two defendants from the drugs conspiracy charges. They also requested for the police officer presiding over the investigations to make a referral for the two clients into the NRM. The police are one of the listed authorities classed as 'first responders' authorized to make such a referral (lawyers do not have the authority to do so). This request did not go well. Chadi recalled: 'The prosecution made a submission, literally scooping at us, laughing in our face, saying that it was inappropriate to use the language of human trafficking in this context. They refused to agree to it'. The judge too supported the prosecution's position, insisting that he did not believe that the defendants were victims of human trafficking. Yet, Chadi was determined not to give up. While, on a Monday morning in September 2019, the prosecution opened their case, Chadi continued to work behind the scenes. The list of 'first responders' authorized to make a referral into the NRM included the Salvation Army, a Christian charity that has been given a government contract to provide support to victims of human trafficking. Chadi reached out to the Salvation Army who, in turn, agreed to make the referral for Williams and one of his co-defendants.

A few weeks later, while the trial was well under way, the NRM returned the first part of its two-step decision making process, the so-called 'reasonable grounds decision', stating that they indeed believed both Williams and his co-defendant to be victims of human trafficking and modern slavery. In light of this decision, a new trial date was set for February 2020, four months down the line, when the NRM's final decision—the 'conclusive grounds' decision—should have come through. Chadi was confident that the decision would come back positive for his client. He was right. In early February 2020, ten days before the new trial was scheduled to start, the NRM communicated its 'conclusive grounds decision' that both clients had been found on the balance of probabilities to be victims of human trafficking and modern slavery at the time of the offending behaviour in question. Chadi was ecstatic, expecting the charges for his client to be dropped once and for all. But once more, it turned out that he had hoped too soon: the day before our first phone call, during which Chadi had described this trial as 'utterly shambolic', the prosecution announced that they would continue with the case. The trial was set to start a week later in Portsmouth Crown Court, in the town where Williams and his co-defendants were accused of having conspired to sell drugs coming from South London.

On the morning of the opening of the trial, Chadi and I had arranged to meet on the 7am train leaving London for Portsmouth from Waterloo train station, a busy station on the banks of the river Thames. As I walked into the train station, I was reminded that this is where I had met Angelique a few months prior to talk to her about her son, who had never been recognized a slave by the official system (Chapter 4). When I stepped on the train that morning, Chadi was already sitting at a window seat, with a take-away plastic coffee cup and his laptop placed on the small table in front of him: a typical pose for defence lawyers, who never had enough time in a chronically underfunded criminal justice system to prepare their clients' cases and would therefore use any free moment to research documents, liaise with solicitors, and finalize their own submissions. As soon as I arrived, Chadi moved his bag from the seat next to him, indicating for me to sit down, and to look at his laptop. He was keen to show me the 'positive conclusive grounds decision' and the accompanying assessment of his client's 'state of vulnerability and exploitation', as he put it. The document was several pages long, containing the initial so-called 'reasonable grounds decision', submissions from a social worker and a police officer, and a detailed summary of his client's background under the heading 'modern slavery'. I took notes on the information provided under the 'modern slavery' section, reconstructing them later in bullet points:

- Williams grew up in London at his mother's flat with his siblings. His mother was a single mum and struggled with working long hours and keeping the family together. Williams's father was deported when Williams was young. Williams spent a lot of time at his grandmother's flat who lives on the same block where his mum had an apartment.
- The suspect (Max) lives on the same block of flats. He is known as a gang member to the police and has previous convictions for drugs and GBH. He is known to be aggressive. Williams met the suspect through his grandmother.
- Williams did not have the money for a bike, and he was upset about this. The suspect offered him his bike and Williams accepted. One day, he left the bike outside the shops, and it got stolen. Williams was too afraid to go to the police to report the theft. When the suspect found out, he was extremely angry, and he subsequently took Williams to Portsmouth in his car and left him in a flat. Williams had to sleep on the sofa in the flat and he was made to handle money. He was not given proper food. On a second occasion, the suspect picked him up and another young female and they were driven back to Portsmouth. This time, they were put in a flat where they were given beds, although the flat was sparsely furnished. Before he could be made to do anything, the flat was raided, and he was arrested.
- Williams had no bag, change of clothes, or toiletries on him when he was found. Williams did not go to the police for fear of retaliation because the suspect was acting very aggressively and threatened to get at his mother and siblings.
- Williams and his siblings are known to have connections/be in a gang and Williams was expelled from school at the time of the events in question.

As we chatted on the train, Chadi informed me about his plan. His first call would be to ask the court, prior to the jury being sworn in, to 'stay proceedings'—that is, to discontinue prosecution against his client. He would ask the court to discharge his client on the basis of an 'abuse of process' argument, an exceptional power to '"stay" an indictment if the court is of the opinion that to allow the prosecution to continue would amount to an abuse of process of the court' (Crown Prosecution Service, 2023). This determination relies on the Crown Prosecution's above mentioned four-limb test on the (non) prosecution of victims of human trafficking and modern slavery. If successful, this argument would result in the discharge of his client before the start of the trial. This would be the most desirable outcome for his client, not least because it would save him from having to sit through a potentially long, drawn-out trial—it having been set to run for five weeks. Failing that, Chadi would advise his client to stick to his 'non guilty' plea, to proceed to trial, and to run the s.45 defence under the *Modern Slavery Act*. Under this second scenario, he would bring the matter of his client's exploitation to the jury, who would then be entitled to return a verdict of 'not guilty'. Chadi was confident that the *Modern Slavery Act* provided a strong framework within which to understand clients like Williams not as perpetrators, but as victims in need of protection by the court.

Chadi asked me what I thought of his plan. Would I care to read his skeleton argument, he asked, once his submission was ready? And did I know of any official guidelines or authorities that had pursued a similar line of thought that he could cite in the court? I nodded and referred him to some recent policy documents. Chadi got animated at this point. 'This is it', he said. 'How can they prosecute someone like my client when the law has been designed to move away from criminalizing? The legislation is trying to move forward on how the courts and law enforcement acknowledge vulnerability'. But his outrage was paired with excitement, too: this was a real opportunity, he said, to push the boundaries of the law, and to work towards a legal system that recognized vulnerable individuals as victims. 'It's like in the case of domestic violence victims or sexual grooming cases', he said, echoing the narrative of Matt, the youth worker who we came across in the last chapter. 'Nobody used to believe that they were victims because their refusal to speak up was considered to be proof of their untrustworthiness'. Similarly, for Chadi, the reluctance of clients like Williams to tell the police about what they had been subjected to as part of their involvement in county lines was only further proof of their vulnerability, and of the court's duty to protect them. 'We are making the courts change the way they look at defendants', Chadi said.

The excitement that came through in Chadi on the train ride to Portsmouth that morning was not unusual. He was one of numerous criminal defence barristers I met who saw themselves as driving a cultural change in the courts, as pioneering the application of a policy that was only now beginning to be used in drugs trials. This is not to say, of course, that considerations of vulnerability were altogether new. As we have seen, like the frontline professionals in the last chapter, Chadi too insisted that there were important parallels, including with 'domestic violence cases' that the law had refused to recognize for a long time. What is more, while clearly seeing himself as a legal pioneer in some ways, Chadi was keen to show that he was acting on precedent: he reminded me that there was an 'established line of case law' concerning victims of cross-border human trafficking, allowing those who had been trafficked across national borders to evade punishment where they had been forced to commit offences. But the authority on county lines cases was still scarce, if not non-existent. What, then, happened when barristers like Chadi tried to use such reasoning in relation to defendants in county lines cases? To answer this question, we need to step inside the courtroom, to see how defence and prosecution lawyers become embroiled in arguments over what precisely constitutes the tipping point of exploitation—or when an individual has crossed the threshold from being a victim of exploitation to becoming a criminal deserving of punishment, once more.

'Splitting hairs between different vulnerabilities'

As soon as we got to Portsmouth Crown Court, Chadi offered to speak to the judge on my behalf, asking for permission to have me attend and take notes during the trial. This was readily granted. As I sat down in the empty public gallery, waiting for the judge to open the morning's session, I had time to take in the defendants, who were brought into the secured dock one-by-one by security staff. There was Williams, Chadi's client, a young Black man with an Afro. He held his face in his hands, looking visibly anxious and distressed. Chadi would later tell me that Williams was utterly exhausted when he arrived in court: he had already been up for hours because he was held on remand in a prison several hours' drive away, where the prison van picked him up at 3am in the morning to drop him and other prisoners off at different courthouses. Next to Williams, and separated by uniformed security officers, were his co-defendants: Campbell and Marshall, two young Black men who had been working alongside Williams on the drugs line; and James, an older white drug user with a nervous twitch and a frail constitution. It was his flat that had been 'cuckooed' by the drugs line. The final defendant, Max's girlfriend, was not present, having obtained permission by the court to remain absent following a doctor's note that her mental health was poor. Chadi would later describe the defendants as an 'assortment of vulnerabilities': 'one of them is a drug addict who can't properly walk; another a victim of domestic abuse; and then the three runners are clearly just vulnerable kids that were exploited'.

This, however, was not the prosecution's view. They insisted that all the defendants had wilfully and jointly taken part in a fully-fledged criminal enterprise, performing crucial roles in a profit-making business. In fact, when it came to Williams, the prosecution's position had not changed since the last trial. The lead prosecutor, a middle-aged white man with a heavy build and a nasal voice that betrayed his class privilege, insisted that proceedings should continue. However, as explained above, the CPS requires the court to work through a four-limb test when aiming to prosecute those who may have been victims of human trafficking and slavery, which involves the following considerations: whether the individual in question is a victim of human trafficking and modern slavery; whether the defence of duress applies; whether there is clear evidence of s.45; and if there is, whether it is still in the public interest to prosecute. In Williams's case, there was no dispute about the first two questions of the four-limb test: he was a victim of human trafficking and modern slavery, having received his 'positive conclusive grounds decision' by the NRM, and duress was not relevant in this instance. The legal arguments were focused on the last two questions of the test, with much of the discussion centring on whether Williams had been 'exploited' in line with the wording and meaning of the s.45 defence—which, as mentioned above, would require the jury to return a 'not guilty' verdict.

The prosecution raised a number of points. They argued that the decision of the NRM had not been based on 'cogent evidence', claiming that the information provided by the Single Competent Authority (SCA) as to the frequency of Williams's trips to Portsmouth did not square up with the available phone evidence that had been extracted from mobile phone companies and analysed by a phone analyst (see also the next chapter). While according to the SCA, Williams had only been to Portsmouth twice, in fact, phone data showed that he had been there on more occasions. In other words, Williams had lied about the number of trips he had made, trying to diminish the extent of his involvement in the drugs trade. This lie, according to the prosecution, went to show that the NRM's assessment as to Williams's vulnerability in particular, and their decision in general, could not be 'trusted'. Further getting to the question as to whether the defendant could run the s.45 defence, the prosecution told the court that Williams had consistently downplayed his own involvement in the drugs trade. Williams had multiple convictions for battery and robbery, thus showing that he was a well-versed criminal. He had also appeared in drill music videos in which the rappers had glamorized violence and drugs. The prosecution further cited the line from the NRM decision that Williams was believed to have 'gang involvement'. While the cogency of the decision as a whole was in question, they argued that elements of the assessment showed that Williams had led a very different life than that presented by his defence team.

Importantly too, the prosecution used information as to Williams' believed 'gang involvement' to construct a narrative of 'joint venture'. This is not the first time we have come across this strategy: in Chapter 4, we saw how the prosecution in the murder trial of K.S. and A.B. had systematically emphasized that both defendants had been 'in it together'. Similarly, here, the prosecution argued that the defence had erred in presenting Max as a 'violent and abusive exploiter' and Williams as 'his victim' when, in actual fact, both defendants had occupied significant roles in the drugs trade. Thus, Max and Williams had not been antagonists [with Max acting as Williams's exploiter] but 'part of the same enterprise, they know each other, they are from the same social group, and they have come down [to Portsmouth] for the same common purpose'. Williams was described as a 'lieutenant to Max' rather than simply an 'exploited runner', having gone from the lowest job of 'running' the drugs to holding them in the safety of flats. Finally, in relation to the fourth limb of the test, the prosecution stated that given that the charge in question was a serious offence known to cause 'much damage to the community', it would be in the public interest to prosecute this case. 'County lines causes misery to towns like this one', the prosecutor said, tapping into the racialized and racist imagery of provincial towns under threat at the hands of 'urban gangsters' (Chapter 2).

Chadi had hoped to avoid entering a discussion around the 'cogency of the NRM decision', he told me on the train that morning. Now that he had to, though, he was keen to remind the court that even if the decision was not legally binding, a certain level of 'institutional deference was due' to a body that 'in the name, is the *single competent* authority [. . .] for determining who is a victim of human trafficking'. But he also made several substantive points in his rebuttal. For one, he told the court, there were no inconsistencies in his client's account. Contrary to what the prosecution called 'lying', his client had always been truthful to the police in his statements about the number of times he had been in Portsmouth, even if this had been differently recorded by the NRM. But more so, even if he had failed to disclose the full extent of time spent away from London, this should not disqualify the decision as such. Citing some of the policy documents and reports on criminal exploitation that I had shared with Chadi upon his request, and echoing some of the voices of frontline professionals that we came across in earlier chapters, he continued to tell the court that it was 'an established finding in the literature on county lines that victims were often untrusting of authorities and prone to hiding the extent of their involvement'. As he told the court:

> The Crown [the prosecution] in their assessment invite your honour to not view Mr Williams [and his co-defendant] as victims of trafficking based on certain indicators—so for example they point to music videos or defendants lying—and it's true that on a base or initial understanding 'the perfect victim' in quotes does co-operate with the police, the perfect victim doesn't lie . . . but the *Modern Slavery Act* was put in place to move past that idea. Taken individually these indicators may point to lying or not collaborating but they must be viewed in the context of the relationship with the trafficker. So, when you put that umbrella relationship with [Max] which the Crown describes as evidence of gang culture, lying, not co-operating, it makes more sense to see them as being exploited. That is the perverseness of the decision to prosecute in this case. And so, lying and non-cooperation are indicators of being scared, of being groomed into a sense of mistrust from authority, it doesn't make Mr Williams less of a victim, in particular if he is sixteen at the time.

In this sense too, the prosecution had misrepresented a picture of 'common purpose' between Max and Williams. To argue that Williams could not be exploited because he was not a 'runner' selling on the streets but rather was told to stay in the flat and guard drugs was to 'split hairs between vulnerabilities': all that mattered is that he was performing these roles in the first place because he had a debt to pay off, and with no control or choice over his own actions. On the prosecution's own account and as derived from phone evidence, Max had been in contact with his defendant nearly 1,000 times in the space of five days while Williams was in Portsmouth. This indicated, Chadi exclaimed, 'not a relationship of trust but one of control'. Similarly, the very fact that his client had criminal convictions was not a sign of his criminality but of his vulnerability, or 'evidence of immaturity and also that you are vulnerable, [that] you can be used as expandable labour'. All of this, combined with the fact that the offences had occurred several years ago; that a significant amount of time and public money had already been wasted on this case; and that the very reason for the *Modern*

Slavery Act was to better protect victims who might otherwise fall through the gaps, meant that it could not possibly be argued that it was in the public interest to prosecute this case.

The legal dispute between prosecution and defence had revealed a central tension: the impossibility of pinpointing the moment when an individual goes from being a victim to becoming a perpetrator, in a context where 'exploitation' was legally vague and had no objective referent in the 'real' world. As Carvalho et al. have recently argued, while modern slavery is often presented as a coherent, easily intelligible phenomenon, there are 'hints' of a more 'complex reality' even in official policy documents and representation, 'from the very imprecision of what constitutes [modern slavery], to the recognition that there is a plethora of types of exploitation and that [modern slavery] constitutes a "hidden crime"' (Carvalho et al., 2024: 6). As the frontline professionals profiled in the last chapter said, determining whether or not a person was victimized then came down to 'professional intuition' or their 'sixth sense'. But depending on whose 'sixths sense' was prioritized, a client's participation in a criminal enterprise could constitute either evidence of their being an 'exploited' victim or, alternatively, a perpetrator. What is more, in trying to come up with definitional clarity, lawyers had to fall back onto 'proxys', again not unlike the frontline professionals in the last chapter, that curiously fused 'moral' assessments with technocratic ones—a defendant's attitudes and behaviours, including their propensity to lie, their relationship with the authorities (including how strained and hostile this was), their involvement in music videos, phone traffic data extracted that showed the frequency of calls and text exchanges, and, as we will see below, expert assessments.

Lawyers were open about the difficulties of 'getting it right'. Like the police officers we saw in Chapter 2 who spoke of how the picture was not always 'black and white', they too recognized that the matter was open to interpretation. But once a legal ruling had been made, open-endedness went out of the window. Five days after the legal arguments had begun, the judge gave his ruling. He sided with the prosecution. The judge reiterated the point that it is not within the jurisdiction of the Single Competent Authority to make the decision to prosecute, but rather within the jurisdiction of the Crown, and that the Crown were therefore entitled to conclude that the decision of the SCA was not based on 'cogent evidence'. He ruled that the 'prosecution have applied their mind to the correct law and guidance', reaching decisions that 'are not improper'. He concluded that 'in my view, this is not a case of an abuse of process but I bear in mind as ever there is still a defence [of exploitation] available to the defendants and that in the event of conviction, a reduction of the sentence will be available on the basis that they were exploited'. The judge's ruling concluded the day in court. Williams was taken down to the holding cell in the basement of the courthouse to wait until the prison van would collect him in the evening to take him back to prison, only for him to be dropped back off again some twelve hours later. It never came to that. The same afternoon, when Chadi went to see Williams in his holding cell, Williams told his lawyer that he had decided to plead guilty.

Chadi was disappointed: he had wanted the case to proceed to trial so that his client could run the s.45 defence. Travelling home on the train, Chadi was withdrawn, his bubbly smile gone. For the first time since I met him, he did not want to speak, looking quietly out the window. 'I feel so drained', he said to me after a while, avoiding eye contact. 'It's like you have the laws in place that are meant to change the way the system approaches vulnerabilities, and then the laws just get ignored, they don't get applied, and why not? Because the system is crying out for punitivism, the system is not ready for this change'. Chadi told me that he had tried to reason with Williams that afternoon, telling him that they could still win the case. But Williams was adamant that he did not want to continue. Asked why this was, Williams said that he could not 'take this anymore': waking up at 3am every morning to the sound of a shouting officer; driving in a van with other prisoners, like cattle, to the court; sitting behind a secured dock with a thick panel that prevented him from being able to hear the proceedings properly; and returning to prison at 9pm to find that his personal belongings had been taken or stolen by cellmates. He had even started taking his belongings with him every time he came to court, in a shoulder-strap bag. But this was exhausting. And why should he keep doing it? At the end of the day, he could still be found guilty by the jury.

Williams's case had revealed a more general truth: namely, how difficult it can be for defence lawyers to push the court's understanding of the tipping point of exploitation, as prosecutors and judges continue to see young men like Williams as criminals deserving of punishment. This becomes even more evident when we turn to the case of Miller and co-defendants, a county lines trial where the defendants not only faced drugs charges, but also human-trafficking charges under the *Modern Slavery Act*. Here, the same individual appeared on one account as an exploited slave, and on another, a human trafficker or slave master, thus turning slavery into a veritable 'hot potato' for the courts.

Masters or slaves?

On 27 January 2019, the *Mail Online*, one of Britain's major right-wing tabloid papers, published an article with the headline 'county lines gang boss aged just 17 "enslaved" two 16 year-old-girls and forced them to sell heroin and crack cocaine on the street by stuffing drugs in their bras and mouths' (Camber, 2019). The article featured a photograph of the 'county lines gang boss', a young Black male named Odain Miller, the 'first ever juvenile in the UK to go on trial charged with modern slavery' (Camber, 2019). According to the article, Miller had 'recruited' two sixteen-year-old girls from South London during a chance encounter, together with his co-defendant, eighteen-year-old Peace Alaka. Miller and Alaka had then introduced 'the girls' to the line's 'ringleader', another eighteen-year-old named Reis Bandhall. The girls had been taken from London to an unknown location in Maidstone, a town in Kent, about an hour's drive from London, where they 'had been locked in a flat and ferried in taxis by Miller and his gang to peddle drugs'. The operation was finally 'smashed' following a police raid of a drug user's flat, where Miller was found inside, having swallowed 'a staggering seventy-eight wraps of drugs before his arrest'. In the same flat, the police also retrieved a samurai sword and a Sim card that had been bent in half. Bandhall and Alaka were arrested shortly after. Miller and his two co-defendants were now on trial for both drugs and human trafficking under *The Modern Slavery Act 2015*.

Fast forward six months, to June 2019. I found myself sitting on a landing, separated from the courtroom below by a thick glass wall. I had come to Woolwich Crown Court, a high security court in South London that had become the state's preferred trial venue for terrorism offences. It was also the setting where Miller and his co-defendants would be retrialed. Through a befriended barrister, I had been able to locate Miller's trial in the Crown Court database and learned that the original trial (mentioned in the *Mail Online*) had collapsed and been scheduled for a retrial, though I did not yet know why. It was the retrial that I was attending that day. Upon arrival in court, I was not welcomed with open arms: the usher told me immediately that the judge 'was not in favour of anyone from the media attending'. My insistence that I was from the University and not from the media did not make a difference, and I was informed that I would only be allowed to sit in the upstairs landing, not in the courtroom itself. She also reiterated that I would not be able to get my laptop out for purposes of note taking. Once up on the landing, I realized that my banishment made it impossible for me to follow the proceedings: the heavy glass wall separating the landing from the courtroom severely restricted my vision of the court, and I could not hear anything being said. Frustrated, I sat in my chair for two hours, trying in vain to make sense of a drawn-out discussion between the judge and lawyers happening below me.

During the lunch break, I decided to introduce myself to one of the defence lawyers in the hope that they could update me about the morning's session and make a case to the judge for my being able to sit in court. I quickly went downstairs and waited outside the courtroom's front door. Soon after, one of the barristers, a forty-something year old man with a tanned face and styled, black curly hair, came outside. This turned out to be Ossie, Miller's lawyer, a criminal defence barrister from London. I would learn later that, as the child of Turkish-Cypriot working-class immigrants, he had first trained as a barber before going on to study law. Like Chadi, he was passionate about helping those less privileged than him. I introduced myself to Ossie and explained that I was doing research into the use of modern slavery legislation by the Crown Courts. Seemingly bemused, perhaps even a little flattered by my unexpected introduction, Ossie wondered how I knew about Miller's case. When I mentioned the *Mail Online*, his face contorted into a grimace. 'That article is a pile of rubbish, it doesn't even tell you half of what is going on', he exclaimed, explaining that there had been a reporting ban on Miller because he was a minor; the *Mail Online* had waited for him to turn eighteen, publishing the story on his birthday. '[The article] did not say anything about the fact that my client is actually a trafficked victim himself. Imagine getting that as your eighteenth birthday present'.

Would I like to come for a coffee? Ossie asked, and together we made our way to the court's cafeteria, a windowless room lit too brightly by ceiling lights, where we sat down on uncomfortable metal chairs in a quiet corner. He started talking immediately. Ossie was appointed as Miller's defence barrister about a year ago. He felt passionate about this case which, he repeated, had been completely misrepresented by the *Mail Online*. He began to fill me in. The initial trial against Miller and his co-defendants opened six months ago in Woolwich Crown Court, in front of the same judge as the one presiding over the trial today. Shortly after the opening, Ossie and his co-defence lawyers received an NRM notification that Miller was believed to be a victim of human trafficking and modern slavery. Alaka and Bandhall also received a 'positive reasonable grounds' decision shortly after. In the face of this news, the judge decided to discharge the jury, and the trial collapsed. A couple months later, the NRM issued its 'positive conclusive grounds' decision, confirming that on the basis of probabilities the defendants were victims of human trafficking and modern slavery. As with the case of Williams, the prosecution still decided to proceed with the charges, arguing that the NRM decision was not legally binding on the court.

Ossie pulled up the NRM decision on his laptop for me to see. It detailed the history of a young man whose life had been marked by challenges. Born in Jamaica, Miller had come to England aged six or seven, under circumstances that were unknown, the suspicion being that he was 'trafficked' into the country. He had grown up on an estate in South London, and faced domestic abuse, school exclusions, and placements in care homes. At age fifteen, he became involved in county lines, and was found to have been exploited; having incurred a drug debt, he was sent to locations across the country to work off his debt. That morning in court, Ossie presented his submissions to get his client discharged, using an 'abuse of process' argument similar to what Chadi had tried for Williams. 'We have an absolutely ridiculous situation here', he exclaimed, 'where one body of the government have said that my client is a slave and another body of the government, the CPS, accuse him of [being the perpetrator of] exactly the same crime!' I nodded, and could not help but think that there was another deep irony at stake: the first-ever juvenile to be charged with a modern slavery crime was a young Black man who was himself a descendant of enslaved people, having come to Britain from its formerly largest plantation colony, Jamaica.

Indeed, the NRM had been vague about the timing of when the exploitation of Miller and his co-defendants was said to have taken place, leaving the prosecution to argue that the decision was not relevant for the charges they were facing now. In light of this ambiguity, the judge requested a 'reconsideration of the NRM decision' that morning, meaning that the Single Competent Authority was now asked to supply further details on the timing and period of exploitation. Until this was supplied, the judge would adjourn the proceedings. Luckily, the waiting period proved not to be too long: the SCA's 'reconsideration' came three days later, with different answers in relation to the defendants. It determined that in Miller's case, the exploitation had indeed continued at the time of the offending behaviour in question. In relation to the other defendants, the wording was more cautious and less favourable, stating with respect to Alaka that they could not say when the exploitation had started and when it ended, and, in relation to Bandhall, that he stopped being exploited when he turned eighteen (and hence shortly before the said offending had taken place). In light of this news, the prosecution announced that they would drop all charges against Miller but continue the case against Alaka and Bandhall. Their respective defence lawyers, in turn, decided to not run an 'abuse of process' argument, but to proceed to trial.

The trial started the day after. This time, having previously been introduced to the judge by Ossie as a 'law professor from the LSE[4] doing research on modern slavery', I was given permission to sit in the courtroom and could therefore properly follow the proceedings. Bandhall, a young man of South Asian heritage, and Alaka, a young man of Nigerian heritage, were being charged alongside Cook, an older white man from Maidstone and a taxi driver, with human trafficking under s.2 of the *Modern Slavery Act* 2015. This provision states that 'a person commits an offence if the person arranges or facilitates the travel of another person (V) with a view to V being exploited'.[5] In addition, all defendants had been charged on four counts of possession of Class A drugs with intent to supply alongside a fourth defendant, a man called Bond, an older white drug user. The prosecution told the court the 'agreed facts': here, we had a number of defendants who together had been running the 'Walter line', a county lines drugs line going from London to Maidstone. Bandhall, Alaka, and Cook were drug dealers on the line. Bond was a drug user who was known to his co-defendants because it was his socially rented property that had been 'cuckooed' by the others. In the last chapter, I argued that quasi-criminal proxis such as 'cuckooing' act as new forms of classificatory knowledge that, in the name of safeguarding the vulnerable (here the 'cuckooed victim'), also enable more policing. We can see this logic at stake here, for it was his 'cuckooed status' that had resulted in Bond being charged with drugs offences.

As in many of the other trials discussed in this book, the prosecution constructed a narrative of 'joint venture' between the co-defendants. The prosecutor told the court that all defendants had been acting together in what was a highly profitable business that came at the expense of the 'two girls' and the local community in Maidstone. The prosecution told the courts that the defendants, while jointly organizing their criminal

[4] The LSE (London School of Economics) was my institutional home at the time of the trial.

[5] The provision further specifies that it is 'irrelevant whether V consents to the travel', and that a person arranges or facilitates V's travel with a view to V being exploited only if 'the person intends to exploit V during or after the travel', or 'the person knows or ought to know that another person is likely to exploit V'. Exploitation is defined under s.45 of the Act, which states, as explained above, that the defendants knew or ought to have known that the victims were under the age of eighteen, and that age was one of the reasons the victims were targeted.

enterprise, had performed distinct roles within the operation. Bandhall was the ringleader of the line, holding the phone and directing calls to others, typically from the safety of London flats. Alaka was his 'left lieutenant', doing the daily work of supervising the line. Cook and Bond were said to have 'lesser roles' in the criminal enterprise, being responsible, respectively, for hosting and for transporting the drugs and their dealers. Bandhall was presented as an entrenched 'gangster' and a 'street-wise, practiced liar'—evidenced by his nick name 'Big Reeks' ('a gangster name'), his involvement in drill music videos, and his history of previous offending. Alaka, who had no history of criminal offending, had shown his criminal propensity by repeatedly refusing to accept offers of help on the part of professionals to exit his 'lifestyle'. In particular, he had gone straight back into drug dealing after being caught 'red handed' by the police, showing his utter disregard for the authorities. Copious amounts of phone evidence were shown to the jury proving 'traffic' between the defendants and the victims. Witnesses were called, including the two victims who confirmed being introduced to Alaka and Bandhall, being driven in a taxi by Cook, staying in Bond's home, and being sent out to sell drugs.

At the close of their case, the defence barristers made a submission of 'no case to answer' for the human-trafficking charges, an application made to the judge to dismiss the case due to lack of evidence for the defendant to answer. The defence's argument rested on a narrow technical point, namely that the prosecution had failed to prove under s.2 of *The Modern Slavery Act* 2015 that the defendants knew that the victims were under the age of eighteen, and that age was one of the grounds on which the victims had been chosen. The defence argued that the evidence given by the prosecution as to the age of the victims was of a 'very generic nature', and that there was insufficient evidence from which to infer the defendants' knowledge of the girls' age. The judge, having at various moments expressed his concern that 'utmost care' ought to be exercised in this 'new area of law', concurred, asking the jury to return a verdict of 'non guilty' for the human-trafficking charges. Following this decision, the judge carefully avoided using the term 'human trafficking', speaking instead of the 'indictment'—anticipating, as he told the lawyers while the jury was out, that the defence would run the 'modern slavery defence' for the remaining drugs charges. 'It would be too confusing for the jury to get their head around the fact that they should acquit for modern slavery but then the defendants are running a defence under modern slavery', the judge warned.

For Alaka's and Bandhall's defence lawyers, the judge's direction that there was 'no case to answer' in relation to the human-trafficking charges was a big relief. It meant that their clients had been 'let off' the most serious charge, one that in theory (though rarely in practice) came with life in prison, and that they believed carried a huge moral stigma (see Chapter 7). But if the defence lawyers celebrated this outcome, it had also betrayed, once more, the impossibility of pinpointing modern slavery. From the start, the trial had been marked by twists and turns, including a conflict between two government bodies (the Single Competent Authority and the Crown Prosecution Service) as to the defendants' status as either victims or perpetrators; Miller's sudden discharge on all counts; and the judge's legal direction to acquit all remaining defendants of the 'indictment' that he felt could not be mentioned by name for fear of confusing the jury. It was this messiness, and the unpredictability to which it gave rise, that Ossie had in mind when he said that modern slavery has become 'a hot potato' for the courts. And yet, as I will discuss momentarily, while Alaka's and Bandhall's defence lawyers celebrated their clients' acquittal for human-trafficking charges, they subsequently struggled to convince the jury that their clients had indeed been 'exploited' under the s.45 exploitation defence with regard to the drugs counts. Their clients, who had been found to be 'modern slaves' by the NRM, were hence turned back into drug dealers, as the jury found them guilty.

A gateway for racialized punishment, once more

Having spent close to six weeks in court by the time the judge issued his direction of 'no case to answer' for the human-trafficking charges, I had had plenty of opportunities to chat with the defence lawyers in the breaks. While the prosecution refused my request to talk on several occasions, after Ossie's departure I grew close to the remaining defence barristers representing Alaka, Bandhall, and Cook. The mood was good between the co-defending parties, especially between Alaka's and Bandhall's barristers, who both intended to run the s.45 'exploitation' defence. Like Ossie, they were of the opinion that none of the defendants should be facing trial in the first place: For them, the single most defining feature of their clients was their shared vulnerability. Alaka and Bandhall were two minoritized youth from London who had been working at the bottom rung of a drugs economy that kept them indebted to others higher up in the chain. Cook, according to his lawyer, was a 'vulnerable chap from a social housing estate' with a 'history of drug abuse'. And Bond was himself a 'cuckooed' victim who, on his lawyer's account, should have never been charged with a crime because he was clearly exploited (and indeed, we saw in the last chapter that this is how frontline professionals conceptualize 'cuckooing'). As one defence lawyer put it, 'This case is ridiculous: So, you have a group of kids where nobody can decide if they are victims or perpetrators, you got a poor chap who has a drug abuse problem, and a vulnerable adult whose flat was taken over'.

After the prosecution formally closed its case, it was the defence's turn to present their evidence. This was also the moment when Alaka's and Bandhall's respective lawyers put forward their defence that their clients had been exploited by people higher up the chain within the meaning of s.45 of the *Modern Slavery Act*, and that this exploitation had not 'stopped' at the time of the indictment. Bandhall told the court that he had only been dealing drugs because of his debts, that he had been injured and received death threats by others higher up the chain, and that he was terrified for his life and that of his parents. 'Big Reeks', he maintained, was not him as claimed by the prosecution, but rather his boss, the very person to whom he was indebted and who had threatened him. Bandhall's father was called as a witness; he was an elderly, frail man who broke down in court as he recalled occasions when his son had come home after episodes of being missing, looking hungry, dirty, and unkempt (echoing the despair and voices of the mothers we came across in Chapter 3). Alaka, too, maintained that he had been working off a drug debt. A social worker told the court that Alaka had the distinct appearance of being 'groomed', he was 'overall dirty, and not flashy at all'. The jury were also given a much-redacted report by a modern slavery expert who had been instructed by Alaka's lawyer, and who, mirroring the language of technocracy we came across in the last chapter, gave the jury a 'list of indicators' to use in assessing Alaka's vulnerability to having been exploited.

Both Bandhall's and Alaka's defence lawyers further maintained a central point: that there was no fundamental difference between the girls, presented as victims in this case, and their own clients, presented as perpetrators of serious crimes. Being similar in age to the girls at the time of the indictments (Bandhall only two and Alaka one year older, respectively), and occupying similar roles at the bottom rung of the drugs economy, there was little that set the girls apart from the defendants, except for their gender. Moreover, the girls' relationship to Alaka and Miller had been one of flirtation and friendship rather than coercion and control; in fact, messages retrieved from their phones proved the amount of banter that had characterized their relationship. Perhaps most importantly, both Alaka's and Bandhall's defence lawyers relied on an email written by a London Metropolitan police officer investigating the case. The officer sent the message to a social worker who had been working with the girls, stating that the police had been unable to get one of them to make a statement, and urging the social worker that 'hopefully you will have more success encouraging [her] to give a statement—*we are really keen for her to be victim [rather] than a suspect*'. For the defence, the fact that the police had so blatantly stated their preference for the girls to be 'victims rather than suspects' was evidence of the police's bias. Indeed, it showed, in the words of Bandhall's barrister, that the police had 'struck a deal' with the girls that came at the expense of Bandhall and Alaka.

In late August 2019, nearly three months after the trial had begun, closing speeches were made. The prosecution made one last attempt to cement their image of Bandhall and Alaka as 'gangsters', with Bandhall as the 'central cog in the wheel'. Incorporating the defence's argument that the defendants had not been at the top of the chain, the prosecution conceded that there had been people above Alaka and Bandhall. But while Bandhall was not 'an enormous, international, top-of-the-three master mind', he had been at the top of 'this particular county line', he *was* Big Reeks, deceiving and lying to the authorities, tricking others into working for him, and trying to get away with it. Bandhall's defence lawyer, in turn, pleaded with the jury to not accept the prosecution's portrayal, to recognize that Bandhall was a 'victim of criminal exploitation'. Referring once more to the email written by the police officer to the social worker, she put it to the jury that the police had decided to treat the 'girls as victims because they are more sympathetic to the jury'; to the police, she argued, Bandhall had never been more than a 'young Black ethnic male carrying drugs' and hence a 'a criminal'. It therefore made no sense to argue that Bandhall had suddenly 'jumped ship from the "exploitation ship" to the "I'm going to make loads of money" boat'. Pleading that 'we are not going to let police make the decision because we know that the police take an easy way out, and so we have [*the Modern Slavery Act*] for you to decide', she told the jury that they were the 'gatekeepers':

> When prosecution say to you 'this is all a big lie', 'a lie up to his eyeballs', '[Bandhall was] climbing the drugs career ladder': have a think about what is really going on here. What's really going on here is a young lad

> who has through no fault of his own ended up in the wrong place at the wrong time aged fourteen. And from that point onwards his life has not been his own because he has been exploited and made a victim and he has been prosecuted even though he clearly is a victim. Ladies and Gentlemen, I am going to ask you to show Bandhall that there are people who listen, people who care, [that] you have listened and heard evidence, and [that] you accept he is victim and that prosecution haven't been able to show that he isn't, show him that for once even: when alarm bells are all ringing so loudly you are not going to ignore it, you are going to listen.

In the end, it seemed that the jury had not 'listened', at least not in the way the defence had pleaded. The jury found Bandhall guilty of all four drugs counts and Alaka of two of the four drugs counts. Alaka's barrister would later give me his interpretation as to why Alaka had been let off on two of the four charges: the jury had accepted that Alaka was 'exploited'—presumably by his co-defendant Bandhall—when he initially went from London to Maidstone (the period of time relating to the first two drug counts). But following his arrest by the police and return to drug dealing, they must have concluded that he stopped being a victim and had become a perpetrator (hence finding him guilty of the two remaining counts). The third defendant, Cook, was also found guilty of two drugs counts, while the fourth defendant, Bond, was the only one to be acquitted of all charges. The judge gave Bandhall a prolonged drugs sentence, arguing that he had played a 'significant' (albeit not a 'leading') role in the Walter line. He accepted that Bandhall had 'been initially exploited', but that he 'had gone up the ladder', and even though he was 'not enjoying the financial benefits of what is a profitable business', he was driven by the 'promise of a comfortable life'. He told Bandhall, '*You were in the process from being the exploited to becoming the exploiter*' (my emphasis). He sentenced him to five years in prison. Alaka, being placed by the judge in a lower yet still significant role, was sentenced to three years.

I was never given the opportunity to debrief the outcome of the case with Bandhall's defence lawyer. When I met with Alaka's defence lawyer a few weeks after the trial, however, he told me he felt that from the get-go, the trial had been stacked against the defendants. He was keen for me to know that he only thought the highest of his defendant: a young man from South London who played the drums at his African church every week and who was enrolled in a plumbing course at a local college, Alaka was someone who 'should have been spared the criminal justice system'. Echoing the views of other defence lawyers that I spoke to, including Chadi from Williams' trial, Alaka's lawyer felt that the trial's outcome was indicative of the criminal courts' difficulty in recognizing boys and young men like his own client and Bandhall as victims rather than as 'gangsters', and hence as perpetrators. The courts, he told me, were not ready for a complicated defence like the 'exploitation defence' under *The Modern Slavery Act*, for all the jury could see was 'a Black defendant in the dock and they automatically think that he must be guilty'. Furthermore, we could say that the judge himself fell into the same trap. Having initially acquitted the defendants of human-trafficking charges, he also found in his drugs sentencing that Bandhall had gone from being 'exploited' to becoming 'the exploiter', thus returning to the very language of exploitation that he had sought to keep out of this trial.

In the last chapter, we looked at how frontline workers' efforts to institutionalize a culture of safeguarding operate as techno-moral forms of governance that intensify the state's pre-emptive reach into the lives of individuals believed to be 'at risk'. In this process, we also saw that individuals become excluded from the protection of the criminal law, as they are made the subjects of state coercion even before they have been (or without ever being) charged with a crime. This chapter has discussed the other side of the coin: even where the criminal law's protection is extended to this demographic, and the ambit of legal victimhood gets 'stretched', this works to re-entrench the state's hold over some of the most over-criminalized populations. Thus, when defence lawyers insist on their defendants' rights by mobilizing the Crown Prosecution Guidelines on victims of human trafficking and modern slavery or by raising the s.45 'exploitation' defence during trial, they create spaces for legal protection that were not available in the same way to this demographic of defendants before. But if this creates new legal possibilities, the opposite is also true: slaves can be turned back into 'gangsters', cuckooed victims into perpetrators, and drug dealers into human traffickers in a game of 'hot potato' between judges, lawyers, and different government authorities. In this process, lawyers too engage in forms of techno-moral governance as they fuse highly moralized assessments of 'exploitation' with technocratic data from cell sites, expert witnesses and bureaucratic bodies like the NRM.

The defence lawyers I spoke to experienced these trials as having to swim against the tide of deeply entrenched punitive cultures that enveloped prosecution, judges, and the jury, often with predictable outcomes for their clients. This should not come as a surprise: institutional racism is ripe at all levels of the criminal justice system, including in the higher echelons of the judiciary (Lammy, 2017; Monteith et al., 2022), where its workings point to the uneasy continuity between colonial battlefields, plantations, and current legal regimes of racialized governance (Gilroy, 1987; Fatsis, 2021). But I would go even further: defence lawyering too is complicit in the punitiveness that they see themselves as fighting against. Thus, they too, when running an 'abuse of process' argument or when invoking the s.45 defence in front of the jury, build their legal arguments on an assumed dichotomy between victims and perpetrators, slaves and slave masters, and whose fallacy I and others have highlighted (McLean et al., 2020; Moyle, 2019; Marshall, 2024). When declaring their client's innocence within the logic of the law, they too assume that the figure of the 'exploiter' or 'trafficker' exists, for their arguments merely displace the figure of the perpetrator from their client onto someone else. Ultimately, then, all judicial actors reproduce the story of redemption considered in Chapter 2 that sees Black and working class youth as in need of saving from their own kind, for their own good.

Judged from this perspective, we can conclude that the legal battles we considered in this chapter become yet another conduit for state domination as the story of modern slavery as emanating from within racialized and working-class communities is repeatedly enacted and confirmed: through prosecutional narratives that present defendants as 'gang members' who exploit others more vulnerable than themselves; through judges who rule that defendants have gone from being 'exploited' to becoming 'the exploiter'; and through the defence lawyers themselves who, in trying to get their clients acquitted, reproduce the very binary of good and evil, and hence the terms of state domination. Once more, then, like with the frontline professionals we considered in the last chapter, the impetus to do 'good' and to 'care' acts as a mechanism for liberal order building that works to entrench and produce an excess of state power. But if in the case of frontline professionals, the outcome of such liberal order building is the (pre)emptive policing of classed and racialized communities, then when it comes to the criminal courts, state power is enacted in its most repressive form: through the deprivation of liberty, potentially for life, in the case of a human-trafficking conviction. In the next chapter, I will take this analysis further by turning to a crucial question: who, in the eyes of the law, constitutes the new slave-master—the very antithesis of liberal freedom?

7 'More than Just a Drugs Crime': Prosecuting Modern Slavery in Drugs Cases

Introduction

In the spring of 2019, Glodi Wabelua, the young man we have encountered at different points in this book, stood trial for human trafficking alongside Michael Karamera and Dean Alford, in Inner London Crown Court. The defendants had been running three county lines drugs operations going from London to Portsmouth, the sea-side town we encountered in the last chapter, situated about an hour and a half's drive from the capital city. Yet, this time the defendants were not on trial for drugs, having already been convicted of conspiracy to supply Class A drugs a few years prior. Rather, they had been charged with human-trafficking offences under the predecessor of the *Modern Slavery Act* 2015.[1] The prosecution's case was that Karamera, Alford, and Wabelua each used phone numbers associated with the drugs lines to arrange and facilitate their victims' travel from London to Portsmouth with a view of exploiting them. Alford was charged with three counts of human trafficking; Karamera with two; and Wabelua with one. All of the victims, except for one adult, were teenagers—described by the prosecution as 'children'—aged between fourteen and seventeen. The three defendants were twenty-one at the time of the offending behaviour in question.

[1] The defendants were charged under s.4(1)(a)(b), *Asylum and Immigration Act 2004* (which is now largely replicated in s.2 of the *Modern Slavery Act 2015*) because the offending in question had taken place before the *Modern Slavery Act 2015* had come into force. However, because the *Modern Slavery Act* replaced the *Asylum and Immigration Act*, this trial is considered a precedent-setting case.

Drugs, Race, and the Politics of Modern Slavery Law. Insa Lee Koch, Oxford University Press.
 DOI: 10.1093/9780198899631.003.0007

Knowing that I was interested to attend upcoming modern slavery trials, a befriended barrister sent an email on my behalf to members of her Inn.[2] Kate, the lead prosecutor, immediately responded, 'I have a case starting in two weeks. You are welcome to come'. A tall, white British woman with a confident demeanour and forceful presence, Kate was a senior barrister in the business of both defending and prosecuting. This case, however, was different from anything she had done before. It was a test case that would use human-trafficking law in a situation that had not been foreseen by its legislators: to prosecute county lines drug dealers who relied on runners to move drugs and to conduct sales within Britain's national borders. The prosecution knew that their case would not be easy to prove. None of the child victims had agreed to act as witnesses, forcing the Crown to proceed with a victimless prosecution, with the exception of one adult witness. The bulk of the prosecution's case was based on thousands of phone entries, called call data records (or CDRs), that showed patterns of movement of phones (and hence of individuals) and of communication between the victims, defendants, and drug users based in Portsmouth.

It worked. Nearly three months after the trial's start date, the three defendants were convicted. In the aftermath of the trial, the media spoke of 'a landmark case' (BBC, 2019; Dalton, 2019; Guardian, 2019). The case had made precedent, proving that modern slavery legislation could be used to tackle what the government has designated a national threat—county lines—as 'more than just a drugs crime'. But if the unfolding media narrative presented this as an unequivocal victory in the fight against evil, a logical extension of a law that sought to protect individuals from undue suffering, then the trial and its history had also revealed a more complicated story, one at the heart of the last chapter: how the commitment of professionals to do 'good' was continuously thwarted by the difficulties they encountered in pinpointing the meaning of inherently slippery concepts like modern slavery, trafficking, and exploitation. Here, I take these recurring themes as my point of departure to ask several questions: What does it take to construct county lines as 'more than just a drugs crime'? How is this 'more'—the criminal excess, so to speak—construed in terms of the language of human trafficking and exploitation? And what does the prosecution of

[2] All barristers are members of a professional organization called an Inn; there are four Inns in England and Wales. My own academic membership in one of the Inns facilitated access to senior barristers and helped establish trust with lawyers.

drug dealers, no longer just under drugs legislation but now under modern slavery laws, teach us about statecraft in contemporary Britain?

Like the law enforcement and frontline workers, lawyers, and judges we encountered in the last two chapters, the prosecution in this precedent-setting case was driven by what policy sees as a noble pursuit: the impetus to protect vulnerable individuals. And yet, as my ethnography with the prosecution team shows, the investigations were riddled with difficulties. Virtually all professionals involved not only struggled to graft singular logics of victims and perpetrators onto what appeared as messy social relations, but changed their assessment as to who exactly was to be seen as a victim, and who should be prosecuted for drugs and/or human trafficking. These difficulties carried over into the trial, where phone data provided strangely sterile evidence in lieu of actual voices from the identified child victims. I argue that the difficulties that pertained to this precedent-setting case, from its investigation through to the trial stage, do not merely evince technical challenges in prosecuting modern slavery cases. Instead, such problems bear witness to a political project-in-the-making that has resurrected the image of an ultimate enemy within. In Britain today, the impetus to protect vulnerable individuals has thus conjured the figure of the law's unfathomable 'other'—the modern-day slave master who has been projected onto the bodies of racialized and working-class youth.

In previous chapters, I already introduced and discussed Glodi's perspective on the trial. Here, I draw upon ethnography with investigative officers and prosecuting lawyers in the case. I was the first, and to my knowledge, the only researcher to have been given access to this trial as it was unfolding in real time, having been lucky enough to make the acquaintance of Kate, the lead prosecutor, who generously took me under her wing. Being invited to sit in the actual courtroom, in the row directly behind the prosecution's bench (rather than being confined to the public gallery at best), my presence was inconspicuous to the judge, legitimized by its very association with the prosecution and hence the state. This gave me a freedom I had not enjoyed before: to come and go as I pleased; to acquire copies of the jury bundles (which I had never seen first-hand before); to take notes on my laptop during trial; and, perhaps most importantly, to have access to the prosecution's back office. It was in the back office that I also met several other high-ranking government and law enforcement staff, including the officer-in-case, whose voice appears in this chapter. Before going into my ethnography, I will first discuss the legal context which made this trial possible.

Modern slavery as a prosecution tool

While the case of Karamera, Alford, and Wabelua was unprecedented in the emerging modern slavery jurisprudence, the impetus to prosecute did not come from nowhere. As we saw in Chapter 2, inherent in the logic of redemption that presents vulnerable communities as in need of saving for their own good is a drive to come down hard on their perpetrators—variously labelled as 'slave drivers', 'enslavers', and 'human traffickers'. For example, in an early government report entitled *Modern slavery: How the UK is leading the fight* (Home Office, 2014), published in the lead up to the *Modern Slavery Act 2015*, then Home Secretary Theresa May announced that 'we are taking steps to ensure slave drivers never think that the UK is a safe space to operate in, and that victims of slavery are not ignored. To anyone involved in slavery let me be clear—we will track you down, prosecute you and lock you up, with your assets seized and confiscated'. The report outlined provisions to be implemented to tackle perpetrators, including: consolidating and simplifying existing modern slavery offences into a single Act; increasing the maximum sentence available to offenders to life imprisonment; creating an independent Anti-Slavery Commissioner to drive improvements; strengthening powers to recover sizeable profits that traffickers and slave masters make; introducing vital tools to restrict the activity of criminals convicted of modern slavery offences; and providing powers to enable police and border forces to act where it is suspected that human trafficking is taking place on board vessels at sea (2014, p. 4).

The Modern Slavery Act 2015 put these commitments into force. Most fundamentally, the Act specifies the offences of slavery, servitude, forced and compulsory labour (s.1), and human trafficking (s.2). For the purposes of my analysis, human trafficking is the relevant offence. Under s.2, a person commits the offence of human trafficking if he or she 'arranges or facilitates the travel of another person (V) with a view to V being exploited'. Further, s.2 specifies that it is 'irrelevant whether the victim consents to the travel'. Importantly, however, a person arranges or facilitates V's travel with a view to V being exploited only if 'a. the person intends to exploit V in any part of the world during or after travel; or b. the person knows or ought to have known that another person is likely to exploit V in any part of the world during or after travel'. The meaning of exploitation is further defined within s.3 of the legislation. It includes, amongst other examples listed, 'securing services etc from children and vulnerable persons in circumstances where another person uses or attempts to use the person . . . having chosen him or her for that purpose on the grounds that a. he or she is a child, is mentally or physically ill or disabled, or has a family relationship with that particular person, and b. an adult, or a person without the illness, disability, or family relationship, would be likely to refuse to be used for that purpose'. The maximum punishment for a human-trafficking offence is life in prison.

Importantly, under part 2 of the *Modern Slavery Act*, an individual convicted of a modern slavery offence can face further civil restrictions upon release from prison. In Chapter 5, we considered the possibility of civil orders, including the Slavery and Trafficking Risk Orders (STROs) for individuals who have not been convicted of modern slavery offences as well as Slavery and Trafficking Prevention Orders (STPOs) that a court can hand down to an individual after conviction under the Act. The logic of these orders is said to be preventive, i.e. such orders are meant to protect potential victims from psychological and physical harm. Here, we are concerned with STPOs, or with orders that can be made following conviction under the Act. An application for an STPO can be made under s.14 of the 2015 Act as part of the sentencing exercise for an offence (or, alternatively, at any time following conviction for a modern slavery offence, where justified to a magistrate's court by a defendant's actions following their conviction). The only prohibitions that a court is allowed to make are 'those which the court is satisfied are necessary for the purpose of protecting persons generally, or particular persons, from the physical or psychological harm which would be likely to occur if the defendant committed a slavery or human trafficking offence' (s.17(2)). The period over which an STPO has effect must be at least five years or 'until further order'. Breach of the order constitutes a criminal offence, punishable with imprisonment.

As county lines activity has become linked to modern slavery in law enforcement practice and public discourse, so the government has made commitments to bring the perpetrators of county lines to justice under modern slavery laws. The key offence under the *Modern Slavery Act* for purposes of county lines is that of human trafficking (s.2); the emphasis being on the movement that comes from 'the transportation of drugs from city centres, along distribution lines and out to the counties' (Davies et al., 2021). In 2018, Duncan Balls from the National Police Council made this connection explicit in an interview with the BBC:

> *The Modern Slavery Act* brings a different dimension and it's an innovative approach in terms of how we use the legislation to tackle county lines. So, previously drug dealers would have been looked at for drugs

> legislation, or if they were committing violence, it would have been offences around the use of that particular violence. How we are using Modern Slavery Act legislation is it goes one step further, in that what it is saying is that to commit your crimes, you are trafficking young children, you are trafficking vulnerable people to then obviously undertake your criminal activity, and that then gives us additional tools and that gives additional options for the court, for example, around sentencing that we can then exploit as well.

In 2017, the Home Office officially recognized exploitation in county lines as a form of modern slavery (Cooper et al., 2017). Prosecutions soon followed suit. The first cases reported in the media were that of twenty-one-year-old Zakaria Mohammed from Birmingham, who was sentenced to fourteen years for trafficking children aged fourteen to fifteen to conduct drug deals from a 'cuckooed' flat in Lincoln (Gayle, 2018), as well as the case of Mahad Yusuf (aged twenty) and Fesal Mahamud (aged nineteen), who were convicted of forcing a nineteen-year-old woman to transport drugs from London to Swansea in Wales (Slawson, 2018); Yusuf and Mahamud were sentenced to nine and ten years, respectively. Both cases never went to trial, since all the defendants pleaded guilty. The case of Dean Alford, Michael Karamera, and Glodi Wabelua followed the year after; these defendants did not plead guilty, at least not initially. Being the first ever jury-led trial in the emerging county lines jurisprudence, this case was precedent-setting. The media have regularly reported on more convictions that have followed since, many of them involving young men in their early-mid-twenties (reflecting the point once made to me by a high-ranking Metropolitan police officer, that the average age of a county lines trafficker is twenty-three) and Black and minoritized defendants as well as more recently, white drug dealers racialized as 'gang' members.[3]

Notwithstanding these recent convictions, academics and think tanks have bemoaned the slow uptake of modern slavery legislation. In his foreword to the 2019 report entitled the *Independent Review of the Modern*

[3] On the latter point, see for example the following press releases: https://www.south-wales.police.uk/news/south-wales/news/2025/march/two-cardiff-men-have-been-jailed-for-drug-and-modern-slavery-offences/ [accessed 2 April 2025]; https://www.heddlu-de-cymru.police.uk/news/south-wales/news/2023/aws-aug/men-who-exploited-teenagers-jailed-for-drug-and-modern-slavery-offences/ [last accessed 2 April 2025]; or https://www.merseyside.police.uk/news/merseyside/news/2025/january-2025/man-jailed-for-12-years-for-modern-day-slavery-and-drug-supply-offences/ [last accessed 2 April 2025].

Slavery Act 2015, MP Frank Field welcomed the legislation, but lamented that 'sadly too few convictions are being handed down for the new offences under the Act and too few Slavery and Trafficking Prevention and Risk Orders are in place to restrict offender activity' (Home Office, 2019). Echoing a similar sense of frustration, Alicia Heys from the Modern Slavery Wilberforce Institute (a research unit funded by the Home Office), drawing on the Crown Prosecution's database, points out that between 2017 and 2019, sixty-four adult offenders were sentenced for modern slavery and human-trafficking offences. However, when measured against the fact that 22,756 potential victims of modern slavery were entered into the NRM during the same time frame, this shows that 'the Modern Slavery Act is yet to meet its goal in ensuring that offenders are held to justice with suitably severe punishments'.[4] Finally, a House of Lords committee tasked with the role of reviewing the *Modern Slavery Act* restated in its 2024 report that prosecution rates remain 'low at around 1.81%' (against the average of 7 per cent prosecution rate for all crimes), the figure representing the number of defendants being prosecuted with victim referrals through the NRM process, including those who do not consent to enter it (House of Lords Modern Slavery Act 2015 Committee, 2024, p. 38). The same report urged the government to 'prioritise prosecutions in its modern slavery strategy', with a focus on treating victims 'as exploited individuals' (2024, p. 45).

Existing analyses into prosecutions under the Act have then tended to present modern slavery prosecutions as a self-evident good in the fight against suffering endured by exploited victims. Some important exceptions exist (e.g. Craig et al., 2019; Broad and Gadd, 2023; Fudge, 2025). But on the whole, to the extent that criticism has been made, it has tended to focus on mounting practical challenges faced by prosecutors, including: the complex nature of the crime, such as those involving 'polycriminality' (defendants' involvement in multiple crimes simultaneously); lack of resources and specialist investigative capacity; low awareness among prosecutors and judges; and lack of victims' engagement with police investigations (Edgington, 2021; The Centre for Social Justice and Justice&Care, 2022; Centre for Social Justice and Justice&Care, 2024; House of Lords Modern Slavery Act 2015 Committee, 2024). As a recent report published by the Modern Slavery

[4] 'Prosecutions Under the Modern Slavery Act', Wilberforce Institute, University of Hull, https://www.hull.ac.uk/research/institutes/wilberforce/prosecutions-under-the-modern-slavery-act [accessed 14 October 2023]. Note that these figures relate to all prosecutions under modern slavery legislation, and not just to county lines specific offending.

and Human Rights Policy and Evidence Centre at the University of Oxford points out, challenges 'relate to *implementation* of the existing framework, as opposed to gaps or deficiencies in the law itself' (2024, p. 27 emphasis in original). And yet, statements to this effect—typical as they are of the technocratic faith that has accompanied the modern slavery agenda—also gloss over the fact that these interventions are never self-evident or neutral. As previous chapters showed, under the guise of neutrality and objectivity, professionals routinely authorize highly politicized decisions that further entrench classed and racialized inequalities within and beyond the criminal justice system.

Indeed, both the previous chapter and the ethnographic literature more broadly remind us that the criminal courts are not neutral settings but places where entrenched power relations, suffused by racism (Gonzalez Van Cleve, 2016), dominant gender stereotypes, and class prejudice, become reproduced through legal narratives (Conley and O'Barr, 1990) and legal story telling (Waller, 2024). This is not to say that the staff who populate Britain's courts are passive agents who merely reproduce relations of domination. As Dewey et al. have argued in their ethnography of gun crime prosecutors in the US South, such 'sweeping generalizations and claims to truth' can easily lose sight of the complex cultural and relational assemblages of actors, knowledges, and practices that comprise the everyday context in which prosecutors carry out their duties (Dewey, VandeBerg, and Webb, 2024, p. 3 ff.). And yet, it is imperative to recall Gilroy's classical account of how criminal courts reproduce images of Black law-breaking through the staging of 'the law's majesty, conveyed as much by the judge's kindly efforts as by his power to punish and to imprison'. It is this 'majesty' that has the capacity to show the nation to itself, for 'adherence to the law symbolizes the imagined community of the nation and expresses the fundamental unity and equality of its citizens' (Gilroy, 1987, pp. 128–129). It follows that when the subject of the law is Black law-breaking, it is also this racialized 'other' who emerges as the antithesis of the nation, even where the defendants prosecuted include those otherwise racialized as white.

Here, taking my cue from these insights, I am interested in the deeply political, if perhaps unintended, effects of turning modern slavery cases into 'good law'. To do so, I analyse the process of precedent-making in Britain's first-ever successful modern slavery case in a jury-led county lines trial. As my ethnography shows, in a context where the line between 'exploited victims' and 'criminals' is vanishingly thin, where professionals struggle to draw this distinction, and where victims refuse to appear as witnesses in court, a finding of modern slavery often comes down to winning an interpretive contest over technocratic data that provides a strangely sterile approximation of the complex and contested social relations at stake. Ultimately, we will see that the court's faith in the possibility of such technocratic assessments to prove 'more than just a drugs crime' has enabled the making of a new kind of enemy within, namely the modern-day slave master in the body of the Black and working-class young man. In what follows, I first turn to the pre-trial history as told to me from the perspective of the officer-in-case; second, to my own court-based ethnography of the final trial; and third, to the precedent it set.

'A never-ending saga'

'This has been a never-ending saga', Simon laughed when I asked him to tell me about the history of the trial. 'Before it started, I didn't have any grey hairs and look at me now!' Thirty-something, white, British, and the father of two young children, Simon was a detective inspector at the London Metropolitan Police's Trident unit, the police squad originally set up to investigate 'Black on Black gun crime' in the capital city. He was also the officer-in-case in charge of the overall investigation concerning the case of Michael Karamera, Dean Alford, and Glodi Wabelua. I met him on one of the first days of the trial, when Kate introduced us to each other in the prosecution's back office, a stuffy room adjoining the courtroom where the trial was held. Simon, his colleagues, and a junior barrister spent much of their time in this room, where—hidden from public sight—they helped prepare evidence for the days ahead, which included responding to the many last-minute requests that came from the defence lawyers in this trial. I had quickly warmed to Simon and his easy manners and self-depreciating sense of humour, which provided a sharp contrast to the formalized and hierarchical environment of the court. During break times, we would chat about our respective jobs, family lives, things that had happened in court that day, and the environmental protests led by the group Extinction Rebellion that were happening on the banks of the nearby situated river Thames.

Like Kate, Simon would often make references to the fact that the trial had a complicated and protracted history, one that he promised he would tell me about 'once everything is over'. This happened in June 2019, a few months after the convictions were secured. Simon had been extremely busy since the end of the trial; on his own admission, he had been travelling 'all over the country delivering training sessions' to law enforcement about the most important lessons that had come out of this case. He was also in the process of writing a manual on county lines and modern slavery investigations for the College of Policing—the professional body for the police in England and Wales—that would be published later that year. Eventually, however, Simon came to meet me at my then University office near Holborn station, in the centre of London. In one of the teaching rooms on campus, he got out his laptop, pulling up the PowerPoint that he normally used during his presentations to law enforcement. As he clicked through slides showing photographs of the defendants and victims, as well as of confiscated drugs and visuals of the phone schedules that had been extracted from call record data, he began to speak, pausing at times to give me the time to type notes on my own laptop, asking me at others to stop typing when something was 'off the record'.

'It all started back in 2014', Simon began, initially with a phone call. 'His team' at the Trident unit, a former Metropolitan Police unit originally established to tackle 'gang' crime within the city's Black communities (chapter 2), received a call from their colleagues in the London Metropolitan police informing them that thirteen teenagers had gone missing. The teenagers were from Lewisham, a predominantly working-class borough south of the River Thames with a high immigrant population. It soon emerged that the original numbers needed correcting, the number of missing children was sixteen, and the teenagers were from both Lewisham and Croydon, another multiracial and working-class neighbourhood in South London. The teenagers were subsequently found dealing Class A drugs in Portsmouth, a place that none of them had any prior connections to. At the time, it had not occurred to any of the professionals to treat the teenagers as anything other than straightforward drug dealers: this was 2014, the year before the National Crime Agency would identify county lines as an emerging threat, and the language of safeguarding had not yet been popularized in relation to those involved at the bottom rung of the drugs trade. All the teenagers were charged with possession of Class A drugs with intent to supply, and pleaded guilty. Some received suspended sentences, others went to juvenile detention facilities.

This could have easily been the end of that 'job', as Simon referred to it, had it not been for a larger investigation into drugs conspiracy that he and his colleagues at Trident decided to undertake. At this stage in the investigation, little was known about the drugs networks that the teenagers had been part of. Specialized police officers now began carrying out undercover police work, including buying drugs off runners in Portsmouth. Gradually, a fuller picture emerged: the teenagers had been part of a larger drugs network dominated by three drugs phone lines—the Mitch, Fly, and Holiday lines—that supplied Class A drugs from London to locations outside the capital city, including to Portsmouth. The teenagers had been doing the most dangerous work of transporting drugs from London to Portsmouth, staying in drug users' homes and other places for days on end, and selling the drugs directly to users. By now, the language of county lines and exploitation was beginning to appear on the policy landscape. Simon and the other investigative officers began to feel that at least some of the teenagers fitted the description. He recalled: 'We felt strongly that some of the children who had been convicted [of drugs charges], well they were actually exploited and we had erred in prosecuting them, and we felt that the drugs legislation wasn't strong enough [to get at their perpetrators], and that there must be a way to punish this crime more severely'.

Importantly, undercover investigative work also revealed the identities of individuals who the police believed to be in control of the phone lines, including those of three young men aged twenty-one at the time: Michael Karamera, Dean Alford, and Glodi Wabelua. All three had grown up in South London, were known to each other, and had collaborated on the deal lines (though the extent of that collaboration would remain in dispute throughout the trial). With histories of drug offending, the three young men were also well known to the police, having each served time in youth detention facilities and later adult prisons for prior convictions. Simon's 'theory' was that they too had once started off as runners, possibly as exploited victims, but at the time of the offending 'they would have risen the ranks', and knew exactly what they were doing. All three had been, at the time of their arrests, in control of the main 'deal line', the phone number associated with their respective drugs lines. As such, they were in a position to command others, sending them out to do the most dangerous work of transporting the drugs from London to Portsmouth, and selling the drugs to users on the streets whilst themselves staying in the relative safety of their own flats, typically in the capital city, and away from Portsmouth.

The investigation team began focusing their attention on Karamera, Alford, and Wabelua. Over and above the drugs conspiracy investigation, the team were 'keen to find an offence that matched the crime'. Simon recalled how they started 'shopping around' for legislation, until they came across human trafficking:

> I did a load of research and found this piece of legislation. [My boss] and I had a number of meetings and he said "these kids are exploited, what can we do", we were also looking at child abduction, all this different legislation, I just came across this piece of legislation [the *Asylum and Immigration Act 2004*], I didn't know what specifically to look for, I was just trying to find something that matched. After a number of re-writes, we had—we had a lot of victims, it was difficult to investigate . . . for my investigators to understand, for me to understand, to get them the case to where it needed to be . . . We were left to muddle our way through it.

However, they were still a long way from being able to charge the young men with human trafficking. The team faced challenges around every corner. At the policing level, the commitment to pursue this investigation was low, not least because it required police to work together across counties and hence across police forces, which police are not in the habit of doing. 'The truth is no one wanted to do it', Simon said. 'It's quite complicated to investigate, it's cross police borders and there is little awareness of what trafficking is'. The Crown Prosecution Service (CPS), the principal body conducting prosecutions in England and Wales, also did not want to hear about 'trafficking' for the first year and a half, this being an unprecedented use of human-trafficking legislation. Finally, there was the problem of securing witnesses. As we have seen, many of the identified runners—now recast as victims—had already been charged and convicted of drugs offences, and served community sentences and prison time. Nobody had entered them into the National Referral Mechanism at the time or suggested that they should be safeguarded. Simon recalled: 'We wrote to the original children on the job, and we said to them we think we got it wrong, and that they should not have been convicted. We wanted to secure them as witnesses'. None of them replied. Simon summed it up: 'It was all a mess. At that point it was the first case of its kind, no one had ever been charged with trafficking within a county lines setting, within the UK, and the law is very badly written!'

In September 2014, the Crown Prosecution Service decided to split the case—that is, to separate the drugs conspiracy charges for Alford, Karamera, and Wabelua from the human trafficking—on the basis that there was insufficient evidence for human trafficking. Simon recalled how disappointing this was for the team: 'From a trial view, it makes no sense, you have to try to keep the charges together to have a stronger case'. Still, they had no choice. The drugs conspiracy case was scheduled before

Woolwich Crown Court in June 2015. There were fifteen defendants on the indictment in total, some of them runners, others drugs users whose flats the dealers from London had occupied or 'cuckooed' (see Chapter 5), and Alford's and Karamera's respective girlfriends. 'It was a massive case', Simon recalled. 'The room was full of lawyers, there were so many people in the room, we couldn't even all fit in'. Wabelua pleaded guilty. On the first day of the trial, Karamera and Alford claimed the defence of duress, and the trial was adjourned to October that year. The prosecution was able to prove that the defence had been fabricated, having tapped the defendants' phone lines in prison. The trial was set to start again. By this point, all the defendants except for four had pleaded guilty. In February 2016, Karamera and Alford were convicted and sentenced to ten and eleven years, respectively. Wabelua was sentenced to five years in light of his early guilty plea.[5]

While the drugs conspiracy trial was on its way in Woolwich, work continued on the human-trafficking charges. By now, Kate had been instructed by the Crown Prosecution Service as the lead prosecution. She was a blessing for the investigative team: committed to the trafficking investigations, she researched the legislation and case law diligently. The team went through the evidence produced by an instructed phone expert about patterns of communication and movements of handsets (the physical phones) and phone numbers that had been recovered during the drugs investigations. Around the same time, T.A., who was roughly the same age as the defendants, disclosed to the police that he had worked for the Fly line as a young adult. He explained that he had been introduced to Karamera through a mutual contact while living in sheltered housing, agreed to work for him, and was sent to Portsmouth. He incurred a drug debt when a user robbed him of his drugs. When he told Karamera that he wanted out, he found himself threatened and held at gunpoint by a group of males. T.A. subsequently tried to rob a supermarket to recover the drug debt but was arrested, charged, and sentenced. Like the other original children who had gone missing, he was never entered into the NRM mechanism at the time. Simon felt that T.A. had been wrongfully treated as a perpetrator when he was 'clearly a vulnerable chap who had been exploited'. T.A. would later become the only witness in the human-trafficking case, and give evidence against Karamera.

[5] [2018] EWCA Crim 1432.

Alford, Karamera, and Wabelua were officially charged with human-trafficking offences in October 2016, more than half a year after being convicted of drugs conspiracy at the Woolwich trial. All of the trafficked victims were children, teenagers aged between fourteen and seventeen, with the exception of T.A. Simon recalled visiting Alford in prison to charge him: 'He was really friendly', Simon laughed, 'and said really nice to see you! I told him, "are you joking, we are just doing our jobs, and we have decided to charge you for human trafficking"'. But once more, difficulties abounded. The case was listed to appear in Southwark Crown Court in August 2016. Three days before the start of the trial, the prosecution received a notification from the defence informing them that they were planning to run 'an abuse of process argument' (an exceptional power to 'stay' an indictment if the court is of the opinion that to allow the prosecution to continue would amount to an abuse of process) on the basis that the prosecution were allegedly trying to re-convict the defendants on the same facts that had featured in the drugs conspiracy case in Woolwich. The case was transferred to the Old Bailey, one of England's oldest criminal courthouses. The defence lost their argument, the judge ruling that the prosecution had in fact separated out the victims by presenting an entirely different set of runners in the drugs conspiracy trial from the ones that appeared on the human-trafficking indictment.

A new trial date was set, this time back in Woolwich Crown Court for January 2016. Yet, once more, it did not go ahead as planned. At the close of the prosecution's case, the defence made a submission of 'no case to answer' (to dismiss the case due to lack of evidence), asserting that the prosecution had failed to prove 'recruitment' of the victims in line with the wording of the legislation. The trial collapsed. After some hesitations and heated consultations between the prosecution team and the Crown Prosecution Service, the prosecution decided to appeal the decision. Much to Simon's relief, the Court of Appeal (the second highest court within England and Wales), decided in the prosecution's favour in *R v Karamera* [2019] 1 WLR 4716. From Simon's perspective, the ruling had made several important points, including that 'recruitment' was not necessary to prove; that the age of the victims was only one of the factors that needed to be proven; and that the prosecution did not have to prove a lack of consent on the part of the victims or any element of coercion. It also ruled that the prosecution did not depend 'on the ability to call the individual said to have been exploited or the target of their exploitation' [61]. Simon recalled what an important victory this final point had been for them: 'This gave us the opportunity to continue with a victimless prosecution', which was the only way to proceed given the child victims' refusal to act as prosecution witnesses. The stage was set for the final trial saga, to be heard in Inner London Crown Court in 2019.

After five years of investigation, a bevy of Crown Prosecution lawyers, a major drugs conspiracy trial, several collapsed trials for human trafficking, and a judgment from the Court of Appeal, the road was finally clear. And yet, all the trials and tribulations had betrayed deep confusion that was set to stay: confusion over how, exactly, involvement in county lines could be portrayed 'as more than just a drugs crime'; what constituted good evidence of 'exploitation' in the absence of victim statements; and who should, in the first instance, be identified as a victim and who was a perpetrator deserving of punishment not only under drugs legislation, but human-trafficking law. In the next section, I analyse how these issues continued to haunt the Inner London trial. While the trial resulted in the convictions of Karamera, Alford, and Wabelua, it also revealed, once more, the murky nature of this precedent. Not only was the finding of human trafficking largely dependent on a technocratic assessment of phone evidence in the absence of victim statements on the part of the child slaves, but as Wabelua's forceful counter narrative proved, the legal storytelling around the phone evidence was highly contested.

The Inner London trial: prosecuting without victims

The human-trafficking trial opened on a cloudy morning in April 2019, in front of Judge Karu, a former prosecutor and unusually, a female judge of South Asian origin. I was waiting for Kate to meet me outside the courtroom. Despite getting everything ready for the prosecution's opening, Kate came to look for me as soon as she heard I had arrived. Carrying her wig in her hand, revealing her blond hair, and her long black gown flowing around her, she quickly sat down on a chair next to me. 'Have a read through this', she said as she passed me a bundle of A4 pages. 'This is our opening. I'll tell you where to sit when you're ready'. Almost as quickly as she had come, she was gone again. I tried to concentrate on the pages in front of me, but was distracted by the comings and goings of the barristers. Ten minutes later, Kate was back, taking the bundle off me again and asking me to follow her into the wood-panelled courtroom, where she motioned for me to sit directly behind her on the bench. From my position in the middle of the courtroom, I could take in the people around me: the sea of lawyers, six for the defence and two for the prosecution; the jurors' bench, still empty; and, when I turned my head, the defendants behind me in the secure dock. These last were three young Black men with alert faces, dressed smartly in white shirts and dark trousers, separated out by security guards on either side of them.

There was much that had already been given as 'established facts' thanks to the drugs conspiracy conviction secured at Woolwich Crown Court some three years prior. As the prosecution told the court, there was no question about the three defendants' involvement with the Fly, Mitch, and Holiday lines, nor was there any doubt that they had access to, and made use of, the main phone numbers associated with these respective drugs lines. But what the prosecution had to prove this time was the 'trafficking element', that these convicted drug dealers had also trafficked the runners—or 'couriers', as the prosecution tended to call them—with a view to exploiting them. Six children in total were identified, as well as T.A., the only adult victim. Their case, the prosecution told the jury, was that T.A. was a vulnerable adult who had willingly acted as a runner. They did not have to prove, however, that the children were especially vulnerable, 'there being strong public policy reasons for why children need protection from themselves'. They only had to prove, in accordance with the law, that a person without the youth of the alleged victims would have been *likely* to refuse to be used for drug running, not that they would have *definitely* refused if they were older.

Karamera was the first defendant on the indictment, having been charged with three counts of human trafficking, including with respect to T.A. In the first week of the trial, T.A. was called in as prosecution witness. I never got to see him in person, nor did the jury: he gave his evidence behind a screen and from a video link being sat in a different room, having been granted these special measures upon the prosecution's request. His evidence mirrored what he had disclosed to the police earlier: he told the court about being introduced to Karamera via a mutual contact who came to the homelessness hostel where T.A. was living at the time, and being sent to Portsmouth on several occasions. Asked by the prosecution if he had wanted to sell drugs for Karamera, T.A. said that he had not initially minded. However, things took a different turn when he was robbed of his drugs in Portsmouth. He wanted to leave but was told he had to pay off his debt. His fear increased when he was told to come to a South London flat, and, upon arrival, was confronted by a group of youth wearing balaclavas who tormented him, forced him to take his clothes off, and pulled the trigger on a gun (that turned out to be fake, though T.A. didn't know this at the time) held to his head. After T.A. finished presenting his evidence, the prosecution called a number of professionals, including a staff member from the homelessness hostel T.A. used to live in, a psychologist, a youth support worker, and a probation worker. The professionals variously spoke about disclosures that T.A. had made to them, emphasizing his 'distressed' appearance, learning difficulties, volatile emotional state, underlying psychological conditions, and early childhood traumas.

When I saw Simon shortly after T.A.'s testimony, he seemed pleased. 'He did really well', Simon said, referring to how T.A. had inhabited his 'victim role'. 'I think the jury could really see how vulnerable he was'. The remainder of the prosecution's case would be much more challenging. In the absence of any of the child slaves being willing to testify in court, the prosecution had to solely rely on thousands of phone data entries, called call data records (CDR). As the jury would hear in due course, for every call, text, or internet and/or application use, there is a record of the 'cell' (mast) that is connected to the event in question. By extracting this record from network providers, phone experts were not only able to establish communication patterns between phones, but could also make inferences about phone locations and movements as well as the co-location of different phones in particular places. The prosecution relied upon this data to make a number of points, including: that on many occasions, the defendants had sent out mass texts to drug users in Portsmouth to advertise their drugs (and indeed, some of these texts had been retrieved from drug users' phones and were read out to the jury); that typically following these mass texts, the defendants' phones would be in contact with the victims' to arrange drug deals and to control their every step and movement; that defendants and victims had met up on several occasions to exchange drugs and money; and that the victims had travelled from London to Portsmouth.

The evidence was presented by a cell site analyst who had retired from his previous work commissioning electronic warfare equipment, radio systems, and mobile network operators to become an expert phone witness in trials. A stocky man perhaps in his fifties with a receding grey hairline, nondescript grey suit, and glasses, he looked the part of a technocratic expert. As he patiently answered the prosecution's questions in an attempt to simplify the thousands of phone entries for the benefit of the jury, the days began to stretch out in front of us. There was an increasing sense of boredom as bundle after bundle containing pages and pages of CDR data were handed out to the jury, providing a quantified picture of 'trafficking' in lieu of victims' own voices. More than once, I heard defence lawyers complain that the prosecution was 'too attritional', and even the judge expressed concerns that 'we are losing the jury' over too much phone data, asking the prosecution to summarize patterns of CDR as opposed to talking the jury through every single phone schedule list. Kate, however, stood her ground, insisting that this information was necessary for the jury to get the 'full picture'. In the end, it took weeks for the phone evidence to be completed. Kate was visibly relieved when she was able to close the case: 'They say the prosecution's case is at its strongest at the start of the trial', she said with a wry smile on the day the prosecution closed its case, 'and the defence's case at the close of the prosecution'.

The defence now opened its case. Karamera, the first and only defendant to have had a victim give evidence against him, was the first to take the stand. Speaking with a confident voice, he denied having ever said anything about a drug debt to T.A. or having any knowledge of the subsequent threats he had been subjected to by the group of 'masked youth'. Conversely, he told the jury about his own childhood, including having been moved into state care at a young age, and struggling 'to fit in' with his peers. At the end of his evidence, the prosecution made an application that Karamera had created 'false impressions' by emphasizing his difficult upbringing, all the while not saying a word about the serious offences that he had been convicted of in the past. The judge concurred with the prosecution, granting permission for the prosecution to cross-examine Karamera on his previous convictions. The cross-examination that followed was tense. Just as Kate had been meticulous about her presentation of the phone evidence, so she now launched into hours of merciless questioning, visibly frustrating Karamera, fixating on his past convictions and life as a criminal. To everyone's surprise, halfway through Karamera's cross-examination, Alford, the second defendant who had been following Karamera's cross-examination from the dock, asked for a special dispensation from the judge. He changed his plea to guilty that same day. Karamera followed suit immediately, having not even finished his testimony.

The next day, the mood in the prosecution's back office was jubilant. I had not been in court the previous day, and the officers joked that 'I had missed all the action'. For the prosecution, Karamera had been 'the main guy', as Simon said, and his conviction as well as that of the second defendant had been secured. They put the success down to Kate's expert cross-examination strategy that had broken two of the defendants. Now only

Glodi Wabelua, the third defendant, was left. Wabelua's defence lawyer had submitted an application that the jury should be discharged on the basis that the guilty pleas of his co-defendants would bias the jury against him. To the prosecution's relief, the application was refused by the judge. Still, even on the prosecution's own account, Wabelua's case was somewhat different from that of his co-defendants. As Simon reminded me, Wabelua had received a substantively shorter conviction for the prior drugs conspiracy charges, having pleaded guilty to them from the outset. Moreover, unlike the first two defendants, Wabelua had only been charged on a single count of human trafficking involving a sixteen-year-old youth called M.W. Finally, the phone evidence suggested that Wabelua had travelled with M.W. from London to Portsmouth. This would make it easier for him to argue that he had believed the victim to be older than he was, rebutting the prosecution's position that, in accordance with the law, he had chosen his victim based at least partly on the belief that he was a minor.

The atmosphere was tense as Wabelua, a tall, dark-skinned young man with cropped hair and in a tight white shirt that revealed his toned body, took the stand. I wondered if the jury had the same question as me: would this defendant also pleaded guilty under the pressure of the prosecution's merciless questions? First, however, it was his turn to give his account. Led by his defence lawyer in a short but pointed evidence-in-chief, Wabelua told the court in a calm voice that he was the first person to put up his hands when he knew he was guilty; that's what he had done when charged with drugs. This time, however, it was different. 'I never understood about the trafficking bit', he told the court. 'The drugs bit—sure. But *not* the trafficking bit'. He told the jury that very much like M.W., the sixteen-year-old victim he was said to have trafficked, he had been working on behalf of someone else. It was his boss who had given him the deal line—the handset with the deal number—on days when Wabelua was working, who had asked him to take orders from drug users, and who had asked him to meet with M.W. as someone who might be willing 'to work for him'. He told the court he never thought about M.W.'s age, but would have estimated him to be eighteen, nineteen years old, based on how he presented himself: M.W. was a tall guy, confident in his manners, who clearly knew what he was doing. 'My job was not to question him about his background', he told the court, 'but to explain the job to him'.

The prosecution's cross-examination was merciless, once more. Kate told Wabelua that the 'prosecution do not accept that you had a boss', that the 'boss' was in fact, a mythical figure, a figment of Wabelua's imagination, mirroring the prosecutional narrative that we already came across in the human trafficking and drugs charges against Bandhall, the young South Asian man in Chapter 6. Taking him back to the cell evidence that the jury had seen a few days prior, the prosecution insisted that Wabelua had solely been in control of the phone line. Wabelua, for his part, explained that he did not 'own' the deal line, that he was only 'holding it' on the days when he was working for his boss, and that he could not remember, based on the phone traffic listed on the schedules, whether he had been working on the phone on the days in question. He explained that in the recorded phone traffic between the deal line and M.W.s' phone, it had not necessarily been him on the other end of the phone (as he only had the deal line on the days he was working), and that even when it had been him on the other end, he had used the phone for a range of communication purposes, including for drugs sales but also other things—for instance, to check in and to trade banter. Once more, the mood was getting visibly tense, Wabelua growing tired of the prosecution's questions and Kate's at times ironic interventions. The following extract was representative of the sense of frustration that came through in the long hours of cross-examination of Wabelua [W] by the prosecution [P]:

> W [interrupted by prosecution]: . . . can I just finish my sentence please [Pause]. I am not glorifying the fact that I sell drugs or the world that I am in, unfortunately for me, I grew up in it and it's just around me, but one thing I am not, I wouldn't pick someone for their vulnerability or because of their age because I think I can bend them to my rules and however way you put it, that's not me, that's not my character, that's not me at all.
>
> P [in a mocking voice]: "Unfortunately for me, I just grew up in it", is what you just said to the jury . . .
>
> W [interrupting]: . . . By that I mean . . .
>
> P [interrupting, cutting voice]: Bear with me, let me finish. "Unfortunately for me I just grew up in it". How old were you when referring to this?
>
> W: I am just walking to it from the young days on the estate, there is things I am seeing . . .
>
> P [ironic voice]: Yeah exactly, exactly . . .
>
> W [sounding frustrated]: Can I finish you keep saying 'exactly' . . . I don't, I have committed crimes, I know that I am always the first to put my hand up if I am wrong, if I have to do time, I will sit to do it. [But] I never understood about the human trafficking bit, I never exploited anyone.

At the close of Wabelua's evidence, his lawyer made an application that the jury be read a statement that M.W., the youth that Wabelua was said to have trafficked, had given the police when arrested with drugs on him. In the statement, quoted verbatim in court while the jury were sent out, M.W. told the officer 'that he knew exactly what he was doing and the dangers around it . . . that he was simply doing it for the money and no one had told him to sell drugs'. Wabelua's lawyer argued that while under the law consent of the victim was not a defence, it nonetheless provided 'relevant context as to the question of whether Wabelua knew he was under the age of eighteen'. The judge refused the application, arguing that to show the jury the statement would mean to 'place the cart before the horse'. The statement did not go before the jury.

The jury retired. There was nothing left to do but wait for their verdict. Simon and the other officers started packing up the back office, shredding the phone schedules and other documents that would no longer be needed, and carrying out plastic bags filled with empty crisp and chocolate bar packages, soft drink bottles, and other rubbish that had accumulated in the office over the previous months. When a day and a half later the jury had still not reached a verdict, the judge announced that they would be allowed to reach a majority verdict of 11:1. On 12 April 2019, the jury announced their guilty verdict for Wabelua with a majority verdict. A month later, the judge sentenced Karamera to five years, Alford to four years, and Wabelua to three and a half years of imprisonment, to run concurrently with the drugs sentences they were already serving. She also granted the prosecution's application for a Slavery and Trafficking Prevention Order (STPO), imposing wide ranging restrictions upon the defendants' movements, freedom of association, and daily life upon release.

The Court of Appeal subsequently struck down many of the terms of the civil order, ruling that the terms had not been necessary and disproportionate. It retained, however, the following provisions: that the defendants do not own more than one mobile phone handset, SIM card, or computer; that they notify the police at the nearest police station of any devices in possession; that they must not contact by any means, directly or indirectly, their co-defendants; that they must not own or be insured to drive a vehicle of which they had not notified the police; that they must 'not drive, escort or arrange the travel of any person under the age of 18 in any vehicle save for family members, the parents of whom must be told of these convictions'; and that they must disclose their home address to the nearest operational police station within seven days of moving. The Order would remain in place until 2027, and breach of any of the conditions mentioned would make the defendants immediately liable to imprisonment, even after their release from their drugs and trafficking convictions. As we will see in the next chapter, when Wabelua, the third defendant, was seen as in breach of the final provision of the Order, he became once more the object of police attention, leaving him, to this date (June 2025) waiting for any indication as to whether he would have to go back to prison.

On the eve of the jury verdict, I was out for a drink with the officers, having been invited by the prosecution team to mark the end of a saga. Kate had told me that she just needed to 'finish some stuff' and would join us shortly. We had gone to a nearby pop-up park with street food stalls and micro-breweries, the bright colours and hipster ambience hitting me as strangely off. More and more officers turned up. Some of them I had never met, and even Alford's defence lawyer had come to raise a glass; for him too, this marked the end of years of protracted legal dispute. Kate eventually turned up. This was the first time I saw her outside the Court, without her long black gown; unlike with the officers and the more junior barristers, with whom the lines between the court and 'outside' world had been crossed, Kate had never invited me to join her for lunch during the trial. As with Simon and some of the other officers, I had grown to like and respect her over these past few weeks, having spent so much time in their presence. As she took a seat next to me, a beer bottle in her hand, I saw a disquiet in her that had remained hidden in the court room. She said quietly, 'This is not about celebrating, you don't celebrate when people are sent to prison. Especially for me this is not easy because I am so often on the defence side'. She sighed, adding that this was a bit different, though. 'This is about protecting the vulnerable, and if this case goes to protect vulnerable individuals in the future, then I have done my job'.

Acting on precedent

The conviction against Karamera, Alford, and Wabelua had established a new precedent in English law: that county lines cases can indeed be prosecuted as 'more than just a drugs crime'. By putting the crime of 'exploitation', as the prosecution often referred to the human-trafficking offence, at the heart of county lines, they had shown that the real crux of these cases was not the drugs element, but the trafficking of vulnerable persons, in particular of children, who were seen to need protection, sometimes or perhaps even *especially* from themselves. Both the conviction and the use of civil orders upon conviction were a means of meeting this overwhelming objective. Such was the sense that 'good' had been done that even Alford's defence lawyer had joined in for the drinks on the eve of the verdict. In fact, as we saw in Chapter 5, the defence lawyer would later be commissioned by law enforcement to write national guidance on the use of STPOs and STROs, and that was published with the National Crime Agency (Davies et al., 2021). I too was invited to act as an independent consultant for this guidance, something that I agreed to do only after a lengthy conversation with Angelique (Chapter 8), one of the mothers introduced in Chapter 3.

And yet, while 'good law' had been made according to a range of experts and professionals involved in this case, none of them were under any illusion that the precedent would be easy to act upon: the realities of prosecuting modern slavery offences would remain hard, resource intensive, and extremely time consuming. I was told repeatedly by law enforcement that the Crown Prosecution Service (CPS) is still reluctant 'to touch these cases' as they are considered too difficult; that lack of awareness and knowledge among CPS lawyers adds to these hurdles. But even if the hurdle of getting past CPS is passed, prosecutions often remain riddled with difficulties as victims are reluctant to speak, causing the evidence to be based on call data and expert witnesses alone. Asked about the difficulties they anticipated in bringing future prosecutions, law enforcement would repeatedly come back to this key problem. We have already seen how this difficulty was present in the trial of Karamera, Alford, and Wabelua, where none of the identified child victims had been willing to speak. Prosecution and defence lawyers had different explanations as to why that had been the case. While the prosecution insisted that the victims had been too fearful to come forward, anticipating retaliation from their perpetrators, the defence lawyers argued that the victims were not really victims: there was little, if any, difference between the victims and the perpetrators, and the victims had had no interest in collaborating with the very agencies that had already convicted them of drugs crimes a few years prior.

Indeed, the impossibility of pinpointing the line between victims and exploiters, between slaves and human traffickers, has also been evident in the prosecutions that have followed in the wake of the convictions secured against Alford, Karamera, and Wabelua. I conclude by turning to the most recent proceedings that I was able to follow: the case of twenty-year-old Itman Ismail and, rather unusually, his female co-defendant, twenty-eight-year-old Amarie Nixon. The basic facts of the case were widely reported in the news at the time (BBC, 2021; Humphries, 2021; itvNews, 2021). On 24 January 2020, the pair was stopped in a car in Torquay, a few hundred miles from their respective London homes in what is called the West country, with two male teenagers in the back. The teenagers were found with 191 wraps of heroin and cocaine that they had swallowed, which were within their bodies. But this was not all. According to the BBC, the 'couple clocked up nearly 11,000 miles in seven different hire cars over four months making at least eleven trips to Devon and Cornwall, where they set up base in Airbnb houses' (BBC, 2021). Ismail and Nixon were charged with trafficking four boys aged fifteen and sixteen for purposes of exploitation. Nixon was also charged with, and admitted to, conspiracy to supply heroin and cocaine and possession of a mobile phone while in prison.

The relationship between the two defendants, dissected at length during the trial, had been a complicated one. Prior to becoming involved in criminal activity, Itman Ismail herself, originally a Somali refugee who had grown up on the East Coast of England, had been working for a care group supporting vulnerable young adults, including 'ex-gang' members. Indeed, what seemed to make the case so shocking for the media was the fact that Ismail, a university graduate, held 'a position of trust and was specifically trained and responsible for protecting and safeguarding young people' (itvNews, 2021). While working for the care group, Ismail met Nixon, a service user and a young Black man from South London with a history of criminal offending. Things took a wrong turn when Nixon and Ismael fell in love and started an intimate relationship. Ismael left her job as staff member for the care group. Through Nixon, she was introduced to drug dealing and soon started working alongside him. The prosecution told the court that each of them had performed a distinct role in what was nonetheless 'a joint business'. While Nixon was heavily involved in the drug operation, part of which 'made use of youth for transporting and running county lines', Ismail was 'involved in [the] hiring and driving of cars and booking accommodation while the runners were in Devon'.

By the time I learned about the case from a law enforcement official working for the Metropolitan Police force, convictions against the two defendants had been secured. I was, however, able to attend the sentencing. This time, I joined the court online, it being the height of the COVID-19 pandemic, and most gatherings were conducted in a hybrid manner. As far as I could see on the screen, the courtroom was largely empty, the defence lawyers and two defendants having joined via online link from their respective prisons. However, the prosecutor, a white British man with a deep nasal voice, was there in person, addressing the judge who also sat in the courtroom. The prosecutor was the first to speak. His speech was short. He reminded the court that this was a highly successful drugs business run by adult criminals whose 'success had depended on the exploitation of vulnerable children'. He emphasized that both defendants had been acting together, thus highlighting the joint nature of the co-defendants' action in what we have seen throughout the cases is a typical move on the part of prosecution. Citing the case of Karamera, Alford, and Wabelua, he furthermore stated there was good precedent for the case at hand, a precedent which had proven that exploitation was a severe crime indeed.

The defence lawyers followed next, each making pleas for mitigation. Ismail's defence lawyer tried to mitigate the narrative of a 'joint venture' presented by prosecution. Thus, he emphasized his client's vulnerability by comparing her position to that of her co-defendant and insinuating that the latter had groomed her. Prior to meeting Nixon, her lawyer told the court, Ismail had been of an upright moral character, with no criminal convictions or any other run-ins with the law. Her relationship with Nixon had been her first intimate relationship and one that she had entered in defiance of her family's wishes. It was Nixon who had introduced her to drug dealing, something she knew nothing of. With nobody else to guide her, and being estranged at this point from her own family and brothers, Ismail had been sucked into criminality against her own best interest, becoming more and more embedded until it was too late. Nixon's defence lawyer came next. He emphasized a different story of vulnerability, one that highlighted his client's own childhood. Having joined online from what I can only assume were his legal offices, with his stature framed by a golden chandelier and a heavy-framed painting in the back, the space betrayed the very privileges that Nixon's defence lawyer asked the court to confront when he pleaded with them to put themselves in the shoes of his client. As he was speaking, the internet connection became unstable, so some of his words may have been misinterpreted in my process of reconstruction. I transcribed as follows to the best of my abilities:

> It is right to say [from] the involvement of multiple agencies from the age of eleven onwards, [Nixon] had himself been referred to as a modern slave on numerous occasions. Your honour it is right to say that every adult derives their package of tools from their childhood experience. It gives a template which is difficult to understand from the recognition of middle-class rather privileged individuals. There is inevitably a disconnect between those involved in the criminal justice system and the individuals like Nixon.

> His background is shocking. He grew up on [an] estate in north London where violence, drugs death, intimidation, murder, and misery were really the only thing that were consistent in his life. You may have noticed recent reports of two further deaths involving stabbings of fifteen-year-olds. They were from the same estate. I notice again that background is increasingly typical for young Black men growing up where they did. As a result of it, the only form of love came from gang culture which he inevitably felt drawn to. He would be seen by people like me perhaps as groomed from an early age into criminal gangs that surrounded it. But the reality is [that] growing up where he grew up there was really only one way forward. It is apparent that these offences are something of an inevitability.
>
> It is right to say that the involvement of the other young people [victims] in this case that they—like him [Nixon] had been corrupted long before Mr. Nixon became involved with them and they—like him—had been utilized by people far more serious than any of them to fulfil their greed. At least one of them was involved in the county lines organizations into which Mr. Nixon became involved as a victim from an equally young age and it is right that one of those victims is currently on remand for murder. The world Mr. Nixon found himself in is one that up to his eighteenth birthday applied as much as to each of the victims identified in this case. I ask your honour to consider him as being himself at the time of the offences not out of being a child, not being far away from all the influences that he had been objected to as a child, all of the fear, all of the intimidation. *This places him only just one step above those [slaves] for whom he is to be sentenced* [my emphasis].

There is much in the mitigation speech given by Nixon's lawyer that is worth unpacking, for it resonates with the themes I have emphasized in this book: from the structural suffering that young men like Nixon are assumed to have been exposed to—represented in the lawyer's portrayal of his upbringing on a housing estate—to the ways in which defence lawyers, too, become complicit in the stigmatizing and damaging language of 'gangs' and its racializing and racist connotations. Crucially, the speech also showed, once more, how Nixon's own history of involvement in the drugs trade was hardly distinguishable from that of the identified victims. In fact, Nixon's defence lawyer was trying to emphasize this similarity between victims and criminals, exploited individuals and their exploiters, when he told the judge that his client had himself been identified as a slave by the NRM; that his 'offences were something of an inevitability' for 'young Black men growing up where they did'; that he, like his victims, had been 'utilized by people far more serious than any of them to fulfil their greed'; and that, taken together, this only placed Nixon 'one step above those for whom he is to be sentenced'.

The judge rejected most of what the defence had put forward, instead drawing heavily on the prosecution's line of storytelling. Holding that this was a case of 'a mutual thing, a true criminal partnership', with each defendant drawing 'confidence in wrongdoing from the other', he disagreed with the defence lawyers' accounts of two individuals who had themselves been deeply vulnerable at the time of their offending, in part at the hands of each other. The judge held that Ismail had moved from 'apparently performing charitable work with vulnerable and marginalized youth to working cold heartedly in criminal exploitation of potentially vulnerable and marginalized youth', while Nixon, for his part, had 'started from experiencing many bad things to doing many bad things and calculatedly exposing other youths to many bad things'. He did take into account, he said, as relevant mitigation that both defendants had shown 'true remorse' while on remand in prison, and that they had tried to better themselves through education. However, it could not be overlooked that we were dealing with a very serious crime, and one that he would not be willing to sentence them for lightly. The judge sentenced Ismail to five years, taking into account her lesser role in the criminal enterprise and her guilty plea, and Nixon to seven years and nine months in prison. Precedent had been acted upon, confirming that those who on their own lawyers' account were no different from the slaves they were said to have trafficked could be punished as slave masters.

The return of the slave master

In the aftermath of the trial of Karamera, Wabelua, and Alford, major newspapers stepped forward to celebrate the conviction as a precedent-setting case in the emerging modern slavery jurisprudence on county lines. For example, *The Guardian* newspaper, speaking of a 'landslide' conviction, quoted Duncan Balls, then deputy assistant commissioner, saying that the 'use of modern slavery legislation is an important aspect of targeting those criminal networks who exploit vulnerable children and adults to maximise their profits from drugs supply. Today's convictions sent a clear message that we will utilise all legislation nationally to suppress county lines activity' (Guardian, 2019). In a similar tone, *The Mail Online*, Britain's leading right-wing online tabloid paper, defined the case as a 'milestone' decision and cited Simon, the Detective Inspector who had been the officer-in-case in the trial: 'This is the first trial of its kind and my hope is that in being successful in this test case, we are sending a message to drug dealers who engage in this pernicious behaviour that we are after them'. He added, 'This case will pave the way for human trafficking legislation to be used to prosecute those individuals who use and recruit young people as part of county drug supply lines' (Aldersley, 2019).

Since the conviction, and when acting upon precedent, statements to this effect have been repeated time and again by senior government officials, law enforcement staff, and the courts. And yet, this public narration of the modern slavery tale in relation to county lines dealers jars with my own ethnographic observations. In particular, the anxieties, insecurities, and unpredictability that characterized the investigations and trial process is silenced by the celebratory and linear tale of bringing perpetrators of modern slavery to justice. As my work with the investigative officers and prosecution lawyers has shown, nothing about this precedent-setting case was inevitable. Over a five-year long 'saga', as Simon referred to it, officers struggled to identify victims and to distinguish them from their perpetrators, and many of the agencies—Crown Prosecution staff, police forces, and frontline professionals—offered widely opposing interpretations of these issues. These difficulties carried over into the trial process itself, during which the prosecution was compelled to prove trafficking of children by relying on phone evidence alone, in the absence of any child victim witnesses. In the end, while the case made a new law—that county lines dealers can be prosecuted under human trafficking laws for 'exploitation offences'—these difficulties have continued to mark the prosecutions that have followed in the aftermath of the case.

We can, of course, take the analysis one step further, for it was not just in this prosecution that we have come across difficulties in defining the dichotomy between victims and perpetrators, slaves and enemies. We have seen these dynamics when considering defence lawyers' attempts to run the 'modern slavery defence' in drugs cases, and in frontline professionals' efforts to monitor 'at risk' populations. Crucially, they also featured in Glodi's own retelling of his story in Chapter 2. As described there, I met Glodi shortly after he was released from prison in January 2023, having served half of his human trafficking and drugs sentences. In the time that

Glodi and I have since spent together, he has shed further light on what he meant when, in the course of his cross-examination, he insisted that he was a drug dealer but not a human trafficker. This is a story in which Glodi, from a young age, had been dealing drugs on behalf of others, becoming embroiled in debt relationships and performing different roles within the lower echelons of the drugs trade. True, at the time of his arrest for human trafficking, he had moved from running drugs to holding the phone line. It is also true that he was a few years older than the person he was said to have exploited, and that he knew exactly what he was doing. And yet, in Glodi's account, when he was in M.W.'s position, nobody had ever treated him as a victim deserving of protection.

To some extent, this would not come as a surprise to the many professionals that I spent time with. Throughout this book, police officers and lawyers have all agreed that the line between victims and perpetrators could be vanishingly thin in a situation where the victims had knowingly committed crimes and where perpetrators had often, at some point, been victimized themselves. But, we have also seen these professionals insisting on the possibility of reaching neutral and objective outcomes with the right procedures, trainings, and awareness in place—even where victims refused to speak. As this chapter has demonstrated, prosecution lawyers, too, have frequently displayed such 'techno-optimism' (Acosta, Bruun, and Koch, 2025) when they insist that expert witnesses (who, more often than not, are law enforcement staff) and phone data can help them reach neutral and objective decisions. And yet, I would put forward a different suggestion: that these cases speak of an act of statecraft-making that amounts to more than just a neutral and objective assessment of 'facts' and the law. Far from constituting merely a juridical development proving that county lines activity is 'more than just a drugs crime', the setting of precedent and the cases that followed suit, I argue, have also signified a political project-in-the-making that has conjured a new kind of 'suitable enemy' (Fekete, 2009)—that of the 'modern slave master' into Britain's body politic.

Let me be clear: the language of the 'slave master' is not one that I frequently heard prosecutors, lawyers, or any other professional use. While looming large in the judicial imagination, the perpetrator has remained a strange, unfathomable figure, almost unspeakable in political parlance, as the language of 'slaves' that is so central to policy and media language has not been matched by that of 'slave masters'. Instead, the language used to designate those who are said to stand behind the crimes of exploitation and slavery is that of 'human traffickers' or to a lesser extent, 'exploiters'. While this reflects the wording of the legislation (after all, the offence for which perpetrators are prosecuted is that of 'human trafficking'), we should, once more, not be seduced by technocratic logics or 'expert talk'. Nor should we see the absence of the 'slave master' in mainstream political discourse as a mere oversight. Rather, I suggest that it is precisely the unspeakability—that which cannot truly be named—that makes it all the more visceral, underscoring the sense of an inscrutable evil lurking 'from within'. In his analysis of 'gang' discourses, Patrick Williams points to what he calls the *absent presence* of 'gangs'—as any invocation of the imaginary of 'gangs' has come to act as a transcendental signifier for moral decay to which heavy-handed policing becomes the necessary response (Williams, 2015). Similarly here, the *absent presence* of the 'slave master' is licensing ever new forms of authoritarianism in the name of public protection, ranging from life in prison to draconian civil orders that severely restrict a person's freedom upon release.

Here, then, our story has come full circle: for the impetus to safeguard the vulnerable and protect them from themselves has become the very mechanism that has resurrected, within law, the figure of the ultimate enemy within, the modern-day slave master and the ultimate antithesis of liberal freedom. But there is a further bitter irony that should not escape us. Both the 'slaves' and 'slave masters' who are discovered as in need of either redemption or punishment today hail precisely from among the constituencies whose exposure to a punitive criminal justice system sits on an uneasy continuum with colonial histories of exploitation and enslavement. Thus, in the first convictions secured under modern slavery law in county lines drugs trials, it is precisely the descendants of formerly colonized and enslaved populations who have become embroiled in a legal dispute over slavery, this time as either modern slaves or their masters. To repeat the obvious, this is not to say that defendants racialized as white cannot be prosecuted for modern slavery offences; the available media publications on more recent modern slavery prosecutions have proven just that. But they, too, become racialized in the trial process—a point illustrated in how defendants' were 'blackened', regardless of their skin colour, by virtue of their structural position at trial (see Chapter 6). In the concluding chapter, I then turn to the 'why', 'what', and 'how': to why we are seeing the emergence of modern slavery in state policies in the current (post)colonial conjuncture; what this shows us about state racism; and how solidarity can be built against this state racism from the bottom up.

8
Political Labour at Work

State racism in a post-racial world

The UK government's Commission on Race and Ethnic Disparities recently claimed that institutional racism is a thing of the past, even going so far as to argue that Britain is 'a model for other white-majority countries' (2021, p. 9). This statement came the year after Black Lives Matter protest movements, sparked by the police murder of George Floyd in the US, challenged the enduring realities of police racism and state violence, demanding, amongst other issues, the defunding of the British police. Exploring how these two approaches to political mobilization—both of which posit analyses of institutional racism—came to such different conclusions, Adam Elliot-Cooper (2023) has argued that the liberal anti-racism endorsed by the British government frames racism as a problem of prejudiced individuals or biased policies that can be addressed with diversity training and inclusion initiatives. By contrast, for social movement members who took to the streets in 2020, institutional racism is a historically constituted disciplinary tool central to the reproduction of imperial and capitalist power. This 'thicker' understanding of institutional racism or 'state racism', as I call it here, punctures the liberal mythologies of Britain's self-image as a post-racial nation by illuminating the racial order that its institutions uphold.

The disjuncture between these two different understandings of institutional racism—one grounded in individualized attitudes; the other in the very constitution of imperial and capitalist state institutions—aptly captures the contrast between the British government's modern slavery agenda, on the one hand, and the more complicated story at the heart of this book, on the other. The official tale of redemption central to modern slavery eradication efforts claims to 'save' the most vulnerable in a colour-neutral and even-handed manner. As proof of this claim, professionals might emphasize that *anyone*—regardless of their skin colour, background, or postcode—can be caught up in experiences of modern slavery and exploitation. Moreover, they insist that modern slavery is not about fighting

Drugs, Race, and the Politics of Modern Slavery Law. Insa Lee Koch, Oxford University Press.
 DOI: 10.1093/9780198899631.003.0008

internal 'wars' in the way that the government did, for example, with respect to 'gangs': rather, it is about safeguarding individuals, including some of the most over-criminalized demographics. British academics working on modern slavery policies and law, including those well versed in calls for 'de-colonising criminal justice' (Aliverti, 2021), have similarly been reluctant to introduce the language of race and state racism into this debate, emphasizing instead how state policies that centre vulnerability mark a deeper, if ambivalent, shift away from punitive policing and provide the foundations for reimagining the state 'as a field to facilitate humanitarian praxis'.[1]

On the other hand, if we start from the second or what I call 'thicker' understanding of racism—namely, the realities of a state racism that are denied by and perpetuated through the liberal establishment—a different analytical lens opens up: one which centres the colonial logics of white saviourism that are central to the belief that working-class, racialized, and migrant populations need 'saving' for their own benefit (Day and Bean, 2022). The critical anti-trafficking literature provides a helpful starting point here (Anderson, 2013; Kempadoo, Sanghera, and Pattanaik, 2005; O'Connell Davidson, 2015, 2022; Brace and O'Connell Davidson, 2018; Kempadoo and Shih, 2022). This literature, reviewed in Chapter 2, has shown that neo-abolitionist efforts have not operated as neutral, less even as benevolent interventions. Rather, these efforts on the part of European powers to eradicate modern slavery have, at different points in time, operated in racializing ways, justifying tighter forms of immigration and border controls in the name of doing 'good'. Whether this happened in late nineteenth century Europe at a time of quickly developing capitalism, or 100 years later in the context of an increasingly unequal neo-liberal global order, initiatives that claim to protect the most vulnerable from trafficking and exploitation have controlled, restricted, and disciplined the labour and movements of predominantly working-class and racialized populations.

Modern slavery's most recent 'apparition' (O'Connell Davidson, 2016) on 'home soil' needs to be understood as a continuation of these logics. The issue entered the policy and legislative agenda at a time of heightened fears over uncontrolled and illegal migration, and the perceived threat of global terrorism (Kenway, 2021). But it did not stop there. As Chapter 2 showed, soon after being enacted, *The Modern Slavery Act* became tied up

[1] See for example, Ana Aliverti et al.'s description of their research project *The Vulnerable State: Appraising the Ambivalent Economies of State Power*, accessible at https://warwick.ac.uk/fac/soc/law/research/centres/cjc/research/vulnerable-state/ [accessed 23 October 2024].

with the issue of policing domestic 'enemy populations'. The same kinds of youth previously targeted by the government's 'war on gangs' came to be presented as victims caught up in regional drugs networks of 'county lines' activity. Their movements—connecting cities to provinces via drugs trafficking routes—and their labour—seen to benefit not a formal employer or the market but the illicit economy—became the subject of an emerging moral panic. A dominant government narrative began to take hold, backed up by the media and the academy, which not only presented urban (read Black) dealers as spreading to innocent (read white) places (Bhattacharyya et al., 2021), but reconstructed the same dealers as in need of saving from themselves, for their own good. Chapters 5 to 7 highlighted the pre-emptive policing, monitoring, and prosecutions that became authorized in the name of protecting the vulnerable, giving rise to forms of techno-moral governance that have cemented racial domination—or institutional racism of the 'thick' kind—at the core of state practice.

Why now, we might want to ask. What explains the resurgence of modern slavery rhetoric and policies today? Stuart Hall and his colleagues (2013) remind us that moral panics function as political tools in times of hegemonic crisis. Their analysis was focused on the early 1970s, when a recession, growing unemployment, strikes, and counter-movements were all calling the social 'glue' of the post-war consensus into question. Today's situation is not that different. Thus, the British government has conjured the image of the slave master at a time when entrenched austerity politics and neo-liberal welfare reforms have driven inequality to a new level. As Chapters 3 and 4 discussed, it is these experiences, as well as the workings of a deeply punitive criminal justice system, that have produced widespread social suffering at Britain's margins. In recent years, Britain's social and economic crisis has been further exacerbated by the outfalls from Britain's referendum on leaving the European Union and a global health pandemic. And yet, the state's affront to people's livelihoods, welfare, and freedom is anything but new. The social suffering confronted by the families whose voices have appeared in this book speaks of the afterlives of imperial histories that have long treated Black, minoritized, and working-class communities as sources of extraction, exploitation, and punishment.

Indeed, it was these histories that were laid bare in the protests of the Black Lives Matter movements that took to the streets in the summer of 2020. The year after Glodi was convicted as Britain's first ever 'slave master' in a drugs trial, protestors took to the streets to draw attention to slavery of a different kind: the transatlantic slave trade, its imperial framework, and their afterlives today. While the trigger that ignited these movements was the video of the brutal murder of George Floyd at the hands of US police in May of that year, the protests were not confined to the US. In Britain, once one of the main drivers of the transatlantic slave trade and the world's largest empire, activists laid bare how these histories continued to be woven into society and culture (Klinkert, 2023), including with respect to unequal access to welfare and housing (Bulley, Edkins, and El-Enany, 2019; Bhambra, 2022), racialized policing and incarceration (El-Enany and Bruce-Jones, 2015; Elliot-Cooper, 2021; Elliott-Cooper, 2023), hostile immigration policies (de Noronha, 2020; El-Enany, 2020), and the unequal effects of the covid-19 pandemic (Platt and Warwick, 2020; Katikireddi et al., 2021). Drawing on the country's long tradition of Black power movements in Britain and beyond, activists demanded a systemic dismantling of historically constituted racial state power and abolitionist futures (Day and Bean, 2022; Elliott-Cooper, 2023; Lamble and McElhone, 2023).

As Fudge has argued, in a political climate marked by polarization, economic crisis and widespread popular dissatisfaction, reviving the fight against modern slavery, allowed the British government in 2015 to build cross-party political support and to reinforce 'a narrative of moral authority, liberty, and British exceptionalism' (2025: 169). But this is not all. Rather, I argue that against the backdrop of Britain's on-going denial of its imperial past—a denial that was thrown into sharp relief by movement members and by the state's brutal repression of protests that followed suit—we also need to conceptualize the appearance of modern slavery on the domestic political landscape as an exercise in what Stoler (2011) has coined 'colonial aphasia'. Stoler uses the term to describe how imperial histories can become displaced through processes of 'dismembering, a difficulty speaking, a difficulty generating a vocabulary that associates appropriate words and concepts with appropriate things' (2020, p. 125). As Gapud (2020) has pointed out, dis-acknowledgements of Britain's imbrication in histories of slavery and colonialism happen here not as a consequence of wholesale ignorance, amnesia, or absence of imperial vocabulary (such as when the imperial past is denied or forgotten in public memory). Rather, what is at stake in 'colonial aphasia' is an occlusion or selective invocation of knowledge to serve new ends.

Modern slavery is an example of colonial aphasia par excellence. Here, an imperial vocabulary of 'slavery', 'exploitation', and 'trafficking' has been rewritten not in terms of the singularity of racial suffering inflicted upon formerly enslaved, colonized, and dispossessed populations, but as a contemporary form of evil emanating from within those same communities. It is this rewriting that, in turn, has breathed new life into old racist narratives that present these populations alternatively as hyper dangerous or as vulnerable and as in need of salvation. As this book has shown, this rewriting happens all the time—it happens when professionals present Black, minoritized, and working-class youth as 'colonizing' predominantly white and middle class provinces; it happens when they frame the same young people as both victimized by and as perpetrators of 'slavery' and 'human trafficking' offences; and it happens when they reconceive of 'exploitation' in terms of a narrow idea of juridical suffering at the hands of one another. At precisely the moment when the British state has embraced the fight against slavery, it has done so not to address its history of racial empire and its afterlives in state racism today, but to fight the modern-day slave master in the bodies of racialized working-class youth.

Ten years on from when *The Modern Slavery Act 2015* became law, government initiatives undertaken in the name of fighting 'modern slavery' are proliferating in Britain. For example, in its recent response to a parliamentary inquiry into the Act, the government renewed its commitment to pursuing multi-agency work and law enforcement, calling for driving up prosecutions and convictions (HM Government, 2024). Meanwhile, county lines drug dealers are now not only being charged under 'human trafficking' (s.2), as discussed in Chapter 7, but also under the 'slavery and servitude' (s.1) section of the *Modern Slavery Act.*[2] With respect to 'criminal exploitation' in county lines, a recent study concluded that while the term 'county lines' might be too rigid to account for the existing range of drug dealing practices, 'criminal exploitation in all drugs markets is the primary defining characteristic that should concern policing rather than the shape markets take' (Coomber et al., 2025). In line with this finding, the government also recently announced that it will codify 'child criminal exploitation' and 'cuckooing' into their own offences, turning them from what I have called 'criminal proxies' into legal realities.[3] This legislative and policing drive to protect 'vulnerability' is in tune with an ever-growing proliferation of international policies that take 'safeguarding' as their object of concern—whether in relation to transnational immigration processes

[2] The news recently reported that two twenty-one-year-old drug dealers from London were charged with 'holding a person in slavery or servitude' (Abou-Setta, 2024).

[3] See the government's announcement in this respect at https://www.gov.uk/government/news/child-criminal-exploitation-and-cuckooing-to-be-criminal-offences [accessed 9 September 2025].

(Smith and Waite, 2018), cross-border trafficking initiatives (O'Connell Davidson, 2015; Broad and Gadd, 2022; Carvalho et al., 2025), or security-led and counter-terrorism policies (Heath-Kelly and Gruber, 2023).

These developments show how the logic of salvation is feeding ever more into authoritarian state projects, particularly in a political climate that, since the start of my research, has moved ever more openly to the far-right (Fekete, 2025) and centred logics of white nationalism (Rogaly, 2024). And yet, this is also not the end of the story. The veneer of legitimacy also runs thin on the ground as the interventions now authorized in the name of protecting the vulnerable are experienced by those at the receiving end as 'setting them up to fail'. I want to return, for one last time, to three different sets of actors who, in their own ways, have challenged the state's official tale of salvation: Glodi, the first young man to be convicted of human trafficking charges in a county lines case; the mothers and other close family members who refuse to be silenced in the face of the system's persistent failings; and the ethnographer, who has turned the research process into an act of public advocacy. Across these actors, we can see a kind of counter-hegemonic labour at work as individuals carve out spaces of agency and solidarity that cut across the state's own facile boundaries of victims and perpetrators, of slaves and their masters, constituting everyday, bottom-up forms of resistance to the dominant political logics of our times.

Glodi: 'Train the body, train the mind'

The first time Glodi and I met in January 2023, over lunch in a Turkish Kebab restaurant, he told me how determined he was to move from his old life. The past fifteen years of his life have been dictated by prison, as he served one sentence after another, with only very short stints of time out in between. Now aged thirty, he has been out on license for his most recent convictions, though he still has a Slavery and Trafficking Prevention Order (PTRO) in place until 2027. Glodi was studying towards his lorry license, his first formal qualification that would allow him to pick up driving jobs. But his heart was in something else: he wanted to become a professional body trainer, mentoring young people who were facing challenging times by teaching them about the importance of staying fit. The idea had come to him in prison, when keeping to a strict regime of exercise was the one thing that kept him going. It was also something that he shared with others, having over the years in prison matured into one of the oldest boys on his

Figure 8.1. Glodi at Lewisham Police Station, Europe's largest purpose-built police station and the place where Glodi was taken into custody on several occasions after being arrested. He is wearing a T-shirt displaying his business logo 'GloFitness'.
Source: © Reece Grant 2025.

wing. The 'youngers' were turning to him for mentorship and support. 'I used to train the boys all the time', he told me. 'I used to take them to the gym and it was a good feeling, and I thought I want to do this professionally'. Glodi had a name for his business idea: 'GloFitness', it would be called, with the motto 'train the body, train the mind' (see figure 8.1. for a logo of his business):

Over the following year, Glodi started building a base of followers on Instagram by posting videos of his exercise routines, diet, and training sessions, and he took on his first clients. And yet, building a life post-prison was not an easy task. As I got to know him, I became privy to the multiple challenges he faced. When coming out of prison, he had been placed in a 'halfway house' and told he would stay there for fifty-six days before being allocated to permanent housing. This did not happen: three months passed, and he was still there. Eventually, Glodi found private accommodation without any help from the authorities, but he struggled to pay the bills in what is one of the most expensive rental markets in Europe. His offending history further meant that employers were reluctant to take him on. He signed up for agency work, doing different driving jobs for companies on zero-hour contracts, making the bare minimum he needed to pay his bills. In 2024, through a mutual contact, he was offered a low-level manager position at one of London's local driving departments. Glodi called me, his voice beaming with pride: this would be his first-ever office job and on a decent salary, too! He felt that he had made it. Yet days later his manager told him that his contract would be suspended; he had done some more 'research' into Glodi's past and was concerned that it posed a 'risk to the reputation of the council'. While his job was eventually restored, it left Glodi feeling anxious for days.

But more than anything else, Glodi found that he remains the subject of a criminal justice system whose surveillance mechanisms seem to follow a brutal logic of their own. Glodi's release from prison had been conditional: he had to sign a license agreement that posed restrictions on his daily life, associations, and movements for the protection of the public. In addition, he was bound by the terms of the Slavery and Trafficking Prevention Order (STPO) handed down as part of his conviction for human-trafficking charges. The rules for the license and the STPO were not the same. Nor were the overseeing officers who were dealing with each of these provisions: his license requirements were handled by a probation officer who he had to see on a regular basis, whereas the STPO was directly handled by the police (who only contacted him once about this in his first twelve months out of prison). Glodi found this system confusing, but he tried, to the best of his ability, to stick to the rules. He would regularly sign on at the police station as requested by his release conditions; attend weekly probation appointments; and keep his probation officer updated about any changes in his life.

One day, however, everything was thrown up in the air. In July 2023, armed police in balaclavas and bullet proof vests came to his flat. Glodi had been at work, but neighbours told him that police had banged on the front door before letting themselves into the garden at the back of the house, knocking on neighbours' doors, and informing them that Glodi had a warrant out for his arrest. Glodi panicked. His instinct was to run; he could not face going back to prison again. And what for? He had not done anything wrong since leaving prison. Indeed, the reason for his warrant turned out to be an administrative hiccup that had nothing to do with his own actions. The prison had made a technical error back in 2019, when Glodi was serving a sentence for a drugs offence committed in Scotland (see Chapter 2). At the time, he had been transferred from a prison in Scotland to one in England.

When Glodi was released in England after serving half of his sentence, the decision to release him early should have gone to a parole board in Scotland (which has its own jurisdiction); this, however, did not happen, for unexplained reasons. Therefore, in order to rectify the mistake, Glodi was informed he would have to go back to prison and await the Scottish parole board's decision from behind bars.

Glodi could not believe that an administrative error would cost him his freedom again. He could not rid himself of the feeling that the recall was a deliberate attempt to interfere with his life just at a point when he had managed to get his business launched and was gaining an increasingly influential social media and public presence. While his lawyer tried to reassure him that he would not be in prison long this time, Glodi did not know how long for, what he would encounter in prison, and whether the parole board would decide in his favour. He worried that once in prison, he would get 'into trouble', as he said, not because he was looking for fights but because of the hostile and unpredictable environment that prison was. If this happened, it would jeopardize any right to early release, and Glodi would spend the remainder of his sentence in prison. On the eve before he had to hand himself over to the police, he posted one last time on Instagram for his followers:

> It's a shame that there's a system that talks about rehabilitation but don't know what it takes to actually rehabilitate, I've been told that I have to return back to prison because my paperwork was not done properly because of an administrative error and the only way it can be fixed is for me to return to custody. I'm shock just like everyone else how this has come to be. I've been home 13 months building and progressing after spending many years in prison now I'm been told they didn't do the paperwork properly. I don't know when I'll see everyone again but please don't give up on me, stay training and keep fit! I will try to keep everyone updated!

In the end, his lawyer was right: he was out of prison again within three days. But the relief Glodi felt about being released was offset by the realization that the conditions of his freedom were even stricter than before. His license conditions for his drugs offence had been rewritten, exceeding in their severity even some of the original terms of the Slavery and Trafficking Prevention Order that had been subsequently struck down by the Court of

Appeal for being too draconian (Chapter 7). In addition to imposing severe restrictions on his use of electronic devices, specifying what job he was allowed to perform ('office-focused work'), and requiring him to keep his supervising officer informed about any changes in his residence or employment, provisions included: a duty to immediately inform the officer of any personal relations ('of any friendships, associations, or intimate or domestic relationships'); a ban on approaching or communicating with anyone he knew or had reasonable cause to believe was under the age of eighteen without prior approval by his supervising officer; a ban on entering 'parks, playgrounds, schools, youth clubs or further educational institutes or any other places' frequented by children without the prior approval and subject to any restrictions his supervising officer may impose; and a requirement that any use of social networking sites be subject to prior approval. Now, virtually *anything* could become the reason for an inadvertent recall to prison: stepping into a park; making new acquaintances, friends, or clients; or posting about his business on his Instagram account.

In the summer of 2024, police came to look for Glodi again. He was in the process of moving; the police went to his old address and when they arrived, did not find him there. Alarmed about what the unannounced police visit could mean and advised by his lawyer, Glodi subsequently went to the police station to turn himself in. He was informed that this time there was no warrant for his arrest. Nor were there any records in the police system that indicated that anyone had come to his house. Glodi was told that he was free to go. Then, again out of the blue, in October 2024, he received a phone call from law enforcement. He was told that he had been in breach of his STPO, which required him to report a change of address to the nearest operational police station within seven days. Glodi had never meant to hide his new address from the police: indeed, upon moving, he had immediately notified his probation officer (reporting a change of address also being part of his license agreement for his drugs offence). He had simply assumed that this would be updated in the police database, too. Still, this simple administrative mistake on Glodi's part was no defence. Glodi was called in for a police interview, where he was told that his breach could go back to a judge who would decide on whether he was liable to go back to prison. At the time of this writing in June 2025, Glodi still has not heard back about the outcome of the police interview.

Notwithstanding these setbacks, Glodi is determined to move on. 'Moving on' for Glodi means sharing his own experiences, mentoring others going through similar situations, and providing platforms for forging solidarities. In 2024, he moved into a care home for troubled young men whom he mentors and trains. He also continues to build his business 'GloFitness', reaching out to official institutions to offer his services to young people, including to some of the very institutions he is still battling with: prison authorities, youth offending services, schools. And he connects himself with larger audiences that he might never meet. Building on the success of the story published in the *New York Times*, as described in Chapter 2 (Gebrekidan, 2022), Glodi has consistently engaged in attempts to make his story known, a story that he feels 'the government never told as it was always on their own terms'. Outlets such as *The Guardian* (Garcia, 2024) and *BBC/Radio 4*[4] have given him a sympathetic platform, at times due to my connecting him with these outlets. Most recently, and in addition to running his GloFitness business,[5] he has started also running his own podcast series called GloTalks on YouTube[6] to which he invites people from all walks of life—including ex-criminals, prison officers, and social media celebrities—to share their stories. His dream is to travel the world one day with his Podcast to interview people all over. 'This is not about me talking about myself anymore', he said, 'but enabling others to tell their story, and to realize that whatever struggles they have faced or been through, they are not alone'.

The last time I saw Glodi was in June 2025, in London. We had agreed to meet together with a friend of his, a videographer and photographer, to take pictures for this book—of the different places and institutions that had framed Glodi's life. We started in Inner London Crown Court, where he had been trialled and convicted for human trafficking (Chapter 7), moving onto to Lewisham Police station (figure 8.1.), where he had spent many hours in the custody suites after being arrested by the police. Outside Belmarsh prison, a high security prison in South London where Glodi had served his last sentence, armed police suddenly drove by, jumped out of the car, and confronted Glodi (just after the picture in figure 8.1. was taken). The violence they displayed with their firearms contrasted sharply with

[4] The BBC/Radio 4 production entitled 'County Lines: Their World' can be accessed at https://www.bbc.co.uk/programmes/m0025d4q [accessed 5 September 2025].

[5] Glofitness can be accessed at https://www.instagram.com/glofitnessuk?igsh=MXZhZWZtbmJxbmR5&utm_source=qr [accessed 5 September 2025].

[6] Glotalks can be accessed on apple at https://podcasts.apple.com/gb/podcast/glotalks/id1822086099 and on spotify at https://open.spotify.com/show/4dwZlmQpT0SmqppSU4OdYo?si=TZT9qXM9RE27PUpqle9ktg and on YouTube at https://youtube.com/@glotalks?si=hhj8kDsHW60KbS82 and on Instagram on https://www.instagram.com/glotalks?igsh=bjRmdmNpNG1teHBt&utm_source=qr [all accessed 5 September 2025].

the warmth we had received just before, when going back to Glodi's estate in Forrest Hill—the place where Glodi had moved to when, aged five, he came with his family from Congo. As we were taking pictures in Glodi's old neighbourhood, a stream of people came by—older Caribbean residents, young Black men, and a South Asian shop keeper—hugging him to say hello, laughing, and exchanging words of banter (see figure 8.2.). 'She's written a book about me', Glodi would say proudly to them.

Figure 8.2. Glodi returning to his childhood estate and being greeted by a friend.
Source: © Reece Grant 2025.

Women's advocacy: 'Connection before correction'

When I first began working with women like Valerie, Tami, and Sue, they all shared a predicament: they were desperate to not only get their loved ones out of the illicit economy, but to protect them from a criminal justice system whose logic refused to protect and rehabilitate them. Years later, their struggles continue, if in ways different from before. To give a sense of what this means: Sue, mother of Lee, who desperately protected her son from being moved into a care home after being identified as a 'slave', still spends much time caring for Lee and for his three young children. As a young father, Lee has exited the illicit economy although he continued to be implicated in the criminal justice system for quite some time. K.S., the 'modern slave' whose murder trial I recounted in Chapter 4, was released from prison on license in January 2024. Despite their duty of care, the authorities failed to provide him with accommodation upon release and to give him access to his benefit payments. His older sister Tami not only offered up her couch in the one-bedroom flat that she occupies with her baby daughter, but she continues to advocate for him to have his benefits and housing right enforced. Finally, Valerie's son M., who the authorities had treated as an 'alpha victim' was released from prison on 3 June 2025, on license for another four years. If it hadn't been for his mother's support, he would not have had a place to stay and an interview for training on a construction site upon coming out of prison.

The seemingly mundane forms of advocacy work that women perform at different points in the young men's lives—during their arrest, trial, in prison, or after release—often constitute the only form of support that they receive in a situation where professionals from all walks of life have abandoned them. But as vital as these acts are, they also make these women vulnerable to unwanted state attention and suspicion. Let me turn again to Tami and her brother's trial, with which I ended Chapter 4. There, we saw that her brother found himself charged with joint enterprise murder alongside his alleged 'exploiter' (an older white male he had been working for in a drugs line going from London to Chelmsford). Over the course of the trial, K.S. was repeatedly portrayed as a 'gangster' by the prosecution, an image reinforced by the judge's refusal to admit his NRM decision (which certified that K.S. was a victim of exploitation) for fear of biasing the jury. But more so, his sister's insistence that a counter-story be heard did not lead anywhere. On the contrary, things took a dramatic turn as she (along with me) found herself banned from the courtroom under threat of arrest. She also faced a criminal investigation for alleged juror intimidation. In the end, this turned out to have been a false allegation, but it meant, in Tami's words, that her reputation had been 'tarnished' and that she was banned from entering the court house again, leaving her brother to stand on his own when the guilty verdict was announced.

After K.S.'s conviction in the summer of 2019, he was transferred to one of the country's most notorious youth offending institutions, Cookham Wood prison (the same institution where Glodi served his first drugs sentence as a juvenile), which has been in the spotlight for its high levels of inmate and staff violence and other serious failings (HM Inspectorate of Prisons, 2023, 2024). On her regular visits, Tami grew concerned when learning about K.S.'s time at Cookham Wood. At the time and even more intensely during the pandemic to follow in 2020, it was common practice to keep the boys locked up for the majority of the day in a cell. K.S. was not given access to education and any remedial support despite his diagnosed autism. But she grew most concerned after receiving a phone call from her brother. 'They run this prison like a gang', K.S. told her. He said that a white officer visited him in his cell one day, telling him that he knew he was in for murder, and asked K.S. to beat up some boys on the wing. When K.S. refused, he was the one to suffer. Not long after his conversation with the officer, K.S.'s cell door was left open with no explanation. A group of boys came in and brutally attacked him. It took a while before an officer intervened, but instead of breaking up the boys, he started beating K.S., kicking him to the floor face down and strangling him. After the beating, K.S. was thrown back in his cell and left there.

Tami was shocked. Once more she wrote a litany of emails to professional contacts, drawing attention to the prison's failures to safeguard the youth under the prison's care and to prevent the use of arbitrary power. The tone of her messages gradually became more forceful, as she failed to elicit any responses. She finally wrote the following to the prison liaison officer, asserting that 'my boy won't die on your watch' (and copying me on the email):

> Why my disabled brother has lumps and injuries to his head for stopping a fight. K.S. case mirrors your unannounced audit of failing you can fail all you like just not at the cost of my brothers life or safety [. . .] Tidy up your ship and get your work force in check and the next person who dares to put their hands around my brothers neck will explore

> the criminal justice system and disciplinary as per prison policy. Since you want to ignore me i will go higher than you because even you have someone to answer too and you are allowing peoples children to be hurt while us tax payers are paying for my boy to have his face smashed to the ground and choked.

In the end, she was told that K.S. was the culprit: he had deliberately got into the fight, assaulting the prison officer first, the liaison officer claimed. Dissatisfied with this response, we decided to write to the governor responsible for the prison, asking for CCTV evidence to be made available. Once more, no response. Instead, prison staff began to actively squeeze Tami out. Her booked visits to see her brother were cancelled under the pretext that the prison's visiting hours were already fully booked. When she tried to book again, she was told that as part of his punishment for assaulting an officer, K.S. would not be allowed to see any visitors for five weeks. More troubling still, the prison now started excluding Tami from monthly progress review meetings held to discuss her brother's welfare with a range of professionals. As his appointed guardian, Tami had been going to these meetings. Through K.S.'s social worker, with whom Tami had a good rapport, she learnt that the prison management felt she was 'making up conspiracy theories about racism' and should henceforth be excluded from any professional communication.

In the end, Tami was able to find a solicitor who was willing to take her brother's case on a pro bono basis. The incident was taken to the prison tribunal, which scheduled a hearing date. An internal board reviewed the CCTV evidence that the prison had previously refused to make available, and ruled that K.S.'s cell door had been left open for unexplainable reasons; that he had been attacked by the boys; and that he had not assaulted the officer. It was also found that the officer had used excessive force, and that some of the techniques used to restrain him were unlawful. Yet, no further action would be taken against the officer. Tami felt that things got 'hushed over'. The day after the hearing, K.S. was moved to a different prison. While Tami had been campaigning for precisely that to happen for months now, she had always been ignored. By contrast, this time, the response, and the speed with which it came had been very different. 'When it was to protect themselves and their members of staff they got him out, they're quick', Tami said, with a bitter laugh. 'Very quickly, they got him out of there, so quick that they moved him in the morning and contacted me at the lunchtime to tell me that he'd been moved to a new prison'.

While she had ultimately achieved what she wanted—to get K.S. moved to a different prison—the victory had left a bitter feeling. It had once more brought to the fore the powers of a criminal justice system whose opaque yet openly racist workings not only marked women like Tami as problems, but further delegitimized their experiences as making up 'conspiracy theories about racism'. But just as young men like Glodi refuse to let police surveillance take over their lives, so too do women like Tami insist that the fight against the system only makes them ever more determined to not give up. The letters Tami continues to write to the authorities—including now, years later, to the local authorities with respect to their failure to help K.S. transition back to his post-prison life—are a testimony to her commitment to justice. Tami has also begun training herself in legal vocabulary and become an expert on disciplinary procedures, always reminding power holders of their duty to be accountable. She conducts research on statistics and reads reports in her spare time. At several points, she has told me that her dream is to study towards a law degree so she can take on the authorities on behalf of those who do not have the power to make their voices heard.

Tami is not alone in her refusal to be silenced. Other women use their lived experiences not only to help loved family members, but to connect with others in similar situations and train them in tools of advocacy. Let me turn to Valerie, mother of M. As she sees it, the kind of work that she was doing on M.'s behalf had a name: non-violent resistance, or NVR. She first encountered NVR when her son started disappearing and she was left 'in the dark' by all professionals. While taking a community course on NVR, she understood for the first time that her experiences were part of historical struggles to refuse to allow communities to become divided by dominant powers and to practice civil disobedience in the face of broader injustices—she liked to cite Ghandi and Martin Luther King. To her, practicing NVR meant refusing to be drawn into a destructive system, whether this involved emotional abuse coming from loved ones or harmful policies and laws. In 2020, I saw Valerie open her own business, a registered community interest company that offers NVR training to carers, parents, and also frontline staff. While she insisted that the tools of NVR were useful for anyone, the parents and carers confronting the criminal justice system remained closest to her heart. 'This is about vigilant care', she told me. 'We need to build connections before correction, whether that's with our own children, our community, or our support networks'.

What it meant to build 'connection before correction' was made clear to me as I was able, at various points over the years, to attend and shadow

Valerie's training and mentoring sessions. Sometimes run in community halls, including in anti-racist community centres, other times online, Valerie's sessions take the shape of several weeklong courses. She teaches participants how to build strength in the face of adversity by promoting self-care, using one's networks for support, and not allowing the language of stigma, shame, and criminalization to overtake their lives. But her sessions are also hands-on. As she builds relations with course attendants, she also becomes involved in their struggles, stepping in to do advocacy work usually by putting pressure on professional bodies in the criminal justice system, and on several occasions, referring them to me for further advocacy. Valerie also supplements her training courses with an informal parents' support group. Here, parents and carers come together in a confidential space, safe from any professionals, to be together and, if they choose, to share their stories. There are mothers whose children have gone missing, who share their feelings of despair; carers who talk of being judged and excluded by the authorities; and parents exhausted from the advocacy work they are doing for loved ones.

Spaces such as the parents' group often provide the only community environments in which attendants feel that they are being 'heard'. More than once, I have been told that these groups make family members feel 'safe' talking about experiences of racism without being treated as if they are paranoid or making things up. What is more, by enabling individuals who might otherwise find themselves at different ends of the 'system' (some as 'victims', others as 'perpetrators') find a common language and common ground of fighting an unaccountable and biased system, these spaces act as an organic route for collectivizing struggles beyond the state's binary logic of (un)deservingness, of victims, and of perpetrators, and hence of beginning to imagine in the words of Ida Danewid, freedom 'without, and despite the state' (2023). Valerie herself, having learnt from other people's experiences, has begun using the language of 'systemic failures' to make sense of the struggles she has experienced on behalf of her son over the years. With two other women who I have advocated for too, she produced a 'write up' detailing the chronologies of how their respective children were 'failed' by the system (part of which I reproduced in Chapter 4 in relation to her own son), which she gave me permission to share. As Valerie has built her own networks, she has spoken at policy events, in front of practitioners, and to government officials, including when sharing a platform with me and Glodi at policy events. Calling herself an 'expert by experience', she makes the point that policy change has to come from the bottom up. 'Something has to give', she often says, 'and communities are beginning to rise up'.

Ethnography as political labour

Probably none of the people whose stories I have outlined here—Valerie, Tami, Glodi, or any of the others—would call their labour 'political'. Even Valerie, who teaches others about NVR, would not describe her own calling as political, preferring instead a language of 'resistance' or 'grassroots work'. And yet, for me, this is precisely what it is: a form of political labour that challenges the dominant narrative of salvation by moving beyond its binary logic of victims and perpetrators, of slaves and their masters, and of good and bad. When Glodi insists that he has the right to be treated like a free man; when he works to realize his dream of running a business that helps others 'train the body and the mind'; when he is determined to continue sharing his story on social media at the risk of breaching his license conditions; when Tami refuses to let her boy 'die on the prison's watch' or insists that the authorities have a duty of care towards her brother after his release from prison; and when Valerie preaches the importance of 'connection before correction' and creates spaces for people to come together free of professional intervention and oversight, all of them are defying the idea of redemption for the few. Instead, they show how relations of care can be forged between individuals and communities both beyond and at times in direct opposition to state and official institutions.

I want to conclude by turning to a final set of reflections on how ethnographic work—the research process, the writing that follows from it, and the enduring social relations that come out of it—can also be thought of as a form of political labour, in a situation where speaking the language of institutional racism and state violence is bound to generate backlash. Unlike many other areas of policy making, the case of modern slavery is one where the government has repeatedly welcomed, and actively sought, collaborations with academics, including by making funding available for research investigating aspects of modern slavery and human trafficking, and in some cases even funding entire research institutes attached to universities. Since I started this research, I have on several occasions—often after consulting with mothers like Valerie and listening to their insistence that policy makers 'need to hear' what families like hers have been through—contributed to these policy debates, including by presenting my research to professional networks; acting as an independent consultant for the government's guidance on the use of Slavery and Trafficking Risk Orders and Slavery and Trafficking Prevention Orders in county lines operations (Davies, 2021);

and, most recently in 2024, submitting legal evidence to Parliament in its call for expert reviews of the *Modern Slavery Act* ten years on (Koch, 2024).

And yet, turning research outputs into policy-relevant 'sound bites' is not without its ethical challenges. I worry that by engaging with policy circles, ethnographic work can have the effect of further feeding into the technocratic faith that I have critiqued in this book. By focusing primarily on 'what works', academics can also become complicit in legitimizing the wider modern slavery agenda, their work further legitimizing the fiction of a post-racial world. To give just one example, when acting as an independent consultant for the government's guidance on the use of civil orders under the *Modern Slavery Act* (Davies et al., 2021), I wrote a lengthy response to the draft document. In it, I critiqued the use of civil-criminal hybrids as extending policing mechanisms into society, and expressed my concerns, as per Chapter 5, that this would come at the expense of already disenfranchised and racialized communities. I also expressed my opinion that grassroots initiatives like Valerie's go a long way to promote resilience and rebuild communities from the bottom up. The former arguments never really made their way into the report, while the latter point was reduced to a footnote. Instead, the language of the report is one where the use of these orders is considered a prima facie desirable step, one officially endorsed by the government. My name on the second page of the report, alongside the name of a prestigious UK university that I was working for at the time, means that such guidance has now also been 'validated' by an academic 'expert'.

For me, the more meaningful if no less murky forms of engagement concern the practical advocacy work that I undertake, often by mobilizing my legal training and cultural capital. I would describe these forms of ethnographic involvement as political labour, too—and as contributing to what Ben Rogaly has defined as 'nascent nonelite cosmopolitan practices' outside academic ivory towers (Rogaly, 2020, 2024). Once more, such advocacy challenges enemy constructions in the law by working across the binary logic of victims and perpetrators that is central to the law, creating solidarity beyond or even against the state. Doing such advocacy-driven ethnography can mean different things. It can mean supporting the mothers and carers in doing the work that they already do for their children. It can also mean connecting people. For example, I put Valerie in touch with Glodi; she invited him along to attend an NVR session and further put him in touch with professionals she was working with, while he, in turn, gave her insights into prison life and her son's rights when she struggled to be in direct contact with her son. I also connected Valerie to social movements and activist groups when inviting her to a symposium I co-hosted on 'state racism and criminal (in)justice' with the Institute of Race Relations, an anti-racist organization, in June 2025. Finally, doing political labour can mean helping people make their own stories public. This has included hiring Glodi as a researcher; inviting him on several occasions to teach at my home university in Switzerland (only after a prolonged bureaucratic battle with government agencies); as well as connecting him to journalists.

But doing advocacy work has brought unexpected challenges, making me part of murky ethical entanglements that have at times backfired in painful und counter-productive ways. This is perhaps best illustrated by turning to some of my experiences with ethnographic advocacy. For example, we saw in Chapter 4 how, in the course of K.S.'s murder trial, I wound up taking on a support role for Tami, who acted as K.S.'s legal guardian and the only family member supporting him in the courtroom. Together we came to trial every day, sitting in the public gallery and taking notes on the proceedings. Eventually, however, it became impossible for us to do this. After an 'anonymous' complaint was made alleging that Tami and I were disrupting the court proceedings, soon followed by a juror allegation that Tami had intimidated a juror, we were prohibited from going to trial under the threat of arrest. On one level, this experience illustrates a point that I have made again and again in this book: how processes of racialization and the demonization, indeed criminalization that come with it, can travel or 'leak'—in this case from the defendant in the dock to his sister and the researcher. But if this is true, the experience also made me acutely aware of how my own privileged position—my professional status as a researcher and academic lawyer—gave me a layer of protection not necessarily afforded to those I was advocating for.

Worse even, my efforts to step in seem to have, at times, generated negative repercussions for individuals I was associated with, often over and above my knowledge at the time. Let me illustrate this point by returning to Valerie. During the COVID-19 pandemic, when face-to-face visits to prison were banned, I became very closely involved in prison advocacy work. On one occasion, I became involved in Valerie's desperate attempts to connect M. to a mentor, an ex-prisoner who was running a charity that helps prison-leavers rebuild their lives. The prison initially insisted that it would not be possible to book a meeting because there were only two categories of (online) visits available: social and legal visits. The prison maintained that a mentor visit would fall into neither. I challenged this decision, first by writing to the prison liaison officer and, when this failed to elicit a response, to the prison governor. Eventually, the mentor was given the green light to book an online visit. Serendipitously, this was to take place on Valerie's fiftieth birthday. 'It's a good omen', she said, 'the best birthday present I could have hoped for'.

The morning of her birthday, Valerie called me crying: Her son had phoned her from prison. He had not been picked up by a guard at the arranged time to be taken to the room where the online meeting was set up. Valerie pictured him in his cell, excited to meet his mentor and only realizing after some time that nobody was coming to get him. I offered to write to the governor again to inquire into what had happened that morning. After several weeks' delay, the governor informed me that the matter had been investigated and that he had come to the conclusion that M. himself had declined the opportunity to speak to the mentor, refusing to leave the cell when an officer had come to pick him up at the arranged time. We were given the option to rebook. And yet, the next time a meeting was scheduled, something went wrong again: M. was told minutes before the meeting was to take place that the online equipment was broken and no visits could take place. M. also reported to his mother that he had started being 'punished' informally. Officers on the wing were using pretexts to withdraw out-of-cell-time privileges and calling him names. M. insisted that this was because of us stepping in and 'grassing' the officers with the governor: having become the subjects of an official inquiry, they were now taking it out on M. Valerie was, once more, heart-broken, but insisted that we not push things further for fear of making the situation even more difficult for her son.

Similarly to K.S.'s experience of having the door to his cell left open for 'unexplained' reasons, there was no way of getting to the bottom of what had happened behind the prison walls. At the very least, however, M.'s treatment here shows how advocacy work can have unintended effects at the expense of the most vulnerable. This does not just pertain to the process of doing research; it can become an unintended side effect of writing, too. Let me return one last time to Glodi to explain this point. As mentioned above, Glodi's story has been in the public domain. Prominent news outlets including the *New York Times* (Gebrekidan, 2022) and *The Guardian* (Garcia, 2024) have covered it since his release from prison, and he has appeared on several social media sites, with one of his interviews being broadcast on a

YouTube channel with nearly half a million subscribers.[7] The *NYT* piece, that I had helped initiate by telling Selam Gebrekidan about Glodi's trial in the first place, was his first major coverage. Published under the title of 'He never denied being a drug dealer, but Britain claims he is a modern slave master too', the story immediately had a huge reception. But it was also the cause of backlash, from both conversative and liberal circles. The *Mail Online*, the website of the *Daily Mail* (one of Britain's largest tabloid papers), attacked the piece with its own story, featuring the headline, 'Fury at NYT over another anti-UK story: police and prosecutors slam county lines article claiming modern slavery laws are being "wielded disproportionately" against black drug dealers' (Camber, 2022).

I was one of the 'experts' quoted in the *NYT* piece, where I expressed the argument put forward in Chapter 7 that the application of modern slavery legislation to the case of county lines dealers has conjured the image of the modern-day slave master in the body of working-class and racialized youth. In a public lecture delivered at the University of Oxford the following year (Koch, 2023), I further presented this argument to an audience of academics and some practitioners. Glodi was present at the lecture, our eyes meeting across the hall as I retold his story. Only a few days after my lecture was placed on YouTube, however, armed officers came to Glodi's house, resulting in the episode I recounted above in which Glodi was recalled to prison over an 'administrative error'. The reason given for his recall was that the Scottish authorities never signed off on his early release; convicted for drugs offences in Edinburgh in 2018, he had served half of his sentence, but in an English prison. We also saw above that once out of prison, Glodi was made to sign a new set of license conditions that extended the police surveillance over his life, including making any social media activity subject to official approval. These new conditions not only put his business under the constant gaze of probation officers and police, but also meant that work he undertook with publicists was subject to scrutiny and censoring.

To be clear: there is no way of knowing if there is a direct connection between my efforts and the kinds of targeted surveillance, interventions, and informal punishments suffered by those I advocated for. It is entirely possible, for example, that Glodi's recall to prison and the rewrite of his license conditions in the aftermath of the public lecture I gave and the coverage he received were purely coincidental (though his own lawyer thinks

[7] https://www.youtube.com/watch?v=E0OXBcrIu1s [accessed 5 September 2025].

otherwise). It is equally possible that there is no connection between my public association with Tami and our respective targeting by the usher (and worse even Tami's investigation for juror intimidation); or between my correspondence with the governor on M.'s behalf and the humiliation that he was subjected to by prison officers in its aftermath. I am also aware that any insistence to the contrary might be subject to the same attack as that suffered by the women I have become close to: that these claims are no more than 'conspiracy theories of racism', unfounded in reality or facts. And yet, as has been argued (Machold and Pelkmans, 2011), what makes a theory a 'conspiracy theory' is not the fact that it is necessarily wrong (and definitely not more 'wrong' than any other competing theory), but that it lacks the legitimacy that comes with power. By sharing my experiences of ethnographic advocacy, then, my intention is to clear a pathway towards allowing an alternative set of voices and interpretations of events to be heard—and in so doing, to provide a counterweight to the liberal orthodoxy of a post-racial world that has constituted the dominant 'truth' in contemporary Britain.

Bibliography

Abou-Setta, R. (2024) 'Two Brighton-related slavery arrests as police raid address', *The Argus*, 6 December.

Abu-Lughod, L. (2002) 'Do Muslim Women Really Need Saving? Anthropological Reflections on Cultural Relativism and its Others', *American anthropologist*, 104 (3): 783–790. Available at: https://doi.org/10.1525/aa.2002.104.3.783.

Acosta, R., Bruun, M.H., and Koch, I. (2025) 'Technomoral Governance: From Techniques of Intervention to Technological Innovation in Politics, Policy and Law', *Social Anthropology* [Preprint].

Agozino, B. (2019) 'Humanifesto of the Decolonization of Criminology and Justice', *Decolonization of Criminology and Justice*, 1(1), pp. 5–28. Available at: https://doi.org/https://doi.org/10.24135/dcj.v1i1.5.

Ahdash, F. (2023) 'Countering Terrorism in the Family Courts: A Dangerous Development', *The Modern Law Review*, 86(5), pp. 1197–1231. Available at: https://doi.org/https://doi.org/10.1111/1468-2230.12812.

Aldersley, M. (2019) 'County lines drug gang become first to be jailed under modern slavery laws after using vulnerable children to ship crack cocaine and heroin across UK', *MailOnline*, 14 May. Available at: https://www.dailymail.co.uk/news/article-7028631/County-lines-drug-gang-UK-jailed-modern-slavery-laws.html (accessed: 16 October 2024).

Aliverti, A. (2020) 'Benevolent Policing? Vulnerability and the Moral Pains of Border Controls', *British Journal of Criminology*, 60(5), pp. 1117–1135. Available at: https://doi.org/https://doi.org/10.1093/bjc/azaa026.

Aliverti, A., et al. (2021) 'Decolonizing the Criminal Question', *Punishment & Society*, 23(3), pp. 297–316. Available at: https://doi.org/https://doi.org/10.1177/14624745211020585.

Aliverti, A. and Tawfiq, S. (2025) 'Caring States? Bureaucratic Care, Moral Ideals and Emotional Dilemmas in British Asylum and Policing', *Theoretical Criminology* [Preprint]. Available at: https://doi.org/10.1177/13624806241310446.

Allen, G. and R.T. (2021) *Drug Crime: Statistics for England and Wales*. Research Briefing. UK Parliament: House of Commons Library. Available at: https://researchbriefings.files.parliament.uk/documents/CBP-9039/CBP-9039.pdf (accessed: 15 October 2024).

Amnesty International (2018) *Trapped in the Matrix: Secrecy, Stigma and Bias in the Met's Gangs Database*. London. Available at: https://www.amnesty.org.uk/files/reports/Trapped%20in%20the%20Matrix%20Amnesty%20report.pdf (accessed: 15 October 2024).

Anderson, B. (1991) *Imagined Communities: Reflections on the Origins and Spread of Nationalism*. London: Verso.

Anderson, B. (2013) *Us and Them? The Dangerous Politics of Immigration Control.* Oxford: Oxford University Press.

Anderson, B. (2018) *Let Language Not Betray Us: Immigration, Enforcement and Modern Slavery.* Oxford. Available at: https://www.rsc.ox.ac.uk/news/let-language-not-betray-us-immigration-enforcement-and-modern-slavery-annual-elizabeth-colson-lecture-2018 (accessed: 8 October 2024).

Arias, D. and Grisaffi, T. (2021) *Cocaine: From Coca Fields to the Streets*. Durham, N.C.: Duke University Press.

Atkinson-Sheppard, S. (2024) 'Hyper-agency and County Lines', *Theoretical Criminology*, first published online 8 August 2025.

Axter, S. and Danewid, I. (2025) 'Countermapping the Carceral Security State: Beyond the Imperial Boomerang'. *International Studies Quarterly* 69(4). Available at: https://doi.org/10.1093/isq/sqaf070.

Bale, K. (2012) *Disposable People: New Slavery in the Global Economy*. Berkeley: University of California Press.

Bassell, L. and Emejulu, A. (2018) *Minority Women and Austerity: Survival and Resistance in France and Britain.* Bristol: Policy Press.

BBC (2019) 'County lines dealers jailed in "landmark" slavery case', 14 May. Available at: https://www.bbc.com/news/uk-england-london-48267349# (accessed: 16 October 2024).

BBC (2021) 'Couple jailed for trafficking teens to sell drugs', 28 January. Available at: https://www.bbc.com/news/uk-england-devon-55561327 (accessed: 16 October 2024).

BBC (2024) 'Harun Jama murder: Renewed appeal by Oxford police six years on', *BBC*, 3 January. Available at: https://www.bbc.com/news/uk-england-oxfordshire-67863144# (accessed: 15 October 2024).

Bear, L. (2015) *Navigating Austerity: Currents of Debt Along a South Asian River*. Stanford, California: Stanford University Press.

Bear, L. and Knight, D.M. (2017) 'Alternatives to Austerity', *Anthropology Today*, 35(5). Available at: https://doi.org/https://doi.org/10.1111/1467-8322.12375.

Beyer, J. (2023) 'The Common Sense of Expert Activists. Practitioners, Scholars and the Problem of Statelessness in Europe', *Dialectical Anthropology*, 46, pp. 457–473.

Bhambra, G. (2021) 'Narrating Inequality, Eliding Empire', *The British Journal of Sociology,* 72(1), pp. 69–78. Available at: https://doi.org/https://doi.org/10.1111/1468-4446.12804.

Bhambra, G. (2022) 'Relations of Extraction, Relations of Redistribution: Empire, Nation, and the Construction of the British Welfare State', *The British Journal of Sociology*, 73(1), pp. 4–15. Available at: https://doi.org/https://doi.org/10.1111/1468-4446.12896.

Bhattacharyya, G. et al. (2021) *Empire's Endgame: Racism and the British State.* London: Pluto Press.

Black, L., Seal, L., Seemungal, F., Malkani, B., and Ball, R. (2021) 'Introduction: Legacies of Empire', *Punishment & Society*, 23(5), pp. 609–612. Available at: https://doi.org/10.1177/14624745211040652.

Bonning, J. and Cleaver, K. (2021) 'There is No "War on Drugs": An Investigation into County Line Drug Networks from the Perspective of a London Borough', *The Police Journal*, 94(4), pp. 443–461.

Bornstein, E. and Sharma, A. (2016) 'The Righteous and the Rightful: The Technomoral Politics of NGOs, Social Movements, and the State in India', *American Ethnologist*, 43(1), pp. 76–90. Available at: https://doi.org/https://doi.org/10.1111/amet.12264.

Bosworth, M. (2004) 'Theorizing Race and Imprisonment: Towards a New Penalty', *Critical Criminology*, 12(2), pp. 221–242. Available at: https://doi.org/https://doi.org/10.1023/B:CRIT.0000040259.65158.a5.

Boublil, E. (2024) 'A Critical Phenomenology of Vulnerability: Toward a Paradigm Shift? A Contribution To An Interdisciplinary Trialogue on Vulnerability', *Human Studies*, 47(2), pp. 275–285.

Bourgois, P. and Schonberg, J. (2009) *Righteous Dopefiend*. Berkeley: University of California Press.

Bourgois, P., et al. (2021) 'The Violence of the American Dream in Segregated US Inner-City Narcotics Markets', in D.E. Arias and T. Grisaffi (eds) *Cocaine: From Coca Fields to City Streets*. Durham, NC: Duke University Press.

Brace, L. (2018) *The Politics of Slavery*. Edinburgh: Edinburgh University Press.

Brace, L. and O'Connell Davidson, J. (2018) *Revisiting Slavery and Antislavery: Towards a Critical Analysis*. London: Palgrave MacMillan.

Bristow, E. (1977) *Vice and Vigilance: Purity Movements in Britain Since 1700*. Rowman and Littlefield.

British Transport Police (2024) *Pair jailed for modern day slavery offences after British Transport Police County Lines investigation—London Bridge*. Available at: https://www.btp.police.uk/news/btp/news/in-the-courts/pair-jailed-for-modern-day-slavery-offences-after-british-transport-police-county-lines-investigation--london-bridge/ (accessed: 16 October 2024).

Broad, R. and D. Gadd (2023) *Demystifying Modern Slavery*. London and New York: Routledge.

Brown, K. (2019) 'Vulnerability and Child Sexual Exploitation: Towards an Approach Grounded in Life Experiences', *Critical Social Policy*, 39(4), pp. 622–642.

Brown, K. (2014) 'Questioning the Vulnerability Zeitgeist: Care and Control Practices with 'Vulnerable' Young People', *Social Policy and Society*, 13(3), pp. 371–387.

Brown, K. (2011) '"Vulnerability": Handle with Care', *Ethics and Social Welfare*, 5(3), pp. 313–321.

Brown, K., Ecclestone, K., and Emmel, N. (2017) 'The Many Faces of Vulnerability', *Social Policy and Society*, 16(3), pp. 497–510.

Bulley, D., Edkins, J., and El-Enany, N. (2019) *After Grenfell: Violence, Resistance and Response*. London: Pluto Press.

Caldeira, T. and Holston, J. (1999) 'Democracy and Violence in Brazil', *Comparative Studies in Society and History*, 41(4), pp. 691–729. Available at: https://doi.org/10.1017/S0010417599003102.

Camber, R. (2019) 'County lines gang boss aged just 17 "enslaved two 16-year-old girls and forced them to sell heroin and crack cocaine on the street by stuffing drugs in their bras and mouths"', *Mail Online*, 27 January. Available at: https://www.dailymail.co.uk/news/article-6638087/County-lines-gang-boss-aged-just-17-enslaved-two-16-year-old-girls.html (accessed: 16 October 2024).

Camber, R. (2022) 'Fury at NY Times over another anti-UK story: Police and prosecutors slam county lines article claiming modern slavery laws are being "wielded disproportionately" against black drug dealers', *Mail Online*, 29 November. Available at: https://www.dailymail.co.uk/news/article-11478629/Fury-NY-Times-anti-UK-story-Police-prosecutors-slam-county-lines-article.html (accessed: 8 October 2024).

Carvalho, H. (2020) 'Joint Enterprise, Hostility and the Construction of Dangerous Belonging', *Criminal Justice, Risk and the Revolt Against Uncertainty*. Cham: Springer International Publishing, pp. 115–137.

Carvalho, H. et al. (2025) 'Modern Slavery and the Punitive-Humanitarian Complex', *The British Journal of Criminology*, 65(1), pp. 93–109.

Cheng, J. (2017) 'Humanity's Subtensions: Culture Theory in US Death Penalty Mitigation', *Social Analysis*, 61(3), pp. 73–90. Available at: https://doi.org/https://doi.org/10.3167/sa.2017.610305.

Civicus Monitor (2023) *The United Kingdom downgraded in global ratings report on civic freedoms*. Available at: https://monitor.civicus.org/country-rating-changes/uk/ (accessed: 23 October 2024).

Cioccini, P. and Greener, J. (2021) 'Mapping the Pains of Neo-colonialism: A Critical Elaboration of Southern Criminology', *The British Journal of Criminology*, 61(6), pp. 1612–1629. Available at: https://doi.org/10.1093/bjc/azab041.

Clayton, J., Donovan, C., and Merchand, J. (2015) 'Distancing and Limited Resourcefulness: Third Sector Service Provision Under Austerity Localism in the North East of England', *Urban Studies*, 53(4), pp. 723–740. Available at: https://doi.org/10.1177/0042098014566369.

Cockbain, E. and Tufail, W. (2020) 'Failing Victims, Fuelling Hate: Challenging the Harms of the "Muslim Grooming Gangs" Narrative', *Race & Class*, 61(3), pp. 3–33.

Cohen, S., Fuhr, C., and Bock, J. (eds) (2018) *Austerity, Community Action, and the Future of Citizenship in Europe*. Bristol: Policy Press.

Commission on Race and Ethnic Disparities (2021) *Commission on Race and Ethnic Disparities: the Report*. Available at: https://assets.publishing.service.gov.uk/media/6062ddb1d3bf7f5ce1060aa4/20210331_-_CRED_Report_-_FINAL_-_Web_Accessible.pdf (accessed: 15 October 2024).

Conley, J. and O'Barr, W. (1990) 'Speaking Patriarchy', in *Just Words: Language, Law and Power*. Chicago: Chicago University Press.

Coomber, R. and Moyle, L. (2018) 'The Changing Shape of Street-level Heroin and Crack Supply in England: Commuting, Holidaying and Cuckooing Drug Dealers Across "County Lines"', *The British Journal of Criminology*, 58(6), pp. 1323–1342. Available at: https://doi.org/https://doi.org/10.1093/bjc/azx068.

Cooper, C. et al. (2017) *A typology of modern slavery in the UK*. Available at: https://assets.publishing.service.gov.uk/media/5a822a42e5274a2e8ab57d66/typology-modern-slavery-offences-horr93.pdf (accessed: 8 October 2024).

Cox, S. and Forde, E. (2017) 'County Lines: The children forced to sell drugs', *BBC*, 24 October. Available at: https://www.bbc.com/news/uk-41720980 (accessed: 16 October 2024).

Coomber, R. et al. (2025) *County Lines, Policing and Vulnerability.* Available at: https://vulnerabilitypolicing.org.uk/wp-content/uploads/sites/133/2025/08/county-lines-report-digital.pdf (accessed: 21st October 2025).

Craig, G. et al. (2019) *The Modern Slavery Agenda: Policy, Politics and Practice in the UK.* Bristol: Policy Press.

Crown Prosecution Service (2023) *Abuse of process: Legal guidance.* Available at: https://www.cps.gov.uk/legal-guidance/abuse-process (accessed: 16 October 2024).

Crown Prosecution Service (2024) *Modern Slavery and human trafficking: Offences and defences, including the section 45 defence.* Available at: https://www.cps.gov.uk/legal-guidance/modern-slavery-and-human-trafficking-offences-and-defences-including-section-45 (accessed: 16 October 2024).

Cunningham, C.D. (1992) 'Lawyer as Translator Representation as Text: Towards an Ethnography of Legal Discourse', *Cornell Law Review*, 77(6), pp. 1298–1387.

Dagdeviren, Donoghue, H.M. and Wearmouth, A. (2019) 'When Rhetoric does not Translate to Reality: Hardship, Empowerment and the Third Sector in Austerity Localism', *The Sociological Review*, 67(1), pp. 143–160. Available at: https://doi.org/https://doi.org/10.1177/0038026118807631.

Dalton, J. (2019) '"County lines" gang who forced children to deal drugs convicted of human trafficking under modern slavery laws', 17 April. Available at: https://www.independent.co.uk/news/uk/crime/county-lines-drugs-gang-children-court-latest-human-trafficking-modern-slavery-portsmouth-a8875321.html (accessed: 16 October 2024).

Das, V. et al. (2000) *Violence and Subjectivity.* Berkeley: University of California Press.

Das, V. et al. (2001) *Remaking a World Violence, Social Suffering, and Recovery.* Berkeley: University of California Press.

Davey, R. and Koch, I. (2021) 'Everyday Authoritarianism: Class and Coercion on Housing Estates in Neoliberal Britain.', *PoLAR: Political and Legal Anthropology Review*, 44(1), pp. 43–59. Available at: https://doi.org/https://doi.org/10.1111/plar.12422.

Davies, H. et al. (2021) *Guidance on the use of slavery and trafficking risk orders and slavery and trafficking prevention orders in county lines operations.* National County Lines Coordination Centre. Available at: https://3rblaw.com/wp-content/uploads/2021/10/NCLCC-STPO-STRO-guidance-final-02072021.pdf (accessed: 16 October 2024).

Day, A.S. and McBean, S.O. (2022) *Abolition Revolution.* London: Pluto Press.

de Noronha, L. (2020) *Deporting Black Britons: Portraits of Deportation to Jamaica.* Manchester: Manchester University Press.

Dench, G., Gavron, K., and Young, M. (2006) *The New East End: Kinship, Race and Conflict.* London: Profile Books.

Densley, J., McLean, R., and Brick, C. (2023) *Contesting County Lines: Case Studies in Drug Crime and Deviant Entrepreneurship.* Bristol: Policy Press.

Dewey, S., VandeBerg, B., and Webb, H. (2024) *Gun Present Inside a Southern District Attorney's Battle against Gun Violence.* Berkeley: University of California Press.

Doezema, J. (1999) 'Loose Women or Lost Women? The Re-emergence of the Myth of White Slavery in Contemporary Discourses of Trafficking in Women', *Gend. Issues*, 18, pp. 23–50. Available at: https://doi.org/https://doi.org/10.1007/s12147-999-0021-9.

Dorling, D. (2018) *Peak Inequality: Britain's Ticking Time Bomb*. Bristol: Policy Press.

Eastwood, N., Shiner, M., and Bear, D. (2013) *The Numbers in Black and White: Ethnic disparities in the policing and prosecution of drug offences across England and Wales*. London. Available at: https://www.release.org.uk/publications/numbers-black-and-white-ethnic-disparities-policing-and-prosecution-drug-offences (accessed: 15 October 2024).

Edgington, M. (2021) *Challenges of policing modern slavery*. Ryton-on-Dunsmore: College of Policing. Available at: https://www.college.police.uk/article/challenges-policing-modern-slavery (accessed: 16 October 2024).

El-Enany, N. (2017) *The Colonial Logic of Grenfell, Verso Blogs*. Available at: https://www.versobooks.com/en-gb/blogs/news/3306-the-colonial-logic-of-grenfell?srsltid = AfmBOoo_fgNcZ8cWcb1g4UY6hn2KmWHQwpms_uED8_U-GKx_49734ySn (accessed: 14 October 2024).

El-Enany, N. (2020) *(B)ordering Britain: Law, Race and Empire*. Manchester: Manchester University Press.

El-Enany, N. and Bruce-Jones, E. (2015) *Justice, Resistance and Solidarity: Race and Policing in England and Wales*. London. Available at: https://cdn.prod.website-files.com/61488f992b58e687f1108c7c/61c32db83898d65a864b9483_Race%20and%20Policing%20v5.pdf (accessed: 15 October 2024).

Elliot-Cooper, A. (2021) *Black Resistance to British Policing*. Manchester: Manchester University Press.

Elliott-Cooper, A. (2019) '"Our Life is a Struggle": Gender, Respectability and Black Resistance', *Antipode*, 51(2), pp. 539–557. Available at: https://doi.org/https://doi.org/10.1111/anti.12497.

Elliott-Cooper, A. (2023) 'Abolishing Institutional Racism', *Race & Class*, 65(1), pp. 100–118. Available at: https://doi.org/https://doi.org/10.1177/03063968231166901.

Fassin, D. (2011) *Humanitarian Reason: A Moral History of the Present*. California: University of California Press.

Fassin, D. (2015) 'Governing Precariousness', in D. Fassin and P. Brown (eds) *At the Heart of the State: The Moral World of Institutions*. London: Pluto Press.

Fatsis, L. (2019) 'Policing the Beats: The Criminalisation of UK Drill and Grime Music by the London Metropolitan Police', *The Sociological Review*, 67(6), pp. 1300–1316. Available at: https://doi.org/https://doi.org/10.1177/0038026119842.

Fatsis, L. (2021) 'Policing the Union's Black: The Racial Politics of Law and Order in Contemporary Britain', in F. Gordon and D. Newman (eds) *Leading Works in Law and Social Justice*. London: Routledge, pp. 137–150.

Fekete, L. (2009). *A Suitable Enemy: Racism, Migration and Islamophobia in Europe*. London: Pluto Press.

Fekete, L. (2022) 'Racism, Radicalisation and Europe's "Thin Blue Line"', *Race & Class*, 64(1), pp. 3–45. Available at: https://doi.org/https://doi.org/10.1177/0306396822110.

Fekete, L. (2025) Paramilitary policing against the people: Colonial continuities and the challenge from below. London: *Institute of Race Relations*. Available at: https://irr.org.uk/article/paramilitary-policing-against-the-people-colonial-continuities-and-the-challenge-from-below/.

Feldman, I. and Ticktin, M. (2010) *In the Name of Humanity: The Govenrment of Threat and Care*. Durham, NC: Duke University Press.

Fitzgerald, F. and Munro, V. (2012) 'Sex Work and The Regulation of Vulnerability(ies): Introduction', *Feminist Legal Studies*, 20(3), pp. 183–188.

Forbess, A. and James, D. (2017) 'The end of austerity? Not for the most needy', *LSE British Politics and Policy Blog*. Available at: https://blogs.lse.ac.uk/politicsandpolicy/667070-2/.

Fuchs, S. (2024) *Fragile Hope Seeking Justice for Hate Crimes in India*. El Alto, CA: Stanford University Press.

Fudge, J. (2025) *Constructing Modern Slavery: Law, Capitalism and Unfree Labour*. Cambridge: Cambridge University Press.

Gallagher, A. (2010) *The International Law of Human Trafficking*. Cambridge: Cambridge University Press.

Gapud, A. (2020) 'Displacing Empire: Aphasia, "Trade", and Histories of Empire in an English City', *History and Anthropology*, 31(3), pp. 331–351. Available at: https://doi.org/https://doi.org/10.1080/02757206.2020.1726905.

Garcia, F. (2024) 'From low-level drug dealer to human trafficker: are modern slavery laws catching the wrong people?', *The Guardian*, 18 April. Available at: https://www.theguardian.com/law/ng-interactive/2024/apr/18/county-lines-drug-dealer-to-human-trafficker-modern-slavery-laws (accessed: 23 October 2024).

Gayle, D. (2018) '"County lines" heroin dealer jailed under child trafficking law', *The Guardian*, 4 October.

Gebrekidan, S. (2022) 'He Never Denied Selling Drugs. But Britain Says He's a Slave Master, Too', *The New York Times*, 27 November. Available at: https://www.nytimes.com/2022/11/27/world/europe/uk-drug-dealer-slave-master.html (accessed: 16 October 2024).

Gibson, M. (1986) *Prostitution and the State in Italy, 1860-1915*. New Brunswick, NJ: Rutgers University Press.

Gilroy, P. (1987) *There Ain't no Black in the Union Jack: The Cultural Politics of Race and Nation*. London: Routledge.

Gilroy, P. (2004) *Postcolonial Melancholia*. New York: Columbia University Press.

Gonzalez Van Cleve, N. (2016) *Crook Country: Racism and Injustice in America's Largest Criminal Court*. Redwood City: Stanford University Press.

Guardian, T. (2019) 'Three convicted of trafficking in landmark "county lines" case', 17 April. Available at: https://www.theguardian.com/law/2019/apr/17/three-convicted-of-trafficking-in-landmark-county-lines-case (accessed: 16 October 2024).

Hacking, I. (2006) 'Making up people: clinical classifications', *The London Review of Books*, 17 August. Available at: https://doi.org/https://www.lrb.co.uk/the-paper/v28/n16/ian-hacking/making-up-people.

Hall, S. (1979) 'The Great Moving Right Show', *Marxism Today*, 23(1), pp. 14–20.

Hall, S. et al. (2013) *Policing the Crisis: Mugging, the State and Law & Order*. London: MacMillan.

Hanley, L. (2007) *Estates: An Intimate History*. London: Granta.

Harvey, D. (2007) *A Brief History of Neoliberalism*. Oxford: Oxford University Press.

Heath-Kelly, C. and Gruber, B. (2023) *Vulnerability: Governing the Social through Security Politics*. Manchester: Manchester University Press.

Herring, F. (2023) 'Drug dealers used children to sell heroin and cocaine for them in Northampton', *Northamptonshire News*, 23 July. Available at: https://www.northantslive.news/news/northamptonshire-news/drug-dealers-used-children-sell-8587690 (accessed: 16 October 2024).

HM Government (2011) *Ending gang and youth violence: A cross-government report including further evidence and good practice case studies*. Available at: https://assets.publishing.service.gov.uk/media/5a79e1d1e5274a684690cc73/gang-violence-detailreport.pdf (accessed: 15 October 2024).

HM Government (2014) *Modern Slavery Strategy 2014*. Available at: https://assets.publishing.service.gov.uk/media/5a7e460340f0b6230268a4b1/Modern_Slavery_Strategy_FINAL_DEC2015.pdf (accessed: 21 October 2024).

HM Government (2016) *Ending gang violence and exploitation*. Available at: https://assets.publishing.service.gov.uk/media/5a7f970ced915d74e33f75dc/Ending_gang_violence_and_Exploitation_FINAL.pdf (accessed: 15 October 2024).

HM Government (2018) *Serious violence strategy*. Available at: https://assets.publishing.service.gov.uk/media/5acb21d140f0b64fed0afd55/serious-violence-strategy.pdf (accessed: 15 October 2024).

HM Government (2018b) *Working together to safeguard children: a guide to inter-agency working to safeguard and promote the welfare of children*. Available at: https://wscp.org.uk/media/1161/working_together_to_safeguard_children.pdf (accessed: 16 October 2024).

HM Government (2023) *Working together to safeguard children 2023: a guide to multi-agency working to help, protect and promote the welfare of children*. Available at: https://assets.publishing.service.gov.uk/media/669e7501ab418ab055592a7b/Working_together_to_safeguard_children_2023.pdf (accessed: 16 October 2024).

HM Government (2024) *Government response to House of Lords Modern Slavery Act 2015 Committee report*, 'The Modern Slavery Act 2015: becoming world-leading again'.

HM Inspectorate of Prisons (2023) *Report on an unannounced inspection of HMYOI Cookenwood Prison*. Available at: https://www.justiceinspectorates.gov.uk/hmiprisons/wp-content/uploads/sites/4/2023/07/Cookham-Wood-web-2023.pdf (accessed: 23 October 2024).

HM Inspectorate of Prisons (2024) *Report on an independent review of progress at HMYOI Cookham Wood*. Available at: https://cloud-platform e218f50a4812967ba1215eaecede923f.s3.amazonaws.com/uploads/sites/19/2024/05/Cookham-Wood-web-IRP-2024.pdf(accessed: 23 October 2024).

Holston, J. (2007) *Citizenship in Disjunctive Democracies*. Berkeley: University of California Press.

Home Office (2014) *Modern Slavery: How the UK is Leading the Fight*. Available at: https://assets.publishing.service.gov.uk/media/5a7d5f6c40f0b60aaa294080/Modern_slavery_booklet_v12_WEB__2_.pdf (accessed: 24 October 2024).

Home Office (2018) *Criminal Exploitation of Children and Vulnerable Adults: County Lines Guidance*. London. Available at: https://assets.publishing.service.gov.uk/government/uploads/system/uploads/attachment_data/file/652652/typology-modern-slavery-offences-horr93.pdf.

Home Office (2019) *Independent review of the Modern Slavery Act: Final report*. Available at: https://assets.publishing.service.gov.uk/media/5ce5116e40f0b627de48663d/Independent_review_of_the_Modern_Slavery_Act_-_final_report.pdf (accessed: 15 October 2024).

Home Office (2019a) *County Lines Programme*. Available at: https://www.gov.uk/government/publications/county-lines-programme/county-lines-programme-overview#home-office-programme (accessed: 15 October 2024).

Home Office (2019b) *Independent review of the Modern Slavery Act: Final report*. Available at: https://assets.publishing.service.gov.uk/media/5ce5116e40f0b627de48663d/Independent_review_of_the_Modern_Slavery_Act_-_final_report.pdf (accessed: 15 October 2024).

Home Office (2023) *Guidance Criminal exploitation of children and vulnerable adults: county lines*. Available at: https://www.gov.uk/government/publications/criminal-exploitation-of-children-and-vulnerable-adults-county-lines/criminal-exploitation-of-children-and-vulnerable-adults-county-lines.

Home Office (2024) *Modern slavery: Statutory guidance for England and Wales* (under s49 of the Modern Slavery Act 2015) and non-statutory guidance for Scotland and Northern Ireland. Available at: https://assets.publishing.service.gov.uk/media/66ffde903b919067bb482c61/Modern+Slavery+Statutory+Guidance+_EW_+and+Non-Statutory+Guidance+_SNI_+v3.11.pdf (accessed: 16 October 2024).

House of Lords Modern Slavery Act 2015 Committee (2024) *The Modern Slavery Act 2015: Becoming world-leading again*. Available at: https://publications.parliament.uk/pa/ld5901/ldselect/ldmodslav/8/8.pdf (accessed: 23 October 2024).

Humphries, W. (2021) 'Care boss and lover used boys as drug mules', *The Times*, 29 January. Available at: https://www.thetimes.com/uk/crime/article/care-boss-and-lover-used-boys-as-drug-mules-hkjmc92dh (accessed: 16 October 2024).

itvNews (2021) 'Pair jailed for exploiting vulnerable teens in West Country drug operation', *itvNews*, 28 January. Available at: https://www.itv.com/news/westcountry/2021-01-28/pair-jailed-for-exploiting-vulnerable-teens-in-west-country-drug-operation# (accessed: 16 October 2024).

Irwin, M. (1996) '"White slavery" as metaphor anatomy of a moral panic', *Ex Post Facto: The History Journal*, 5.

James, D. and Koch, I. (2020) 'The State of the Welfare State: Advice, Governance and Care in Settings of Austerity', *Ethnos*, 87(1)(1), pp. 1–21. Available at: https://doi.org/https://doi.org/10.1080/00141844.2019.1688371.

Katikireddi, S.V. et al. (2021) 'Unequal Impact of the COVID-19 Crisis on Minority Ethnic Groups: A Framework for Understanding and Addressing Inequalities', *Journal of Epidemiol Community Health*, 75(10), pp. 970–974.

Kelly, T. (2006) 'Documented Lives: Fear and the Uncertainties of Law During the Second Palestinian Intifada', *Journal of the Royal Anthropological Institute*, 12(1), pp. 89–107. Available at: https://doi.org/https://doi.org/10.1111/j.1467-9655.2006.00282.x.

Kempadoo, K. and Shih, E. (2022) *White Supremacy, Racism and the Coloniality of Anti-trafficking*. New York: Taylor & Francis.

Kempadoo, K., Sanghera, J., and Pattanaik, B. (2005) *Trafficking and Prostitution Reconsidered: New Perspectives on Migration, Sex Work, and Human Rights*. Boulder, USA: Paradigm Publishers.

Kenway, E. (2021) *The Truth About Modern Slavery*. London: Pluto Press.

Kimbell, L. and Bailey, J. (2017) 'Prototyping and the New Spirit of Policy-making', *CoDesign*, 13(3), pp. 214–226.

Kleinman, A. and V. Das (1997) *Social Suffering*. Berkeley: University of California Press.

Klinkert, V.L. (2023) *Tracing Rhodes: An Ethnography of White Ignorance at Oxford University*. SOAS University of London. Available at: https://doi.org/https://doi.org/10.1080/23322705.2023.2222602.

Knight, D. and Stuart, C. (2017) 'Ethnographies of Austerity: Temporality, Crisis and Affect in Southern Europe', *History and Anthropology*, 27(1), pp. 1–18. Available at: https://doi.org/10.1080/02757206.2015.1114480.

Koch, I. (2014) '"A Policy that kills": The bedroom tax is an affront to basic rights', *LSE British Politics and Policy Blog*, 23 September. Available at: 'A policy that kills': The bedroom tax is an affront to basic rights | British Politics and Policy at LSE (accessed: 14 October 2024).

Koch, I. (2018) *Personalizing the State: An Anthropology of Law, Politics and Welfare in Austerity Britain*. Oxford: Oxford University Press.

Koch, I. (2021) 'The Guardians of the Welfare State: Universal Credit, Welfare Control and the Moral Economy of Frontline Work in Austerity Britain', *Sociology*, 55(2), pp. 243–262. Available at: https://doi.org/https://doi.org/10.1177/0038038520936981.

Koch, I. (2023) 'Re-centering the state: On drug trafficking, modern slavery and decolonial endeavours in austerity Britain'. Available at: https://www.youtube.com/watch?v=OI35YWEFC84 (accessed: 16 October 2024).

Koch, I. (2024) *Written evidence for Modern Slavery Act 2015 Parliamentary Committee* (MSA0079). Available at: https://committees.parliament.uk/writtenevidence/129328/pdf/https://committees.parliament.uk/writtenevidence/129328/pdf/ (accessed: 8 October 2024).

Koch, I. (2024) 'From Criminals to Slaves: "Modern Slavery," Drug Trafficking, and the Cultural Politics of Victimhood in Postcolonial Britain', *Current Anthropology*, 65(2), pp. 267–291. Available at: https://doi.org/https://doi.org/10.1086/729537.

Koch, I. and Reeves, A. (2021) 'From Social Security to State-sanctioned Insecurity: How Welfare Reform Mimics the Commodification of Labour Through Greater State Intervention', *Economy and Society*, 50, pp. 448–470. Available at: https://doi.org/10.1080/03085147.2020.1844936

Koch, I., Williams, P., and Wroe, L. (2024) '"County Lines": Racism, Safeguarding and Statecraft in Britain', *Race & Class*, 65(3), pp. 3–26. Available at: https://doi.org/https://doi.org/10.1177/03063968231201 32.

Koram, K. (2019) *The War on Drugs and the Global Colour Line*. London: Pluto Press.

Kudnani, A. (2023) *What is Antiracism? And Why it Means Anticapitalism*. London: Verso.

Lamble, S. and McElhone, M. (2023) 'Over-policed and Under-protected: Why Does Nothing Change?', *Institute of Race Relations News* [Preprint].

Lammasniemi, L. (2017) '"Anti-white Slavery Legislation and its Legacies in England"', *Anti-Trafficking Review*, 9, pp. 64–76. Available at: https://doi.org/10.14197/atr.20121795.

Lammy, D. (2017) *Lammy Review: Final Report. An Independent Review into the Treatment of, and Outcomes for, Black, Asian and Minority Ethnic Individuals in the Criminal Justice System. London*. Available at: https://assets.publishing.service.gov.uk/media/5a82009040f0b62305b91f49/lammy-review-final-report.pdf (accessed: 15 October 2024).

Laub, M.M. (2021) 'Policing Authoritarian Neoliberalism in South London', *Political Geography*, 90, p. 102471. Available at: https://doi.org/https://doi.org/10.1016/j.polgeo.2021.102471.

Laub, M.M. (2024) 'Austerity-driven Policification: Neoliberalisation, Schools and the Police in Britain', *The Sociological Review*, 72(3), pp. 651–672. Available at: https://doi.org/https://doi.org/10.1177/00380261231202649.

Lewis, P. et al. (2012) *Reading the riots: Investigating England's summer of disorder*. Available at: https://www.theguardian.com/uk/interactive/2011/dec/14/reading-the-riots-investigating-england-s-summer-of-disorder-full-report (accessed: 15 October 2024).

Lianos, M. and Douglas, M. (2000) 'Dangerization and the End of Deviance: The Institutional Environment', *The British Journal of Criminology*, 40(2), pp. 261–278. Available at: https://doi.org/https://doi.org/10.1093/bjc/40.2.261.

Loader, I. and Sparks, R. (2017) 'Penal Populism and Epistemic Crime Control', in A. Liebling, S. Maruna, L. McAra (ed.) *Oxford Handbook of Criminology*. 6th edn. Oxford: Oxford University Press.

Local Government Association (2019) *Councillor guide to tackling modern slavery*. Available at: https://www.local.gov.uk/sites/default/files/documents/22.47%20Councillors%20guide%20on%20modern%20slavery%20WEB.pdf (accessed: 16 October 2024).

Local Government Association and Independent Anti-Slavery Commissioner (2017) *Tackling modern slavery: A council guide*. London: Local Government Association. Available at: https://www.cannockchasedc.gov.uk/sites/default/files/site-old/tackling_modern_slavery_-_a_council_guide.pdf (accessed: 16 October 2024).

Loopstra, R., et al. (2015) 'Austerity, Sanctions, and the Rise of Food Banks in the UK', *BMJ*, 350, p. h1775. Available at: https://doi.org/10.1136/bmj.h1775.

Lowndes, V. and L. Pratchett (2012) 'Local Governance Under the Coalition Government: Austerity, Localism and the "Big Society"', *Local Government Studies*, 38(1), pp. 21–40. Available at: https://doi.org/https://doi.org/10.1080/03003930.2011.642949.

Machold, R. and Pelkmans, M. (2011) 'Conspiracy Theories and Their Truth Trajectories', *Focaal: Journal of Historical and Global Anthropology*, 59(15), pp. 66–80. Available at: https://doi.org/https://doi.org/10.3167/fcl.2011.590105.

Makkii, L. (2010) 'Children, Humanity, and the Infantilization of Peace', in M.T. Ilana Feldman (ed.) *In the Name of Humanity: The Government of Threat and Care*. Durham, N.C.: Duke University Press, pp. 58–85.

Marshall, H. (2024) 'Victim as a Relative Status', *Theoretical Criminology* 28(2), 157–174.

McLean, R., G. Robinson, J. A. Densley (2020) *Criminal Networks and Evolving Drug Markets in Britain*. Cham, Swizerland: Springer, 39–51.

Ministry of Justice (2019) *County Lines Exploitation Practice guidance for YOTs and frontline practitioners*. Available at: https://assets.publishing.service.gov.uk/media/63ff45658fa8f527f53ef112/moj-county-lines-practical-guidance-frontline-practitionerspdf.pdf (accessed: 15 October 2024).

Ministry of Justice (2019) *County Lines Exploitation Practice guidance for YOTs and frontline practitioners*. Available at: https://assets.publishing.service.gov.uk/media/63ff45658fa8f527f53ef112/moj-county-lines-practical-guidance-frontline-practitionerspdf.pdf (accessed: 15 October 2024).

Mirza, H. (1997) 'Mapping a genealogy of Black British feminism', in H. Mirza (ed.) *Black British Feminism: A Reader*. London: Routledge, pp. 1–30.

Mitchell, T. (1988) *Colonising Egypt*. Cambridge: Cambridge University Press.

Modern Slavery & Human Rights Policy & Evidence Centre (2024) *Modern slavery policy in the UK: priorities for the UK Government*. Available at: https://modern-slavery.files.svdcdn.com/production/assets/downloads/MSPEC-UKgov-priorities-policy-report-final.pdf?dm=1728388629 (accessed: 16 October 2024).

Monteith, K. et al. (2022) *Racial bias and the bench: A response to the judicial diversity and inclusion strategy* (2020-2025). Manchester. Available at: https://www.intermediaries-for-justice.org/sites/default/files/unimanchesterracejudiciaryreport.pdf (accessed: 15 October 2024).

Moyle, L. (2019) 'Situating Vulnerability and Exploitation in Street Level Drug Markets: Cuckooing, Commuting, and the "County Lines" Drugs Supply Model'. *Journal of Drugs Issues*, 49(4), pp. 739–755.

Munro, V. and Scoular, J. (2012) 'Abusing Vulnerability? Contemporary Law and Policy Responses to Sex Work in the UK', *Feminist Legal Studies*, 20(3), pp. 189–206.

National County Lines Coordination Centre and National Police Chief's Council (2024) *County lines: Strategic threat risk assessment April 2023 to March 2024*.

National Crime Agency (2015) *County Lines, gangs and safeguarding*. London. Available at: https://www.nationalcrimeagency.gov.uk/who-we-are/publications/359-nca-intelligence-assessment-county-lines-gangs-and-safeguarding-2015/file (accessed: 15 October 2024).

National Crime Agency (2016) *County Lines, gang violence, exploitation and drug supply. London*. Available at: https://www.nationalcrimeagency.gov.uk/who-we-are/publications/15-county-lines-gang-violence-exploitation-and-drug-supply-2016/file (accessed: 15 October 2024).

National Crime Agency (2017) *County Lines, violence, exploitation & drug supply 2017*. Available at: https://www.nationalcrimeagency.gov.uk/who-we-are/publications/234-county-lines-violen-ce-exploitation-drug-supply-2017/file (accessed: 15 October 2024).

National Crime Agency (2018) *County Lines, drug supply, vulnerability and harm 2018*. Available at: https://www.nationalcrimeagency.gov.uk/who-we-are/publications/257-county-lines-drug-supply-vulnerability-and-harm-2018/file (accessed: 15 October 2024).

Neocleous, M. (2011) '"A Brighter and Nicer New Life": Security as Pacification', *Social & Legal Studies*, 20(2), pp. 191–208.

Neocleous, M. (2025) *Pacification: Social War and the Power of Police*. London: Verso.

Newburn, T. (2007) '"Tough on Crime": Penal Policy in England and Wales', *Crime and Justice*, 36(1), pp. 425–470. Available at: https://doi.org/https://doi.org/10.1086/592810.

Nijjar, J. (2018) 'Echoes of Empire: Excavating the Colonial Roots of Britain's "War on Gangs"', *Social Justice*, 45(2/3 (152/153)), pp. 147–162. Available at: https://www.jstor.org/stable/26677660 (accessed: 15 October 2024).

Nijjar, J. (2022) 'Racial Warfare and the Biopolitics of Policing', *Social Identities*, 28, pp. 441–457. Available at: https://doi.org/https://doi.org/10.1080/13504630.2022.2056438.

Norris, M. (2024) 'Fresh appeal six years after murder of Harun Jama, aged 16', *Oxford Mail*, 3 January. Available at: https://www.oxfordmail.co.uk/news/24022143.fresh-appeal-six-years-murder-harun-jama-aged-16/(accessed: 15 October 2024).

Office of the Independent Anti-Slavery Commissioner and University of Nottingham Rights Lab (2017) *Collaborating for freedom: anti-slavery partnerships in the UK*. Available at: https://iascmap.nottingham.ac.uk/CollaboratingforFreedom.pdf (accessed: 16 October 2024).

Office of the Independent Anti-Slavery Commissioner and University of Nottingham Rights Lab (2022) *Partnerships for freedom Improving multi-agency collaboration on modern slavery*. Available at: https://www.nottingham.ac.uk/research/beacons-of-excellence/rights-lab/resources/reports-and-briefings/2020/september/partnerships-for-freedom.pdf (accessed: 16 October 2024).

Ofsted (2018) *Protecting children from criminal exploitation, human trafficking and modern slavery: An addendum*. Available at: https://assets.publishing.service.gov.uk/media/5bebe2ac40f0b667b363e279/Protecting_children_from_criminal_exploitation_human_trafficking_modern_slavery_addendum_141118.pdf (accessed: 15 October 2024).

O'Connell Davidson, J. (2015) *Modern Slavery: The Margins of Freedom*. Basingstoke: Palgrave Macmillan.

O'Connell Davidson, J. (2016) 'De-canting "Trafficking in Human Beings", Recentring the State', *The International Spectator*, 51(1), pp. 58–73. Available at: https://doi.org/https://doi.org/10.1080/03932729.2016.1121685.

O'Connell Davidson, J. (2022) *What Do We Know and What Should We Do About Slavery?* London: Sage Publications.

Parmar, A. (2011) 'Stop and Search in London: Counter-terrorist or Counter-productive?', *Policing and Society*, 21(4), pp. 369–382. Available at: https://doi.org/https://doi.org/10.1080/10439463.2011.617984.

Parmar, A. (2017) 'Intersectionality, British Criminology and Race: Are We There Yet?', *Theoretical Criminology* 21(1), pp. 35–45.

Philips C et al. (2020) 'Dear British Criminology: Where Has All the Race and Racism Gone?', *Theoretical Criminology*, 24(3), pp. 427–446. Available at: https://doi.org/https://doi.org/10.1177/1362480619880345.

Phillips, C. and Bowling, B. (2003) 'Racism, Ethnicity and Criminology. Developing Minority Perspectives', *British Journal of Criminology*, 43(2), pp. 269–290.

Phoenix, A. (1997) 'Theories of Gender and Black Families', in H. Mirzwa (ed.) *Black British Feminism: A Reader*. London: Routledge, pp. 63–66.

Pitts, J. (2020) 'That Other Epidemic: A Review of Simon Harding's County Lines', *Youth&Policy* [Preprint].

Platt, L. and Warwick, R. (2020) 'COVID-19 and Ethnic Inequalities in England and Wales', *Fiscal Studies*, 41(2), pp. 259–289.

Powers, T. and Rakopoulos, T. (2019) 'The Anthropology of Austerity: An Introduction', *Focaal*, 2019(83), pp. 1–12. Available at: https://doi.org/10.3167/fcl.2019.830101.

Ramsay, P. (2010) 'Overcriminalization as Vulnerable Citizenship', *New Criminal Law Review*, 13(2), pp. 262–285. Available at: https://doi.org/https://doi.org/10.1525/nclr.2010.13.2.262.

Ramsay, P. (2012) *The Insecurity State: Vulnerable Autonomy and the Right to Security in the Criminal Law*. Oxford: Oxford University Press.

Razack, S. (2020) 'Settler Colonialism, Policing and Racial Terror: The Police Shooting of Loreal Tsingine', *Feminist Legal Studies*, 28, pp. 1–20. Available at: https://doi.org/10.1007/s10691-020-09426-2.

Reynolds, T. (1997) '(Mis)representing the Black (Super)woman', in H. Mirza (ed.) *Black British Feminism: A Reader*. London: Routledge, pp. 97–112.

Robinson, G., McLean, R., and Densley, J. (2018) 'Working County Lines: Child Criminal Exploitation and Illicit Drug Dealing in Glasgow and Merseyside', *International Journal of Offender Therapy and Comparative Criminology*, 36(5), pp. 694–711. Available at: https://doi.org/https://doi.org/10.1177/0306624X18806742.

Robinson, K. and Sheldon, R. (2019) 'Witnessing Loss in the Everyday: Community Buildings in Austerity Britain', *The Sociological Review*, 67(1), pp. 111–125. Available at: https://doi.org/10.1177/0038026118797828.

Rogaly, B. (2024) Commentary on Koch, 'From Criminals to Slaves: "Modern Slavery," Drug Trafficking, and the Cultural Politics of Victimhood in Postcolonial Britain', *Current Anthropology*, 65(2), pp. 267–291. Available at: https://doi.org/10.1086/729537.

Rogaly, B. (2021) *Stories From a Migrant City: Living and Working Together in the Shadow of Brexit*. Manchester: Manchester University Press.

Rogaly, B. and Taylor, B. (2009) *Moving Histories of Class and Community: Identity, Place and Belonging in Contemporary England*. Basingstoke: Palgrave Macmillan.

Scheffer, T. (2010) *Adversarial Case-making: An Ethnography of English Crown Court Procedure*. Brill.

Scott, J.C. (1998) *Seeing like a State: How Certain Schemes to Improve the Human Condition have Failed*. New Haven, Connecticut: Yale University Press.

Seaward, T. (2021) 'Harun Jama "unlawfully killed" in Oxford, inquest rules', *Oxford Mail*, 12 November. Available at: https://www.oxfordmail.co.uk/news/19711815.harun-jama unlawfully-killed-oxford-inquest-rules/#:~:text = A%20TEENAGER%20stabbed%20by%20a,of%20a%20gun%20being%20fired (accessed: 15 October 2024).

Seaward, T. (2023) 'Harun Jama Oxford murder: No new arrests five years on', *Oxford Mail*, 3 January. Available at: https://www.oxfordmail.co.uk/news/23225632.harun-jama-oxford-murder-no-new-arrests-five-years/ (accessed: 15 October 2024).

Shih, E. (2023) *Manufacturing Freedom: Sex Work, Anti-Trafficking Rehab, and the Racial Wages of Rescue*. Berkeley: University of California Press.

Shilliam, R. (2018) *Race and the Undeserving Poor: From Abolition to Brexit*. London: Agenda Publishing.

Shange, S. (2020) *Progressive Dystopia: Abolition, Antiblackness, and Schooling in San Francisco*. Durham and London: Duke University Press.

Shiner, M. et al. (2018) *The Colour of Injustice: 'Race', Drugs and Law Enforcement in England and Wales*. London: StopWatch, LSE and Release. Available at: http://www.lse.ac.uk/News/Latest-news-from-LSE/2018/10-October-2018/Drug-policing-drives-racial-disparity.

Skeggs, B. (1997) *Formations of Class and Gender: Becoming Respectable*. London: SAGE.

Slawson, M. (2018) 'Two men jailed for gang-related human trafficking offences', *The Guardian*, 13 April. Available at: https://www.theguardian.com/uk-news/2018/apr/13/two-men-jailed-for-gang-related-human-trafficking-offences (accessed: 16 October 2024).

Spicer, J. (2020) *Policing County Lines: Responses to Evolving Provincial Drug Markets*. Cham: Palgrave Macmillan.

Spicer, J. (2021) 'Between gang talk and prohibition: The transfer of blame for County Lines', *International Journal of Drug Policy*, 87, p. 102667. Available at: https://doi.org/https://doi.org/10.1016/j.drugpo.2020.102667.

Spicer, J., Moyle, L., and Coomber, R. (2020) 'The Variable and Evolving Nature of "Cuckooing" as a Form of Criminal Exploitation in Street Level Drug Markets', *Trends in Organized Crime*, 23(4), pp. 301–323. Available at: https://doi.org/https://doi.org/10.1007/s12117-019-09368-5.

Steur, L. (2018) 'Contradictions of the "Common Man": A Realist Approach to India's Aam Aadmi Party', in D. Kalb and M. Mollona (eds) *Worldwide Mobilizations: Class Struggles and Urban Commoning*. Oxford, New York: Berghahn.

Smith, K. and Waite, L. (2018) 'New and Enduring Narratives of Vulnerability: Rethinking Stories about the Figure of the Refugee', *Journal of Ethnic and Migration Studies*, 45(13), pp. 2289–2307.

Stoler, A. (1995) *Race and the Education of Desire: Foucault's History of Sexuality and the Colonial Order of Things*. Durham and London: Duke University Press.

Stoler, A. (2011) '"Colonial Aphasia: Race and Disabled Histories in France"', *Public Culture*, 23(1), pp. 121–156. Available at: https://doi.org/https://doi.org/10.1215/08992363-2010-018.

Stone, N. (2018) 'Child Criminal Exploitation: "County Lines", Trafficking and Cuckooing', *Youth Justice,* 18(3), pp. 285–293. Available at: https://doi.org/https://doi.org/10.1177/147322541881083.

Tawfiq, C. (2022) *The State of Homelessness: Authority, Trust and Charity in Metropolitan England.* London School of Economics.

The Centre for Social Justice (2013) *It Happens Here: Equipping the United Kingdom to Fight Modern Slavery.* London. Available at: https://www.centreforsocialjustice.org.uk/wp-content/uploads/2013/03/CSJ_Slavery_Full_Report_WEB5.pdf (accessed: 8 October 2024).

The Centre for Social Justice and Justice & Care (2022) *A Path to Freedom and Justice: A new vision for supporting victims of modern slavery.* Available at: https://www.centreforsocialjustice.org.uk/wp-content/uploads/2022/01/CSJ-JC-A-Path-to-Freedom-and-Justice-a-new-vision-for-supporting-victims-of-modern-slavery-single-pages.pdf (accessed: 14 October 2024).

The Centre for Social Justice and Justice&Care (2024) *Criminal exploitation: Modern slavery by another name.* Available at: https://www.centreforsocialjustice.org.uk/wp-content/uploads/2024/02/CSJ-JC_Criminal_exploitation.pdf (accessed: 15 October 2024).

Ticktin, M. (2011) *Casualties of Care: Immigration and the Politics of Humanitarianism in France.* California: University of California Press.

Timmins, N. (2017) *The Five Giants: A Biography of the Welfare State.* Revised ed. London: Harper Collins.

Townsend, M. (2023) 'Police county lines strategy "cruelly targets" black youth in UK', *The Guardian,* 19 November.

Turner, A., L. Belcher, and I. Pona. (2019) *Counting Lives: Responding to Children Who are Criminally Exploited.* London. Available at: https://www.childrenssociety.org.uk/sites/default/files/2020-10/counting-lives-report.pdf (accessed: 15 October 2024).

Tyler, I. (2015) *Revolting Subjects: Social Abjection and Resistance in Neoliberal Britain.* London: Zed Books.

Tyler, K. (2012) *Whiteness, Class and the Legacies of Empire: On Home Ground.* London: Palgrave Macmillan.

United Nations General Assembly (2021) *Implementation of the non-punishment principle* A/HRC/47/34. Available at: https://www.ohchr.org/en/calls-for-input/written-submissions-received-report-united-nations-special-rapporteur-trafficking (accessed: 16 October 2024).

University of Nottingham (2024) The Rights Lab, *University of Nottingham—Written Evidence (MSA0024).*

Wacquant, L. (2008) *Urban Outcasts: A Comparative Sociology of Advanced Marginality.* Cambridge: Polity Press.

Walkowitz, J. (1980) *Prostitution and Victorian Society: Women, Class and the State.* Cambridge: Cambridge University Press.

Waller, N. (2024) *The legal dragnet Joint enterprise law and its implications.* London: Centre for Crime and Justice Studies. Available at: https://t2a.org.uk/wp-content/uploads/2025/04/The-Legal-Dragnet-Sep-2024.pdf.

Wilde, M. (2022) 'Gatekeeping, Militant Care and Moral Economies of Housing in London', *Ethnos*, 87(1), pp. 22–41. Available at: https://doi.org/https://doi.org/10.1080/00141844.2019.1687540.

Williams, P. (2015) 'Criminalising the Other: Challenging the Race-gang Nexus', *Race & Class*, 56(3), pp. 18–35. Available at: https://doi.org/https://doi.org/10.1177/030639681455622.

Williams, P. and Clarke, B. (2016) *Dangerous Associations: Joint Enterprise, Gangs and Racism. An Analysis of the Processes of Criminalisation of Black, Asian and Minority Ethnic Individuals.* London. Available at: https://www.crimeandjustice.org.uk/sites/crimeandjustice.org.uk/files/Dangerous%20assocations%20Joint%20Enterprise%20gangs%20and%20racism.pdf (accessed: 15 October 2024).

Williams, P. and Clarke, B. (2018) 'The Black Criminal Other as an Object of Social Control', *Social Sciences*, 7(11), pp. 1–14. Available at: https://doi.org/10.3390/socsci7110234.

Willis, R. (2023) *A Precarious Life*. Oxford: Oxford University Press.

Wilson, W. et al. (2021) *Rescue and Response County Lines Project: Supporting Young Londoners Affected by County Lines Exploitation. Year 3 Strategic Assessment.* London. Available at: https://www.london.gov.uk/sites/default/files/rescue_and_response_strategic_assessment_2021.pdf (accessed: 22 October 2024).

Windle, J., L. Moyle, and R. Coomber (2020) 'Vulnerable Kids Going County: Children and Young People's Involvement in County Lines Drug Dealing', *Youth Justice*, 20(1–2), pp. 64–78. Available at: https://doi.org/https://doi.org/10.1177/1473225420902.

Woods, T. (2013) 'Surrogate Selves: Notes on Anti-trafficking and Anti-blackness', *Social Identities*, 19(1), pp. 120–134. Available at: https://doi.org/https://doi.org/10.1080/13504630.2012.753348.

Woolley, S. (2021) 'Our Drug Laws are Racist, and Doctors Must Speak Out—An Essay by Simon Woolley', *BMJ*, 374: n2147. Available at: https://doi.org/10.1136/bmj.n2147.

Wroe, L. (2021) 'Young People and "County Lines": A Contextual and Social Account', *Journal of Children's Services*, 16(1), pp. 39–55. Available at: https://doi.org/https://doi.org/10.1108/JCS-10-2020-0063.

Wroe, L. (2023) 'The Panic Around "County Lines" is Legitimising Expanded Policing Powers', *Novara Media*, February. Available at: https://novaramedia.com/2023/02/09/the-panic-around-county-lines-is-legitimising-expanded-policing-powers/ (accessed: 16 October 2024).

Zedner, L. and Ashworth, A. (2014) *Preventive Justice*. Oxford: Oxford University Press.

Index

For the benefit of digital users, indexed terms that span two pages (e.g., 52–53) may, on occasion, appear on only one of those pages.

Figures are indicated by an italic *f* following the page number.